$H!T JESUS SAYS

RECLAIMING LOVE IN THE KINGDOM OF HEAVEN

IAN MACDONALD

APOCRYPHILE
PRESS

Apocryphile Press
PO Box 255
Hannacroix, NY 12087
www.apocryphilepress.com

Copyright © 2025 by Ian Macdonald
Printed in the United States of America
ISBN 978-1-965646-35-9 | paper
ISBN 978-1-965646-36-6 | ePub

No part of this book may be reproduced, stored in a retrieval system, or transmitted in any form or by any means—electronic, mechanical, photocopy, recording, or otherwise—without written permission of the author and publisher, except for brief quotations in printed reviews.

The author would like to thank Janeen Jones for her excellent editing.

Cover illustration and design by Jeff Kemhadjian.

Please join our mailing list at www.apocryphilepress.com/free. We'll keep you up-to-date on all our new releases, and we'll also send you a FREE BOOK. Visit us today!

CONTENTS

Acknowledgments	vii
Introduction	ix

1. Step One	1
2. Repeat	2
3. The Key to Love? Don't Be a Dick	4
4. Love	12
5. Repent	22
6. Stop, Drop, and Follow Me	29
7. The First True Crazy Thing Jesus Says	38
8. You Are the Flavor of the World	49
9. Shine On, You Crazy Diamond	59
10. Righteousness Straight Up Off the Charts	68
11. The Dude Abides	77
12. Seriously? Don't Be Anxious	85
13. Don't Give Me That Old Wine, I Want Something New	94
14. Living Water	102
15. The Smallest Act of Compassion Is the Best Kind of Welcome	109
16. Reconcile Now, Damn It!	117
17. Yes, You Have to Love All the Assholes, Too	125
18. The Kingdom of Heaven Is a Condiment	134
19. A Few More Thoughts on Seeds and God	142
20. You're Right, It's Not Fair Thanks To God	150
21. You Wanna Talk About Money? Listen to This Shit!	159
22. Pearls, Pigs, and Punk Rock	168
23. Wait—Hate Everything Important In Your Life?	177
24. Where's Your Faith, Dude?	184
25. I Have a Question	194
26. I Have Another Question	200
27. Love Is the Wood, the Nails, and the Flesh	205
28. Love Is the Key That Unlocks It All	215
29. Don't Make It So Hard	224

30. Now What?	232
31. One Last Thing	242
About the Author	243

For Kathleen, Fiona, Colleen, and Sean.

ACKNOWLEDGMENTS

I would like to thank everyone who supported me through this incredible journey. First, my mom and dad—who never flinched at my passions, no matter how wild, loud, or half-cocked they seemed. They never liked my music, but they loved me without condition—and in that love, they taught me how to do the same.

You're reading this book thanks in part to one of my most cherished friends, Janice Bussing, who coached and coaxed these words out of my deepest fears and insecurities. She has consistently pushed and supported me through some of the hardest trials of my life. Thank you for helping me find the strength, courage, and tools to turn my dream into reality.

These words are sharper and kinder thanks to Sara Lawson, the first brave soul to read the manuscript. She kindly wrangled typos and unruly footnotes into a cohesive whole, giving it the professional eye it desperately needed. And to Jeff Kemhadjian—my insanely talented art director and friend—who turned a half-baked cover idea into a stunning work of art.

I'm deeply grateful to my ministerial partners, friends, and colleagues who've widened my vision and understanding of God: Harold Anderson, Dawn Carlson, Tommy Givens, Tom Richard, Bob Walkup, and all my sisters and brothers in the National Association of Congregational Christian Churches.

I owe much of my creative outlook to the teachers who pushed me to see the world around me differently. To my grade school art teacher, Ms. Linda Knisley, who introduced me to Salvador Dalí and gave me permission to color outside the lines. And to the punk and poetic voices who shaped me—Joe Strummer, Exene Cervenka, Charles Bukowski—thank you for giving me language to howl at the moon, call out injustice, and scribble truth in my own crooked voice.

Then there is Kathleen—my beloved muse, my fiercest companion, the love of my life. You have stood beside me through cancer, career pivots, and everything in between. All the words in this book exist because you never let go of my hand and continue to show up everyday to teach me how to love the way Jesus loves.

And lastly, to Fiona, Colleen, and Sean—my co-conspirators in this life—whose stories run through these pages. Through each of you, I've learned that unconditional love isn't just an idea, it's flesh and blood, laughter and tears, late-night talks and everyday grace. This book belongs to you as much as it does to me. Thanks for making me the man I am today.

INTRODUCTION

In 1991, I moved into an apartment just half a block south of Sunset Boulevard in an eclectic neighborhood in the heart of Hollywood. Well, maybe not the actual heart—more like the clogged artery where guitar shops and tattoo parlors stood shoulder to shoulder with Russian bakeries and synagogues. Hasidic men in dark wool suits shuffled past heavy-metal-looking hookers in black patent leather. This was the Hollywood of contradictions and complexity. And I was right there in the middle of it all.

I moved into a one-bedroom apartment in a building that had been around since 1926. It had its share of secrets smudged into its nicotine-stained walls, each one holding stories of famous faces and forgotten souls. Rumor had it that Famous Amos, whose cookie would go on to change the world, lived in my apartment. The building was full of stories—some romantic, others tragic. By the time I arrived, musicians had taken over many of the apartments, including a band with one of the best names in rock 'n' roll history: *Pygmy Love Circus*.

None of the guys in this band were small by any account. Despite their rough, intimidating appearance, they were all surprisingly kind-hearted. They welcomed me into their world, and soon I became part of their circle—which meant invitations to their wild parties, where the nights blurred into mornings. Soon their friends became my friends, including Don, who I thought was their drug dealer. Turns out, he was just their roadie. I guess my assumption was a little correct.

One night, during one of their epic parties, Don approached me with a question that caught me off guard. I would have seen it coming had I remembered that he had recently gotten clean and was committed to turning his life around. He was beginning his journey through the Twelve Steps and was curious about something. For some reason, he thought I would be the one to help. With a little hesitation, Don asked, "Will you go to church with me?" And for some reason, I said yes.

Church was not a foreign place for me. Growing up, I had attended every Sunday. I had participated in youth group and Sunday school. I even had spent most of my childhood attending a deeply religious school. I had faith, but not the words to articulate it. I loved God but didn't know how to express it. And I was pretty sure I knew who Jesus was, even though I didn't really take the stuff he was saying very seriously. But at that point in my life, I couldn't remember the last time I had stepped into a church. I didn't know anyone who went to church. It seemed Don was in the same boat. His question surprised me, and yet, something inside me knew I couldn't back out. So I said yes.

The next morning, slightly hungover but determined, I got up and prepared for our outing. We planned to meet at 9:45, which seemed early enough for a Sunday, but as I stood outside waiting for Don, I couldn't help hoping he would bail on me. Maybe he'd forgotten or chickened out. Still, part of me wanted to go, just to see where this strange journey would lead.

I had walked the neighborhood enough to know that there were two churches nearby. One was two blocks north of our apartment. The other, two blocks to the east. That one had a rainbow flag outside its doors to let the world know it was inclusive to all.

At 9:55, Don pushed through the metal gate of our building, flustered and apologetic. Unwilling to try two new environments at one time, Don and I walked north toward St. Thomas the Apostle Episcopal Church, a beautiful stone structure sitting at the edge of the Hollywood Hills. The service started at 10:30, so we had time to observe the parishioners as they greeted each other with warmth and affection. I still had that gnawing question: Why had Don asked me to be his sidekick? So I straight up asked him, "Why me?"

I didn't think this was an outrageous question. I was not the poster child of Jesus. Nor was I a shining example of sainthood. My halo—if I ever had one—had been lost or left behind in some dark, dingy place. When Don invited me, God knows what was in my system. And only God and I knew all the shit I was doing when others weren't around. So why me? I didn't have to wonder long. Don, lighting a cigarette and glancing at me with a mix of uncertainty and hope, looked me in the eyes and simply said, "You're the only person I know who mentions God without following it up with 'damn.'" That was all he said. It was all either of us said. I stood there stunned as I watched him snuff out his cigarette and walk toward the door.

Who would have thought not saying "god damn" would get you an invitation to heaven? In that moment, I realized that when we show up for each other, God shows up for us in the most unexpected ways. I inhaled a deep, nervous breath. And I followed him in. As we entered the church, my life began to change. It would take years—decades actually—before I would realize that Don's invitation was God's invitation all along. That small voice within us all that whispers, "Come with me." An invitation Jesus extended to his followers: "Follow me and I will make you fishers of people" (Matt. 4:19).

This was some crazy shit to say even back then. But that's what Jesus does. He says shit that catches us off guard and gets us to respond in the most insane of ways. He corners us at the party and hits us with some crazy shit that only allows one of two responses. We can say no. Or we can drop our nets and follow him inside.

When I began a summer sermon series in 2024 entitled, *Shit Jesus Says*, I told those who were in attendance, "If this title offends you, then buckle up. Because the shit Jesus says is offensive. And if you aren't offended or challenged, then why bother?" Many people out there think they know Jesus. They speak about all his wonderful deeds and his amazing grace. They remark that he is the only one who can save you from the pit of eternal hell. I know this because that's what I was taught. Jesus, like God, is to be feared and adored at the same time. In what world does that make sense? Not in mine. And apparently, not in Don's.

That day, we took our first steps into St. Thomas. And I would come to discover a God and Savior who said and did some offensive shit. Like loving the unlovable. Forgiving the unforgiveable. Bringing good news to the poor. Releasing folks from the prisons they've put themselves into. And giving sight to those blinded by their own prejudices, anger, racism, sexism, and all the other shit we do that harms others. Jesus is more than just someone who offends, shocks, or upsets the apple carts of society. He also opens the doors of our hearts and minds and invites us to come with him to see heaven. And his words teach us how to live in this heaven right now.

My favorite 13th-century German mystic Meister Eckhart taught, "There is no need to look for God here or there. He is no further away than the door of your own heart."[*] As Don helped me realize, our hearts can tell an amazing story. Every broken heart, kind heart, gentle, hard, or hardened heart offers a testimony to the world—just as every plant and sunset and speck of sand can express God's love for you. Sometimes the greatest and truest form of worship we can offer to God isn't stepping into a church, but being the visible and tangible expression of God's love and grace in the wilderness we call the world.

The gospels give us numerous examples of how Jesus embodies God's love in all the ways he responds to human need. Stories of healing, forgiving, feeding, and of course, sacrifice—putting others' needs before his own. In Jesus, the word of God truly becomes flesh and blood. He meets us where we are. And brings us back to where we

---

[*] Meister Eckhart, *Selected Writings*, translated and edited by Oliver Davies (London: Penguin Classics, 1994), 199.

need to be. In him and through him, the will of God is proclaimed perfectly. No one is left out.

But I am not convinced that human beings, especially those who claim to follow Jesus, have even come close to trying what is being asked of us. There have been some wonderful people and movements for sure. But Christianity as a whole—I believe—has failed. We need another big Jesus movement. A revolution from our apathy. A kick in the ass that wakes us up and sends us out there.

Imagine if we actually believed this shit Jesus says and applied it to our lives? From the biggest moment to the most mundane, the world would be a much different place if we only took the steps to accept his invitation and go with him—to embrace his way and truly follow him. This could be a transformative movement.

As Jesus pointed out to those who questioned his intentions, it's not enough to honor God with our lips. Our words will fall on deaf ears if we refuse to also honor God with our hearts and hands. True worship—that which is truly pleasing to God—is manifesting God's glory in all that we do. We see this throughout creation. The psalmist writes, "The heavens are telling the glory of God; the firmament proclaims God's handiwork. Day to day pours forth speech, and night to night declares knowledge. There is no speech, nor are there words; their voice is not heard; yet their voice goes out throughout all the earth, their words to the end of the world" (Ps. 19:1–4). And in his letter to the church in Rome, Paul says, "Ever since the creation of the world his eternal power and divine nature, invisible though they are, have been understood and seen through the things he has made" (Rom 1:20). Eckhart echoed the Apostle's sentiment. "A person who knew nothing but creatures would never need to attend any sermons, for every creature is full of God. A book of their own."[*]

Just as we are a reflection of God's glory, we are also an invitation to God's love. The author of the Gospel of John describes Jesus as

---

[*] Meister Eckhart, *Sermon 9*, in *Meister Eckhart: The Essential Sermons, Commentaries, Treatises, and Defense*, translated and introduced by Edmund Colledge and Bernard McGinn (New York: Paulist Press, 1981), 178.

"The Word of God." He uses the Greek word *logos*, which derives from the verb *lego* which means "to say, count, or gather." John uses *logos* to describe Jesus as the living, eternal, divine word of God. His wisdom, reason, and purpose are fully embodied in the Christ—the full expression of God's love made visible in human form. John believes Jesus lives his life as the purest expression of God's love. And as such, he is the exact representation of God's character, which is love.

We can debate until the end of time whether or not Jesus is "The Christ"—the long, awaited Messiah who came to rescue the Israelites from their troubles. But if we believe the shit Jesus says to be true, then the gospel stories make this pretty clear: the way Jesus lives and what he teaches says something profound. I would argue that his entire life is a living testimony to God's greatness and glory.

Those who followed him, who took his words to heart and lived them out as he did, experience true transformation. Katie Hines-Shah argues, "The living word is not just text but must be embodied, meeting God's people today in their deepest need. Our hands belong not over our hearts but at work for our neighbor, if we would have the word take flesh in us."[*] This is exactly what Jesus did as the living and divine embodiment of God's love. When he says, "Come with me," he is not asking us to go to church—he is inviting us to be the Church: to be his body and his love in ways that allow others to see God's love in the flesh.

You might not see yourself as a holy book. I certainly didn't. But my neighbor Don helped me to realize that my words might be the only bible someone reads. And my willingness and friendship might be the only way someone encounters God and discovers their true worth. There will be Dons in all of our lives, people hungering and searching for something greater than the world can offer. You might be that person yourself. Or you might be someone who grew up with faith, but for one good reason or another walked away from it—like I

---

[*] Katie Hines-Shah, "Living By The Word: January 23, Third Sunday after the Epiphany," *Christian Century* 139, no. 1 (January 12, 2022).

did. Whoever you are, and whatever you are looking for, Jesus has something to say to guide your way.

I once read this, written on the outside of an old, weathered church: "Wherever there is life, there is God." And as Jesus showed us with his own life, wherever God is, there is love. So whenever or wherever we gather in love, people get a chance to meet God in the flesh. Our flesh. Our words. Our deeds.

In all the beautiful shit he teaches us, Jesus gives us the words we need to inspire the world to love. His words show us how to create a way of life that transforms the hearts and minds of those around us. His words help us turn the world on its head. His words aren't simply about being happy—they're transformative. Not about finding prosperity, but something greater. The kind of abundance you can't possibly put a price on—love, joy, peace, hope.

If that sounds like some good shit to you, do yourself a favor and read on.

1
STEP ONE

Love. That's it.

2

REPEAT

*"This is the new commandment that I give to you,
that you love one another as I have loved you."*
—John 13:34

Go back a page and reread chapter one until you've committed the entire thing to memory. Chant it like a mantra. Practice it like a drug addiction. Stich it in needlepoint. Tattoo it on your heart. Spray paint it on your brain. Make it a part of every breath you inhale, and I guarantee that it will also be in every breath you exhale. That is how love works. It's that simple. It's that hard.

A good thing to keep in mind is that if this is as far as you read, you will still know everything you need to know to take Jesus' shit seriously. In fact, I will dare you not to read any further until you can honestly say you've got the entire first step memorized.

What's that first step? Love. The second step? Love.

Know it. Memorize it. Live it as if it's the only thing that keeps you alive. Love is life. It is the key that unlocks heaven. Love is heaven. I am not talking about some celestial cloud we are flown to when we die. I am talking about here. Earth. North America. Central Asia. Scotland. Greenland. Poland. Moscow. Vancouver. Pittsburg. A Masai village in Tanzania. A ghetto in São Paulo. The red-light district in Phuket. A house in suburban Los Angeles. Heaven is in you. Heaven is in me.

There is no place that is not God-created, God-blessed, and God-loved. Every space. Every nook and cranny. Everything is a vessel for God's love, to be held or shared. Jesus has ushered in heaven here. And he gives us a foretaste of heaven to come. But he also says not everyone who calls 'Lord, Lord' will be saved (Matt. 7:21).

Yes, you read that right. Those aren't my words—they're Jesus' words. He says shit to get our attention and to get us to put our focus on where it needs to be. And where is that? Out there in the world. Inside your heart. And everywhere in between. Love is needed everywhere. So before you go any further, commit these two steps to memory.

Step One: Love.
Step Two: Repeat.

3

THE KEY TO LOVE? DON'T BE A DICK

*"Do not judge, or you too will be judged.
For in the same way you judge others,
you will be judged, and with the measure
you use, it will be measured to you."*
—Matthew 7:1–2

Would you agree that the opposite of love is hate? If so, then you probably also know it's a little more complicated than that. I can hate mayonnaise, which I really do, but that doesn't mean I can't appreciate it for the condiment that it is. In the same way, I don't like it when someone just assumes I want it on a sandwich. But I don't despise someone who slathers it on their sandwich. I mean, I *do* quietly judge them—it's gross—but that's on me. And here's the thing: that judgment is what I need to work on. The antidote? Acceptance.

It's easy enough to accept someone's decision to spread a glob of gross and disgusting mayo on a perfectly well constructed ham on rye. It gets harder, however, when it comes down to more personal issues like politics or religion. Jesus made it very clear when he said, "Don't be a dick about it." Actually, it was this guy Matt who said that.

He's not nearly as eloquent as Jesus, but he gets the point across. "Don't be a dick, and people won't dick you around."

The law of attraction suggests that if you show kindness you will attract kindness. Or if you are constantly judging others, you will attract judgment on yourself. So don't be a dick. Learn to see people for who they are, even the ones you'd rather write off. That's how love starts—by refusing to build walls between yourself and others.

I think the same holds true with judging others. Do not seek to find fault in others. Instead, seek the opposite. Seek what is good about them. Going back to the mayonnaise example—mayonnaise is a condiment that adds moisture to an otherwise dry sandwich. Some would argue that its flavor complements the ingredients, like the meat and cheese and vegetables. Its texture provides a smooth contrast to the crunch of lettuce and the chewiness of the bread. I have often used mayonnaise as part of the base for something else. So even though I try to avoid it because I don't like its smell, I can find a good reason to keep a jar in my fridge. Again, this is easy to realize when we're considering something inanimate and mundane. But it's not so easy when it comes to people. Or their political preferences.

I think both Matt and Jesus would agree: this is where it is hard not to be a bit judgmental. It's baked into our DNA. Humans use judgment to navigate relationships and understand behaviors. But Jesus isn't calling us to stop making decisions. He's asking us to stop being hypocrites. You know, the whole speck-and-log-in-the-eye thing. You can't help someone see clearly when you're blinded by your own mess. The absurdity of the image underscores the importance of self-awareness: remove your own flaws before pointing out the flaws in others. Jesus doesn't prohibit addressing others' faults, but he insists we do so humbly and with love.

One does not need to look very far to see how hypocrisy has become the norm. In every political season, raincoat sales go up because of all the mudslinging. Politicians love pointing out every flaw and failure of their opponent while conveniently ignoring their own.

In our culture, judgment and hypocrisy are running rampant not just in politics but in religious circles as well. When a culture is obsessed with morally superiority, it's easy to be critical of others. But Jesus calls us to a different standard—a life of humility, self-reflection, and grace. Although it would have been just as easy for him to say, "Don't be a dick," Jesus opted to speak a little more eloquently: "Don't judge, or you will be judged" (Matt. 7:1). It's such a good saying that my dear friend Dawn likes to say, "That needs to be stitched on a tea towel."

Even though Jesus is pretty direct, it's easy for us to ignore his words. And then we risk falling into the same hypocrisy trap as those who tried to entrap Jesus. He criticizes the political and religious leaders of his day for focusing on trivial rules while neglecting justice, mercy, and faithfulness (cf. Matthew 23:13–36). He calls them "blind guides"—people who are quick to enforce the rules on others but slow to look at their own hearts. Today, Jesus might say something like, "Woe to you, senators and sly foxes, who criticize others for not securing borders but refuse to pass the necessary legislation to do so." Or perhaps a little closer to home, "Woe to you who preach against homosexuality while secretly hiding your own dark secret in the closet." Ouch.

We cannot escape life without making critical judgment calls. But we can critique others without condemning ourselves. It begins by acknowledging the huge plank protruding from our own eye before we point out the tiny speck of sawdust from someone else's eye. Again, the absurdity of the image teaches this: you can't help others see clearly if you can't see your own faults. Jesus isn't telling us not to help others with their specks, just address your own "planks" first. Be humble and self-aware, recognizing your own imperfections before judging others. This is a great way not to be a hypocritical dick but to show God's love to someone in need of it.

There's a big difference between Republicans and Democrats when it comes to helping single mothers who rely on welfare programs to care for their children. One side says they shouldn't have babies if they can't afford them. Then it passes laws prohibiting them from terminating unwanted pregnancies. The other side isn't much better by emphasizing bodily autonomy while mandating public health policies. Both sides love to point out the sawdust—without acknowledging the two-by-four protruding from their eyes.

The brilliant Swiss psychiatrist Carl Jung said, "Everything that irritates us about others can lead us to an understanding of ourselves."* Jesus invites us to look within ourselves—at the space between our head and heart where our words and deeds are born. If we take the time to do some honest self-examination, we can change the way we see the world, viewing it through the lens of a compassionate heart rather than one that condemns. Such a heart reminds us that we are all in need of grace and love—essential nutrients for our spiritual health. Renowned German theologian Dietrich Bonhoeffer reminds us, "When I judge, I am blind to my own evil and to the grace granted to the other person."†

You see, Jesus says this shit not to offend us, but to awaken our hearts and minds to the kingdom of heaven that he is ushering in. This kingdom is for everyone. All are welcome. But we must understand that we are worth no more and no less than anyone else. We all have planks. We all have sawdust. Like Paul pointed out in Romans, "We all fall short of the glory of God" (Rom. 3:23). We all need God's love and grace—no matter how big or small our need is.

Our spiritual journey is not a competition; it's about walking together toward God's steadfast love. No one is morally or spiritually better than anyone else on this path. Each of us must look within ourselves before we look at another person with contempt. For it's in our removing of the plank that we clear our vision and change our perspective. Instead of seeing others as objects of judgment, we can see them as God sees us—beloved children made from love for the purpose of love. When we see and understand others this clearly, we become more generous with our love, mercy, and grace. But first, we must learn to see beyond the kind of thinking that separates people

---

* Carl Jung, *Memories, Dreams, Reflections*, ed. Aniela Jaffé, trans. Richard and Clara Winston (New York: Vintage Books, 1965), 247.
† Dietrich Bonhoeffer, *Ethics*, ed. Clifford J. Green, trans. Reinhard Krauss, Charles C. West, and Douglas W. Stott (Minneapolis: Fortress Press, 2005), 146.

into "good or bad" and "right or wrong." We must remove the blinders from our eyes so we can see the divine presence in everyone.

Hebrew scriptures teach us that we are all made in the divine image of God. We all draw from the same source for our nutrients. Any part of us that doesn't produce the fruit of God's love must be removed—starting with that giant, protruding plank. When we see ourselves and others as part of a larger, unified whole, we can move beyond our rigid divisions toward true compassion and understanding. We can become people who stand for peace and justice for all.

Jesus spoke to the folks who would become the Church. But that could be any one of us. He knows that moral superiority is toxic to any community and that hypocrisy will only pollute this sacred space. By helping us to recognize our shared humanity and brokenness, Jesus levels the playing field, allowing us to approach correction with a humble heart of love rather than a smug soul of condemnation.

My mother is a wonderful, kind woman. For most of my life, she's opened her home for countless church potlucks, garden club events, and New Year's Day parties, always preparing many delicious foods for everyone to enjoy. Up until recently, my mother has been a terrific cook—and an even greater critic of those who bring dishes to her parties. She is known to have pointed out when someone else's casserole was overcooked, even though hers was a little too salty. The judgmental critique doesn't fix the casserole or improve her own dish. But it might be the reason she isn't always invited to other people's parties. Jesus calls us to approach others not with condemnation but with humility and love, knowing that we all contribute imperfectly to the "potluck" of community.

In his book, *A Community of Character*, Stanley Hauerwas reminds us that "The church is the body of Christ, constituted by practices that form people who can recognize their need for forgiveness and, therefore, are able to forgive others."[*] To take Jesus at his word is to

---

[*] Stanley Hauerwas, *A Community of Character: Toward a Constructive Christian Social Ethic* (Notre Dame, IN: University of Notre Dame Press, 1981), 101.

reflect his love and grace in every situation. Such a posture deepens our relationship with God and others, instead of pushing them both away. Jesus was pretty damn clear about this when he said, "Love one another as I have loved you" (John 13:34). He isn't saying you should overlook someone's faults or sins. He just says remove the blinders from your eyes and heart, so you can see people the way he sees them and love and forgive them like he does.

This is the kind of shit Jesus says to inspire us to actually love both our neighbor and ourselves (Mark 12:31). He shows us how to do it, so we will mirror his mercy and reflect his grace in ways that exemplify his call to "Forgive and you will be forgiven" (Luke 6:37). Jesus calls us to live a life that reflects his life and teachings. This begins by cultivating a heart of love, by striving to love our neighbors as ourselves. Regardless of how they cook their casseroles or who they vote for, Jesus tells us to love them. In fact, he tells us to love everyone. Love is the way we can extend forgiveness even to our enemies. Jesus invites us to embrace a Christ-centered, nonjudgmental mindset—one that is grounded in the practice of love. This entails learning how to love and forgive others as much as we love ourselves and forgive our own wrongs and shortcomings.

Forgiveness is central to this path—freely forgiving others for their wrongs, no matter the magnitude, forgiving ourselves for our own mistakes, and seeking reconciliation with those we have hurt or who have hurt us. Developing empathy allows us to see others as we see ourselves and to understand that everyone carries their own struggles and perspectives. By putting ourselves in another's shoes, we can respond with compassion and kindness, instead of judgment and hatred.

Jesus' teachings on love and forgiveness challenge us to transcend the divisions and conflicts of modern life, calling for compassion, empathy, and reconciliation. But he's not alone. The ancient wisdom traditions echo this truth. *Wuwei* or "effortless action" is a Taoist ideal that encourages us to live in harmony with the natural flow of life. Such an approach prevents us from imposing our own rigid judgments on a world already brimming with God's presence. It's about letting go and allowing love and grace to organically work their way in.

Jesus knows that judgment is the poison that hardens our hearts, building walls where bridges should be. But when we begin to glimpse the interconnectedness of it all—the way one soul's sorrow mirrors another's—compassion becomes not only possible, but inevitable. It's a recognition of the divine image in every face, even the ones we've been taught to fear. This nonjudgmental love isn't some airy ideal. It's the very heart of the Gospel, the invitation to participate in the divine life, to dwell in the unity that is God's dream for the world.

Jesus says and does a lot of things worthy of being stitched onto a tea towel, most of which could be summed up with this saying: "Do to others what you would have them do to you" (Matt. 7:12). Be a lover, not a dick. Show people kindness, and you will find kindness. Welcome people with open arms, no matter who they are, who they love, or how well they cook. And you will be welcomed.

Henri Nouwen, a Dutch Catholic priest and prolific author, reminded us that "Those you have deeply loved become part of you."[*] Since there will always be people to love, we will always have one another as part of who we are. As the inner community of our heart becomes wider, "the more easily you will recognize your own brothers and sisters in the strangers around you."[†]

To paraphrase Bonhoeffer, Jesus has set out to create a community of the heart—a place where love is abundant, grace is offered freely, and judgment is tempered by humility. Instead of criticizing others, let us look inward, asking God to reveal our planks. Instead of calling out one another's faults, let us examine our own lives first to ensure we are living out God's will for us with integrity.[‡]

Jesus says, "The measure you give is the measure you will receive"

---

[*] Henri J.M. Nouwen, *You Are the Beloved: Daily Meditations for Spiritual Living* (New York: Convergent, 2017), 68.
[†] Nouwen, *You Are the Beloved*.
[‡] Dietrich Bonhoeffer, *Life Together: The Classic Exploration of Faith in Community* (New York: Harper & Row, 1954), 91-93.

(Matt. 7:2). Some call this karma, the principle that what goes around comes around. But it reminds me to be mindful of what God continues to do in my life so that I can be generous with my love and abundant with my grace. It is just one of the many ways we can embody Christ's compassion and help others to feel God's love. Jesus reminds us, "The eye is the lamp of the body. If your eyes are good, your whole body will be full of light" (Matt. 6:22).

Our eyes reflect and reveal our truth, especially the ways we see those who are in need. Just as "healthy" eyes see with purity, hypocrisy blinds us spiritually. Jesus uses another crazy illustration to drive this point home, saying, "If your eye causes you to stumble, it should be cut out and thrown into the fire" (Matt. 5:29). But before things get that drastic, maybe we should just remove the planks from our own eyes so we can see more clearly the way of the one who says, "Blessed are those who are *not dicks to others*, for they will see God" (Matt. 5:8).

4

LOVE

*"But I say to you, love your enemies
and pray for those who hate you."*
—Matthew 5:44

I love my mom.
I love my dad.
I love my wife.
I love my kids.
I love my dog
(and all the dogs and cats and tortoises and pets I've ever had).
I love my sisters.
I love my brother.
I love my mother in-law,
sisters-in-law, and brothers-in-law.
I love my nieces and nephews.
I love my cousins.
I love my second cousins.
I love my cousins who are once and twice removed.
I love my friends.
I love my church.

I love trees that grow fruit for me to eat.
I love pizza, donuts, tacos, fried egg sandwiches,
pancakes, cupcakes, pretty much most cakes,
single malt Scotch whisky, and margaritas—to name a few.
I love coffee.
I love a good comedy.
I love to laugh.
I love to cry.
I love to sit in silence and be in the middle of chaos.
I love massages.
I love the ocean.
I love the beach.
I love road trips and seeing new places.
I love meeting new people and seeing old friends.
I love listening to good music and seeing good bands.
I love playing guitar.
I love being around others who play guitar better than me.
I love the sound of my wife's voice when she sings.
I love learning new things.
I love eating new things.
I love the unexpected.
I love watching basketball.
I love Kobe. I love the Lakers.
I love riding my bike.
I love working in the yard.
I love sharing what I've learned with others.
I love learning from others.
I love the sound of babies babbling.
I love climbing into a bed with clean, warm sheets fresh out of the dryer.
I love the rain.
I love the wind.
I love the sun.
I love night.
I love God.

CHAPTER 4

I love you.

But my enemy?

Why do I have to love the jerk who wants to hurt me or take away the rights of my children?

It seems okay for me to not love things like injustice or criminal activity. But you are telling me I have to love the one who causes it? Jesus, that's some crazy shit.

I do not love weeds. I don't love insomnia. Or dog hair stuck to my socks. And I definitely do not love hatred or bigotry, violence or fear-mongering. But the violent person (or organization) in charge of spewing hatred, bigotry, and fear? I'm working on it.

It's hard to read the sayings of Jesus and find a command to hate someone. It's hard because that particular command is nowhere to be found. But there are some who find a way to work it into his story. Jesus says some wild things, but it's never hate. It's always love. That doesn't sound too crazy to me. We all want to experience the comfort and joy of love. There is a natural longing within us all that seeks relationship and companionship—whether sexual, fraternal, or familial. Even God wants it. Maybe not the sexual part, but if scripture is to be trusted, then God most certainly wants our companionship. And experiencing that kind of connection is a bit more complicated than swiping left on a dating app.

When Jesus says, "Love one another," it's not exactly a Hallmark moment. And it should make us squirm a bit. Because Jesus doesn't tack on a comforting qualifier like, "Love the ones who are easy to love." No. He throws down the gauntlet and asks us to love everyone —especially the ones we'd rather not. The people we label, dismiss, or even despise. That's where Jesus goes. But are we willing to follow?

Let's be honest: loving the easy stuff is, to state the obvious, easy. When something brings you joy, your heart is quick to respond. That first bite of perfectly grilled salmon? Love. Watching snow gently fall on a forest as leaves cling to their last bit of color? Love. The first time you lock eyes with the person who will become your spouse? That's love too—the kind that makes your heart leap without any effort at all. Loving the beautiful, the joyous, the good—these moments feel like grace made tangible. And if we could live in those moments forever, we'd probably never blink for fear of missing the beauty.

But Jesus doesn't let us stay there. He's not interested in the kind of love that makes us feel cozy and unchallenged. He's after something bigger, something deeper. He talks about love with wild abandon: "Love God. Love your neighbor. Love your friends." Then comes the curveball. "Love your enemies and pray for those who persecute you, that you may be children of your Father in heaven" (Matt. 5:43–44). He's not playing around.

It gets even harder when Jesus reminds us why. Again, stating the obvious, it's because God loves everyone—the whole lot of us. That includes the people we wish God didn't love. The coworker who drives you up the wall? God loves them. The neighbor who never waves back? God loves them too. The politicians who make your blood boil and the folks cheering them on? God loves them. The bully, the liar, the criminal, the grumpy DMV clerk—all of them are drenched in God's love. Jesus says it plainly. "God makes the sun rise on the evil and the good and sends rain on the righteous and the unrighteous" (Matt. 5:45). Like it or not, God's love doesn't discriminate. And there isn't a damn thing we can do to change that.

But maybe—just maybe—that's the best news of all. Because it tears down the walls we are all so good at building, the ones that divide "us" from "them." God's love isn't transactional or dualistic. It's not some cosmic reward system for good behavior. It's just love, unrelenting, all-encompassing love. It's all or nothing. Either God loves or God doesn't love. And that's where Jesus keeps pushing us—to love like that.

Of course, that's easier said than done. Loving someone who loves you back? Piece of cake. Loving someone who hurt you, betrayed you, or flat-out hates you? That's where the rubber meets the road. And you can bet that's the kind of love Jesus is most interested in. The kind that breaks your heart open and transforms you in the process. The kind that makes you more human, more like him.

CHAPTER 4

"If you love those who love you, what reward do you have? Do not even tax collectors do the same? And if you greet only your brothers and sisters, what more are you doing than others? Do not even the Gentiles do the same?" (Matt. 5:46–47)

My son loves tennis. And I love watching him love it. There's something about his joy on the court that fills me up. One of the things I find fascinating about tennis is that the court is this meticulously measured space—36 feet wide, 78 feet long, split neatly down the middle by a thin net. It's designed for competition: one side against the other. That's the game. But here's the thing—too many of us think God operates the same way. We picture God on one side of the net, picking favorites, while the rest of us scramble to make sure we're on the right team.

But Jesus tells us again and again that God doesn't play that game. God doesn't choose sides. The sun shines on everyone. The rain falls on all of us. God's love is bigger than our little nets and divisions. So then, why do we keep putting up barriers?

We like our sides. They make us feel safe, even when they leave us isolated. We live in a world obsessed with boundaries—us versus them, left versus right, good guys versus bad guys. Somehow, we've managed to create a Christian tradition that doesn't take Jesus' words seriously. We've built walls, not bridges. Instead of allowing us the freedom to experience life to the fullest, these boundaries and barriers we create are limiting. They limit our movement. They limit our experiences. They limit our joy. They limit our love. The great irony of Christianity these days is how we imprison ourselves instead of enjoying the freedom and liberation God wishes us to experience.

Richard Rohr reminds us that in the early church, Christians were the underdogs—the powerless and the oppressed. They heard Jesus' teachings as pure liberation. He writes, "In the first two centuries, the church was identified by and large with the underclass, the poor and enslaved members of the Roman Empire." Living under violent oppression, "they had no trouble hearing what Jesus had to say as good news."* But then came Constantine, and suddenly Christianity became the empire. The powerless took the reins of power and instead of reflecting God's love, we started drawing lines—heaven over here, earth over there; us over here, them over there. Game. Set. Match.

It's no wonder we struggle to understand the shit Jesus says like, "Be perfect, therefore, as your heavenly Father is perfect" (Matt. 5:48). Come on, man. Who can pull that off?

I always know I'm dreaming when—in the middle of my dream—I see myself in a mirror. The excitement of seeing myself with a perfectly quaffed head of thick dark hair always jolts me awake, where I am still perfectly bald. Why do I need perfect hair—or a perfect body for that matter—to be perfect? Does a perfect nose, or perfect abs, really lead to a perfect life? And who decides what's perfect? Isn't it subjective?

When Jesus calls us to be perfect, I don't think he is talking about the perfection of flawlessness. He's talking about the perfection of love. And this isn't just any love, but God's perfect love. To be perfect like God is perfect means loving like God loves—without conditions and without keeping score.

It means loving the people who annoy us, betray us, hurt us. Jesus says, "Love your enemies, do good, and lend, expecting nothing in return. Your reward will be great, and you will be children of the Most High, who is kind to the ungrateful and the wicked" (Luke 6:35). That's the kind of love that changes everything.

The problem is, we like to put conditions on love. We keep believing there's a net between us and them, a scoreboard to keep track of who's winning. But God doesn't see sides. God doesn't keep scorecards. God only loves.

I saw this quote by Edwin Bliss on a poster in a coworker's office. It read, "The pursuit of excellence is gratifying and healthy. But the

---

* Richard Rohr, "The Non-Violent Manifesto of Jesus," *Another Name for Every Thing with Richard Rohr*, podcast audio, February 23, 2020, accessed November 4, 2022, https://cac.org/podcasts/the-non-violent-manifesto-of-jesus/.

pursuit of perfection is frustrating, neurotic, and a terrible waste of time." It reminds me of the classic joke about the perfectionist who walks into a bar only to immediately turn around and leave because the bar wasn't set high enough.

Jesus tells us to be like God with our love. He says, "Love one another as I love you" (John 13:34). And "Be merciful, just as God is merciful to you" (Luke 6:36). Do that when it's hard. Even to the asshole who annoys you and makes you angry. If you're only nice to those who love you, what good is that kindness? Jesus says, "If you lend to those from whom you hope to receive, what credit is that to you?" (Luke 6:32). He goes on to say, "Love your enemies, do good, and lend, expecting nothing in return. Your reward will be great, and you will be children of the Most High who is kind to the ungrateful and the wicked" (Luke 6:35). This is a bar set high enough for the perfectionist, and yet this heavenly standard is attainable to all. If God offers us endless grace, then we should do the same for one another. If God refuses to put up a wall to divide us, we must also refuse to put up a wall dividing ourselves from God or one another. In fact, the only net God puts between us is a safety net that doesn't let anyone slip through.

I think we make Jesus' words difficult because we don't trust him enough to believe he means what he says. We squirm, we theologize, we argue—but what if we simply took him at his word? What if we approached life with the humility of Christ instead of our incessant need to be right? What if we stopped acting like we're the only ones God loves, the only ones going to heaven? That's the very notion Jesus always shatters.

Jesus invites us to take a deeper look at our own hearts. He invites us to open our eyes wide and see others with compassion instead of contempt. His way tears down the walls and erases the lines we have drawn between ourselves and everyone else. This is what it means to love like God loves. Perfect isn't about our flawlessness—it's about giving our hearts away the way God does every single day. It's about being generous with our grace, our time, and our resources. It's about dropping our judgments and choosing, instead, to love. Everyone. As

Rohr so powerfully put it, "There's no hope for the world if religion remains infantile and incapable of love."*

Jesus doesn't hand us a checklist or a rule book. He doesn't ask us to be the perfect spouse or the perfect parent. Instead, he reveals a way to live perfectly in sync with God's nature—a way of forgiveness, non-retaliation, kindness, and radical love. He calls us to be the kind of community where hatred is met with tenderness, offenses are answered with grace, and everyone's needs are met because no one is left out. This is the way God's kingdom comes—by God's will being done. God's will is simply and undeniably love.

Every word Jesus speaks and every action he takes gives us a glimpse into the heart of God, a heart that doesn't keep score, doesn't compare, and doesn't take sides—a heart that is "kind to the ungrateful and the wicked" (Luke 6:35). God showers us with abundant grace, mercy, and protection—and Jesus knows we can do the same for others. Jesus didn't merely flip tables in the temple; he flipped the entire world on its head. He introduced new paradigms and a new way of being. And he's our proof that, out of great love for us, God comes to us, endures the worst we can throw at him, and then rises to forgive us.

Jesus has entrusted this upside-down kingdom to us—imperfect, messy, inconsistent us. He believes in us. Why? Because he knows we're not the ones doing the heavy lifting—God is. To be perfect as God is perfect means allowing God's love to flow in and out of us, no blockages, no barriers.

Imagine how different the world could look—how different you and I would look—if we let God's love flow through us to everyone we meet. Jesus expands the law not to burden us but to free us, so we can mirror God's love in the way we live. Anyone who's experienced God's forgiveness can forgive others. Anyone who's received God's generosity can give without hesitation. Anyone who's known God's love can love their enemies.

Every time Jesus acts, he gives birth to the kingdom of heaven.

---

* Rohr, "The Non-Violent Manifesto of Jesus."

With every act of compassion, he shows us God's vision for a world ruled by genuine, unconditional love. And he believes we can do the same.

The Bible never says Jesus was the perfect son or a stellar carpenter. But it does tell us he perfectly embodied God's love. Every moment of his life was a living, breathing testament to that love. To follow him is to let God come alive in us. It's not impossible or even as hard as we make it out to be. We all love at least one thing. I love my family, even with all their imperfections. I'm sure you love someone or something as well. Now take that love a little further and expand it to your friendships. It's not that hard. Push it a little further—to the folks you work with or go to school with. Then a little further—to the person next door who plays their music way too loud and way too late.

I used to live in this apartment complex where the only thing separating me from my neighbors was a skinny little driveway. My windows faced an apartment that housed a guy who didn't need a microphone to make his point. His voice wasn't just loud, it was angry. Even with the windows closed, I knew *everything* about this guy's life—his grievances, his arguments, his frustrations. Meanwhile, he knew absolutely nothing about me…or the slow-burning anger growing in my heart.

One day, his phone rang. Of course, he answered it in that same booming voice, but this time, something was different. His words cracked under the weight of grief, and suddenly, this man who I'd only known as a loud, angry presence became something else entirely. Through his tears, I listened as he told someone—his brother, maybe—that his mom had passed away. He broke the news again and again, calling others in his family.

Sitting on the other side of the driveway, something shifted in me. All that anger I'd allowed to fester just dissolved and compassion took its place. This man, whose life had been nothing but an irritation to me, became a human with a pain I could suddenly feel in my own chest. Love your enemy. Pray for those who you despise.

Jesus doesn't say love the lovable only. He calls us to love the loud ones, the angry ones, the difficult ones. He calls us to lean into their humanity instead of our judgment. Let compassion have the final word. When we love our neighbors like God loves us, love is perfected in us. When we prioritize others' needs over our own, love is perfected in us. When we let go of anger and choose peace instead of retaliation, love is perfected in us. When we love like this—when we allow God's love to flow perfectly through us—the world starts to change. Families heal. Communities flourish. Divisions dissolve. And our world starts to look a whole lot more like the heaven Jesus has invited us into.

5
REPENT

"Repent, the kingdom of heaven has come to you."
—Matthew 4:17

Why Jesus? Why follow his way? Why take seriously all the wild, upside-down things he says? Well, I guess that depends on who you ask. Some folks might say, "Because only Jesus can save you from eternal damnation." And sure, if that's true, who wouldn't want to play it safe? But fear as a motivator has a way of leaving people stuck —trapped in a story about punishment instead of freedom, a story about sin instead of grace. And Jesus? Jesus isn't about trapping anyone. He's all about setting people free.

So why do I listen to Jesus? Why do I follow him? I guess my answer is pretty simple: why not? If he saves me from some eternal inferno, great. If not, the way he calls us to live, the hope he offers, and the liberation he embodies still beats any other way I've been told to live. Jesus doesn't lead with fear; he leads with kindness. He doesn't pile on rules and expectations; he invites us to lay our burdens down. He saves us from our shame, our smallness, and our certainty that we're unworthy of love.

Jesus shows us what it looks like to live wholeheartedly with arms wide open, to meet and to claim the divine DNA woven into each of us. He says, "My way is easy. My burden is light" (Matt. 11:30). Of course, this "easy" way of his is not without a cost. Jesus wasn't big on toeing the party line—much less sticking to the script. He didn't always color inside the lines. He spoke his truth. He walked his walk. There are so many stories of Jesus loving the people that no one else would touch. Forgiving them of unforgivable offensives. And defying every system that tried to box him in. That's the deal with Jesus: he's not here to play nice—he's here to turn the world on its head. That's what got him in trouble…and what eventually led to his death.

In 1997, Apple computers launched one of the greatest advertising campaigns of all time. It featured portraits of Einstein, Gandhi, and Martin Luther King Jr. to set their company apart. Each ad began like this: "Here's to the crazy ones. The misfits. The rebels. The troublemakers." These ads celebrated people who dared to see the world differently, who pushed the human race forward simply because they were crazy enough to believe they could. That's how I see Jesus. The original rebel. The ultimate misfit. The one who refused to conform to the status quo. He's the square peg the world tried to cram into a round hole. And when I hear his words, I can't help but lean in, because I know—deep in my bones—that he's onto something.

The ad concludes, "You can quote them, disagree with them, glorify, or vilify them. About the only thing you can't do is ignore them." Call me crazy, but the shit Jesus says is revolutionary. And we ought to pay close attention to every word and syllable. "Because," as the ad reminds us, "the people who are crazy enough to think they can change the world are the ones who do." Jesus thinks different. He acts different. He loves different. That's why I follow him.

Jesus says the kinds of things that make you stop and question everything you thought you knew: "Love your enemy." "Turn the other cheek." "Eat my flesh and drink my blood." He's not pulling any punches. He wants us to think differently, to live differently, and to love in ways that terrify the world. Because loving like that? It disrupts. It heals. It changes everything.

CHAPTER 5

"Repent, the kingdom of heaven has come to you" (Matt. 4:17).

The way of Jesus isn't easy in the sense of being comfortable, but it's easy in the sense of being real—it's aligned with who we were created to be. Jesus calls us into a way of living that cracks us open, freeing us to love as wildly and recklessly as God does. And yeah, it's crazy. But maybe, just maybe, that's the point. To make us crazy enough to push against the way of the world. Because following his way can revolutionize the world.

Jesus has this way of saying things that snaps us out of our haze and shakes our complacency. Like a cold splash of water on our faces. But he's not saying all this stuff to shock us. Jesus isn't some kind of celebrity influencer constantly chasing after reactions for ratings. He's the beloved Son of God. His goal is not to shock but to awaken. His ministry aim is to change and transform us from the inside out. If you haven't felt at least a little uncomfortable—or a little offended—by what Jesus says, then maybe you're not letting his words sink in. Because Jesus doesn't coddle anyone. He calls. He disrupts. He nudges us out of complacency and moves us into the beautiful, difficult business of transformation.

Jesus came to change us. That's how he saves us. But here's the thing: most of us aren't too keen on change. We don't roll out the welcome mat for it. In fact, most of us fight it. We'd rather stick with the familiar—even if it's suffocating us—than face the hard truth that Jesus is asking us to deny ourselves, pick up our cross, and follow him. But Jesus is pretty set on this one particular idea of transformation.

He invites us to step out of the old, to let go of whatever is weighing us down, so that God can move us into something new. Jesus doesn't leave us where he finds us. He invites us to grow, to change, to become more fully alive. Just look at what happened to the fishermen he met and called to be his disciples. When they met Jesus they had no idea that their lives were going to be turned upside down. But for some reason they left their nets, their boats, their whole identity as fishermen, and stepped into a new, uncharted life with Jesus.

Think different. Live different.
Love in ways that disrupt, heal, and change everything.

That's the thing about Jesus. He's always inviting us to let go of what we know so that we can step into what God is doing now. It's never easy. But it's always worth it. Transformation isn't just what Jesus does—it's who he is. He takes what's old, what's broken, what's hopeless, and he breathes new life into it. Then he invites us to do the same—with our lives, with each other, and with the world.

"Repent, for the kingdom of heaven has come near" (Matt. 4:17).

Jesus doesn't waste time. Right out of the gate, he kicks off his ministry telling us to repent. It's the same message his cousin, John the Baptist, had shouted down at the Jordan River. John was baptizing people, part of the cleansing ritual that prepared people to meet God in the temple. Jesus? His work was to show us that we are the temple—that God is already here, dwelling in us, among us, through us.

How do you think people reacted when Jesus started preaching? Some probably dismissed him as another wilderness prophet like John—also a little nutty. But others were drawn in, intrigued, curious. Something about this idea of repentance seemed worth exploring.

Which takes us back to the beginning. What does it mean to repent? Most people will tell you it's about turning from your sins, cleaning up your act, or becoming a better person so you don't spend an eternity slow roasting in a BBQ pit. And let's be honest, for many of us, the word comes loaded with shame, guilt, and fire-and-brimstone finger-wagging. For years, I heard repent as an invitation to self-loathing. That's how many of us were taught. Repent or else.

But Jesus isn't about "or else." He's about love, transformation, and abundance. He isn't trying to scare us into believing so we can get into heaven—that's not what his mission is about. Following his way isn't about obtaining a golden ticket to some celestial paradise. I don't even think he's talking about leaving this world. Heaven, according to Jesus, has come down to earth. It's here. In the very space you are receiving these words.

Jesus doesn't want us to feel bad or beat ourselves up. He has come to wake us up. He wants us to change how we see the world, others, and ourselves. The Greek word for repent, *metanoia*, literally means to "go beyond the mind" or to put it in a more common vernacular, Jesus is saying, "Hey, man. Change the way you think." This isn't a call to grovel. It's a call to grow. Jesus isn't saying this shit to get you into heaven but to get heaven into you. Think different.

That's what makes repentance revolutionary. Jesus isn't asking for a little behavior modification. He's asking for total reorientation, a complete shift in how we live and love and move through the world. He's asking us to let go of our ego, our fear, and all the things we clutch so tightly that keep us from being free. He's saying, "Change your mind so your heart can follow." This is more than simply telling us to stop sinning. Jesus wants us to change our thinking such that sinning is no longer a part of the equation. Jesus knows if we can go beyond ourselves—to make it about God and not us—then not only will we be transformed, but we will be able to participate in the transformation of others as well.

When Jesus calls us to repent, it's not just for our own sake but for the sake of the world. He's inviting us to participate in God's kingdom —to be the light that shines in the dark places and show people their own worth in God's eyes. When Jesus called Simon and Andrew to follow him, he wasn't just calling them to a new way of thinking but a new way of being. "I will make you fishers of people," he told them. He called them to action, to transformation, to living out the kingdom of heaven right where they were.

This is not a warning or condemnation. It's an invitation. A way to see the world differently, to live fully, to step into the kingdom of heaven that's already here.

Jesus wants more from his followers than to simply learn some new social ethic. He wants us to embody and live this new ethic in a way that will shock and offend the world into waking up. He wants an inward change—a change of heart, a change of thinking, a change in the way we see and approach our neighbors. True repentance moves us away from our self-centered ways to a God-centered worldview that challenges the established norms and systems of power we have created.

As Richard Rohr often says, "You cannot *not* live in the presence of God. We are totally surrounded by God all the time and everywhere."* Heaven isn't far away. It's here. It's now. It's in every act of love, every moment of grace, every person we encounter. Jesus is inviting us to see it, to be part of it, and to let it transform us and the world around us.

Jesus is calling all of us to do some radical stuff. His demands haven't changed since James and John dropped their nets to follow this guy, who went around "teaching in their synagogues and proclaiming the good news of the kingdom and curing every disease and every sickness among the people" (Matt. 4:23). Think about those verbs—teaching, proclaiming, and curing. This is how people are able to see that the kingdom of heaven is within their reach.

Until heaven and earth are one, we need to shine the light of Christ onto the darkest of places. We need to proclaim the Good News of God's redemptive love. And we need to make known the glory of God's marvelous works, so others will know they are of value to God.

When I hear Jesus say repent, I don't hear a commandment. I hear incarnation. A call to be a part of God's community in the world, where the kingdom of heaven is revealed. I hear an invitation to be healed, restored, and redeemed—brought back to my rightful place as God's beloved child. And I hear a call from God to live fully and faithfully into that responsibility.

Repentance isn't about earning God's love. It's about realizing we already have it and living like it's true. So open your eyes. Open your heart. And step into the kingdom of heaven that's right in front of

---

* Richard Rohr. *Yes, And... Daily Meditations* (Cincinnati: Franciscan Media, 2013), 71.

you. Reimagining the world through Jesus' radical teachings leads to real change—not just in our own lives, but in the lives of others. His way is not a private spiritual journey; it's a public revolution of love. "The kingdom of heaven has come." It's here. It's now. It's all around us—right in front of you, behind you, beside you. Open your eyes. Open your heart. Step into it. Be part of the transformation God is bringing into the world. Jesus invites us not just to believe it but to live it. When we reimagine the world through all the weird things he says, we can't help but be moved to make real changes and real differences in our own lives and in the lives of others.

Think different. The kingdom of heaven has come. Enter into its glory.

6

STOP, DROP, AND FOLLOW ME

> *Jesus said to them, "Come with me.*
> *I'll make a new kind of fisherman out of you.*
> *I'll show you how to catch men and women*
> *instead of perch and bass."*
> *They didn't ask questions.*
> *They dropped their nets and followed.*
> —Mark 1:17–18, *The Message*

In the fall of 2010, my school counselor handed me a sheet of paper listing all the classes I needed to take for my Master of Divinity degree. Right there, staring back at me, was a word that shook me to my core. It wasn't Greek or Hebrew, though those intimidated me as well. The word was...conversion.

Those who know me know I'm not the street-corner, Bible-thumping type. And thanks to the overly zealous youth ministry I grew up with, I'm not big on shouting at people about Jesus. So I avoided the class until my very last quarter four years later. What a mistake. It turned out to be one of the most transformative classes I'd ever taken. It also wasn't about winning theological arguments or shaming people into belief as I'd feared. It was about learning to tell my own story—the story of handing my life over to God and saying yes to the calling God had placed on me.

There's a story in Luke 5 about Jesus showing up on the docks to convert some people to his way of life, a way of love grounded in God's way of righteousness. And there they are, mending their nets, when Jesus walks up and says, "Hey guys, drop what you're doing and follow me." And they do. I think most of us, if we're being honest, would have ignored this crazy call, pretending to be too busy with work to take him up on this radical invitation. But these four fishermen don't. There's something about Jesus that causes them to change their minds. And as a result, Jesus would forever change the direction of their lives.

You might think any rabbi worth their salt would sit back and wait for disciples to come to them. But Rabbi Jesus does the opposite. He goes out and finds his own. His focus isn't on his status but on the sacred mission God has called him to do—to go out into the world and usher in the kingdom of heaven. While the other rabbis would rather pick and choose from the brightest students from the best rabbinical schools, Jesus goes to the docks, into everyday spaces, and selects ordinary people like you and me.

Simon is one of those ordinary, everyday guys. He's not a scholar or a spiritual heavyweight. He's a fisherman, tired after an unproductive night of backbreaking work, fishing all night but catching nothing. When Jesus arrives, Simon is calling it a day. But Jesus isn't having any of that. He has no time for Simon's pity party. Instead, Jesus asks to borrow his boat. That's it. Their whole relationship begins with Jesus saying, "Hey, you've got something I need."

Now this is an important, often overlooked point in the story. And if we read too quickly, we might miss that Jesus is the one who makes the first move. God always initiates the relationship. And meets us right where we are in the dullness or messiness of our lives. You don't need to be special or extraordinary for God to call you. You just need to show up. That's what Simon, James, and John did—they showed up. And Jesus turned their empty boat into a vessel of abundance.

After teaching the crowd from Simon's boat, Jesus goes a step further. He says, "Let's go out into the deep water. Let's try again." Imagine Simon's reaction. He's exhausted. He fished in these waters all night. He's probably thinking to himself, "Well, this is a waste of time." But for some reason, Simon agrees. Maybe it's the way Jesus asks—maybe it's just desperation. But either way, Simon obeys. And what happens next blows his mind. They catch more fish than their nets can hold. There's so much abundance, it's spilling everywhere.

Another thing we might miss when we hurry through this story is that in Jesus, God not only initiates the relationship but also takes the risk. God puts it all on the table, hoping we'll respond. Simon could have said no. James and John could have clocked out and gone home. But they didn't. They took a chance—and in doing so, they caught a glimpse of God's kingdom breaking into their ordinary lives.

And there's still more happening here. You see, Jesus isn't just calling us to sit in the boat and watch. He's inviting us to get out into the deep, to risk failure, to trust him. Jesus wants us to toss out our nets and see what our faith will yield. That's what Simon and the others do. They go out into the deeper waters where Jesus tells them to go. They do what Jesus asks them to do—"Cast your net over here." And when they do, their eyes are opened. For the first time, Simon sees something holy in this man standing in his boat before him. Overwhelmed, he falls to his knees in repentance. "Go away from me, Lord," Simon says. "I'm a sinful man." Simon doesn't just hear what Jesus has to say—he witnesses what Jesus can do. Seeing it, he believes. His mind is changed. His life transformed.

That's the other thing this story teaches us about this guy. Through Jesus, God illuminates our minds, our awareness and understanding. When we encounter Jesus, we see ourselves—and the world—differently. We see not with our eyes, but with the eyes of God. In the same way, we love not with our hearts, but with the very heart of God.

Simon's encounter with Jesus changes everything. He sees something that he had never seen or experienced before. In this man, Jesus, God has a face Simon can see. A heart he can feel. A voice he can hear. The Jewish philosopher Emmanuel Levinas said the only thing that really converts people is "the face of the other."* He argues that genuine transformation arises through our encounter with the other, where their vulnerability and humanity demand our ethical response. This seems to be the case when Simon sees Jesus, and he will never see life the same way again.

As the story goes, the disciples don't think twice. They just drop their nets and follow. Why do they do that? What is it about Jesus that makes people leave everything behind to follow him?

When Jesus sees Matthew sitting at his tax booth, he doesn't give him a lecture. He doesn't tell him to repent first. He simply says, "Follow me" (Matt. 9:9). And Matthew gets up and leaves everything—his money, his job, even the hatred and scorn people had piled on him because of his profession. No one liked tax collectors back then either. They were seen as sellouts, traitors working for Rome. But something about Jesus made Matthew step away from it all. He chose to leave behind the known, the routine, the security of his life to follow a man who had no place to lay his head (Luke 9:58).

So, what's going on here? What is it about Jesus that draws people in?

Nearly every time he is asked why young people join gangs, Greg Boyle, a Jesuit priest and founder of Homeboy Industries, says that it mostly comes down to broken homes, loneliness, and an aching need to belong. Gangs, as violent as they are, operate on a code and offer a promise: Follow us, and we will protect you. It's the following part that often takes these kids in the wrong direction, but—as Boyle points out—gang members don't join because they're drawn to crime or violence; they join because, for the first time, someone welcomes them, sees them, and makes them feel like they matter. "We all just want to belong somewhere," Boyle writes. "We want to be seen, to feel necessary, to know that someone delights in our existence."†

Isn't Jesus like that? He sees you. He doesn't ask you to clean up

---

* Emmanuel Levinas, *Totality and Infinity: An Essay on Exteriority*, trans. Alphonso Lingis (Pittsburgh: Duquesne University Press, 1969), 213.
† Gregory Boyle, *Cherished Belonging: The Healing Power of Love in Divided Times* (New York: Avid Reader Press/Simon & Schuster, 2024), 55.

your act or get your resumé in order. He sees you as you are and says, "Follow me." It's not about fitting into some religious mold or being good enough. With Jesus, you already belong.

If we're being honest, most of us are followers, not leaders. It's just how we're wired. We want to belong to something bigger than our own ordinary, messy selves. Belonging gives us a sense of purpose and identity. It helps us feel like we matter. That's why charismatic leaders—politicians, influencers, even gang leaders—have such pull. They tap into this deep human desire to belong. Sometimes, that desire leads us in the wrong direction. Sometimes, following can lead to violence, destruction, or heartbreak. But other times, it can transform us.

The disciples didn't overthink it. They just followed. There's no record of Simon or Andrew asking Jesus, "Where are we going? What's the pay like? Do you have a benefits package? They didn't analyze or strategize. They just walked away from their nets and followed him. Jesus doesn't sugarcoat it either. When someone rushes up to him and says, "I'll follow you wherever you go," Jesus replies, "Foxes have dens and birds have nests, but the Son of Man has no place to lay his head" (Luke 9:57-58). In other words, following Jesus isn't about comfort or security. It's about transformation. It's about stepping into a way of life that challenges the status quo and turns the world upside down.

Why would anyone say yes to that? Because they saw something in Jesus that no one else offered. Jesus wasn't like the other rabbis who stuck to the script and quoted tradition. He taught with authority (Mark 1:22). He healed the sick, restored the outcasts, and forgave sins—something only God could do. He wasn't just saying things—he actually did things that pointed to a new reality. The kingdom of heaven was no longer just a far-off dream; it was breaking into the here and now. And people wanted to be part of it.

Someone once asked me if I thought Jesus ever smoked pot. I have no idea why they asked me this, but it intrigued me. I thought for a moment before explaining how I could picture Jesus sitting around at a party where a group of people are smoking weed. I imagine when the joint is passed to him, Jesus takes it—not to smoke it, but to bless it, the way he blesses cups of wine and plates of bread. But I don't think Jesus takes a toke. He just blesses it and passes it on the next person. Only now, things are different. The person who receives the joint from Jesus is also receiving his blessing. And that's where the transformation happens. So that person passes it to the next person without needing to take a hit. Then the next person receives the blessed joint and passes it on. Around the circle it goes until it's back in the hands of the one who blessed it. I imagine that's when Jesus smiles and snuffs it out gently between his fingers.

There is something about Jesus that makes me want to hang out with him. I want to go to parties with him, to sit with him on a mountainside, listening to his teachings and receiving his blessings. Jesus doesn't shame us or nitpick the legality or health benefits of not smoking marijuana. He just comes. And blesses. He accepts us where we are and loves us. The blessings we receive from him—the very love of God—are the very blessings we are called to pass along.

Following Jesus meant stepping into something bigger than themselves. "Follow me, and I will make you fishers of people," Jesus tells Simon and Andrew (Matt. 4:19). It's a strange metaphor, but it gets at the heart of what Jesus is calling them to: a life of purpose, a life of bringing others into this new reality. And as I study the shit Jesus says, I have to ask myself how I am willing to respond to the blessings I receive from him. How will I drop my net and follow Jesus along this way of love and transformation? And what is my net that I need to drop?

For Simon and the others, the nets represented their livelihood, their comfort zone, their old way of life. Your net might look different. It might look similar. Maybe it's a carefully constructed image that attracts the attention of others to notice you instead of the Christ-light within you. Maybe it's a career path that is all about climbing the ladder instead of lifting others up. Maybe it's the security blanket of material wealth, the belief that more stuff equals more happiness. Maybe it's the fear of failing or lies that whisper we're not being good enough, smart enough, or holy enough to make a difference.

Dropping our nets means letting go of all the things that keep us tethered to the shoreline, the things that prevent us from stepping into the deep waters of faith. It means trusting that Jesus is enough, that his abundance will meet us on the boat, on the dock, and even in the water. But it's not just about what we let go of; it's also about what we take up. Getting in the boat with Jesus is a scary proposition. It's scary because we have to risk facing all our insecurities, fears, and doubts. We have to risk going out into the deep where the seas are rough, and the winds push against us. We have to risk letting go of the safety nets we have relied on all our lives.

You might be wondering why people follow Jesus? I think it's because he doesn't just promise transformation—he embodies it. He sees us, loves us, and invites us to be part of something that will outlast and outshine anything this world has to offer. As Boyle writes, "We stand with the disposable so that the day will come when we stop throwing people away."[*]

Again, Jesus says the shit he says not to scare us or shock us. Jesus comes to us to awaken us to the way of God's redeeming love. Following Jesus means stepping into his way of life—a way marked by love, compassion, and radical inclusion. It means seeing the world through his eyes and a heart that breaks for the marginalized and the forgotten. It means being willing to risk comfort and security for the sake of something greater. We drop our nets whenever we make space for others.

Think about Simon's boat for a moment. At first, it's just an ordinary fishing vessel. But then, when Jesus steps into it, his boat becomes a place of teaching, of healing, of abundance. Our lives can be like that boat. When we let Jesus step in, our ordinary becomes extraordinary. Our homes, workplaces, and communities become places where God's love is made real.

When we choose to take Jesus at his word—when we choose to set out and follow him—it means that we too will have to initiate the conversation by showing up in the lives of others. So often, we over-

---

[*] Boyle, *Cherished Belonging*, 93.

complicate discipleship, thinking it requires grand gestures or theological expertise. But following Jesus is really about presence—being there for people in their joy and their pain, in their hope and in their despair. It's about listening without judgment, loving without condition, and walking alongside others as they navigate the messy, beautiful journey of life.

We can also follow Jesus by choosing to live simply. In a world that tells us to chase after more—more money, more power, more recognition—Jesus invites us to embrace less. "You cannot serve two masters," he says. "It's either God or wealth" (Matt. 6:24). When we loosen our grip on material things, we free ourselves to hold onto what really matters: relationships, community, and the abundant grace of God.

And finally, we follow Jesus by being open to transformation. Simon, James, and John didn't know what they were getting into when they left their nets behind. They just knew that what Jesus offered was worth the risk. Their "yes" changed everything—for them and for the world. When we say yes to Jesus, we open ourselves up to that same transformation. We become part of God's work of healing and renewal, right here, right now.

By walking away from their boats, their families, their routines, they stepped into a love so big it would transform and change the world. They discovered in Jesus this undeniable truth: God is love. And Jesus calls us to live out that love in all we do—to be the light, the leaven, the salt, the mustard seed of the kingdom.

Their story teaches us that when we say yes to the shit Jesus asks of us, our lives will never be the same. And that's the whole point of salvation—the reason God initiates a relationship with us in the first place. Like Rohr has taught me, "God is changing the world. But to get everyone and everything there, God needs people who are willing to enter this kingdom and transform it into life—life more abundantly" (John 10:10)."*

---

* Richard Rohr, "The Mind Does Not Like to Change," *Another Name for Every Thing*, podcast audio, January 25, 2020, accessed January 19, 2023.

Jesus moves us from being ordinary, everyday people to kingdom people—extraordinary, beloved children of God. Our nets, once empty, are now filled with the abundance of everlasting life. Through our transformed hearts, God's grace and love spreads like wildfire, igniting hope and renewal wherever we go. All because these ordinary people responded and took the extraordinary risk to get in the boat with Jesus and follow him into this crazy, beautiful, upside-down kingdom.

7

THE FIRST TRUE CRAZY THING JESUS SAYS

He said, "Blessed are you..."
—Matthew 5:1-12

In the opening of his Rule, St. Francis of Assisi simply wrote, "The Rule and the life of the Friars is to live the Gospel." Simple, right? But when he sent his rule off to Rome, the Pope allegedly returned it with a note that said, "This is no rule, it's just the gospel." I can only imagine Francis wanted to reply back with a note of his own, "Well, duh!"

The gospel is life. It's not just for monks—it's for all of us, whether we wear robes or jeans. But somehow, we've managed to complicate it. The truth is so simple, so pure, it's easy for our minds to overthink it, twisting it into little, divisive arguments instead of letting it breathe life into us. And in doing so, we kill the spirit God is trying to bless us with.

I once met a young woman named Maria who, for most of her life, had struggled with feelings of inadequacy and shame. Ever since she was a small child, Maria had been told that she wasn't enough—by society, by her family, and eventually by herself. But one day, while volunteering at a local shelter, Maria encountered a man who had been homeless for years. It seemed it had also been that long since he had seen a bar of soap. Whenever he came in, it always seemed to be time for everyone's break—everyone but Maria. One day the man heard her putting herself down. So he walked over to her and began to share his story. It was a story filled with hope, of how he'd found peace in God's love despite the hardships he faced.

"Look at me," he said with a smile. "I have nothing, but I'm rich in God's mercy." God loves us all, no matter who we are. Or what we smell like. Maria left that afternoon with a deep sense of gratitude, realizing that being poor in spirit didn't mean being without value—it meant being open to receiving God's blessings. Even in our brokenness, Jesus wants to bless us. But will we be open to letting him get close enough to do so?

Despite her insecurities, Maria can teach us an important lesson, one of modern sainthood. She lived the way Jesus teaches us to live—as a blessing for others. Imagine a world where everyone practiced nonjudgmental love, unconditional forgiveness, radical peacemaking, and reconciliation? Imagine how many hearts we could crack open so God's love could pour in. Jesus didn't just come to give us words to repeat; he came to change our hearts so our actions would follow.

St. Francis understood this. He took Jesus at his word: If Jesus meant it, then Francis ought to live it. John's gospel tells us Jesus is the Word made flesh—so his words matter. They're not merely wise sayings or inspiring thoughts. They're a road map to help us navigate our spiritual journey toward love. They're blueprints for living a good life. They're a social commentary, ethical pronouncements, and radical declarations. And when we live these words, we begin to see the world as Jesus does: through the lens of God's love, peace, and justice. We make heaven come alive and all blessings flow.

Look at all the stuff he gives us in the Sermon on the Mount—pretty much the greatest sermon ever preached. It's a master class in how to live a good life—a life that challenges systems of oppression and instead lifts up the brokenhearted, the meek, the merciful, and the peacemakers. Jesus starts with blessings—unexpected blessings.

Not for the rich, not for the powerful, but for the poor, the mourning, the hungry, the merciful. Jesus blesses the people the world forgets, and by doing so, shows us a new way which really is an old way. God's way.

These blessings—what are known as the Beatitudes—are not just nice sayings. They're the foundation of God's kingdom on earth—a kingdom where God speaks directly to us and says, "You are loved. You matter."

For the first time, the ones on the margins—those who have never felt blessed—hear, "You are seen. You are loved." Jesus radically affirms them in their poverty, pain, hunger, and persecution. I imagine those who listened were in shock as they witnessed their world turn upside down. To be poor in spirit or meek gets you nowhere in a culture of competition and fear. But Jesus, who sees the world with God's eyes and loves others with God's heart, blesses those who know what it's like to be excluded and those who don't make it to the top of the ladder. Shocking as they are, his words give us all hope, for the way things are now is not the way they will always be.

In her book, *Accidental Saints*, Nadia Bolz-Weber describes this moment as Jesus giving a blessing to "those who never expected one in the first place."[*] These are people like Eric, a young man who came to our church hesitant and unsure. He confessed, "All this sounds good, but how do I know it's real? How do I know this place is for real?" Eric, like many of us, had trouble believing that a world so broken could really be blessed. And yet, Jesus blesses us anyway—not because we've earned it, but because it's in his nature to do so.

Jesus isn't setting us up for failure or shame. He's showing us a way to participate in the kingdom of heaven knowing exactly what that will entail. Yes, it's a messy, difficult way, filled with doubts, fears, and mistakes. But Jesus knows us, and he still chooses to bless us, even at the cost of his own life. Jesus, as imagined by Bolz-Weber, looks at the crowd and begins "extravagantly throwing around bless-

---

[*] Nadia Bolz-Weber, *Accidental Saints: Finding God in All the Wrong People* (New York: Convergent, 2015).

ings as though they grew on trees."* This is heaven on earth where communities of saints run around blessing one another—paying special attention to those the world doesn't admire: the broken, the peacemakers, the merciful.

James had always been disillusioned with the injustice he saw in the world. As a young man, he wanted to make a difference but didn't know where to start. One evening, he sat down with a group of people who'd been advocating for better healthcare for unhoused mothers. There had been a lot of push back from those on the other side of the issue, and it felt like the opposition was winning. James admitted that he wasn't sure if their work was even worth it. To say he felt discouraged was an understatement.

One of the older activists, Mavis, took James outside and said, "Righteousness isn't about seeing instant results. It's about showing up every day and doing the right thing because it's the right thing to do. God's justice is slow, but it's real." The hunger for righteousness doesn't always get immediate satisfaction, but it always has an eternal impact. Blessed Are Those Who Hunger and Thirst for Righteousness.

St. Francis of Assisi didn't just read the Sermon on the Mount, he lived it. He took Jesus at his word, creating a community that lived into their blessedness by blessing others. Francis believed when Jesus said the kingdom of heaven was near, he meant it—and he chose to live as if it were true. He put in long hours loving those the world overlooked and helping them discover their worth in God's eyes.

> *Jesus says, "Blessed are the poor in spirit,*
> *for theirs is the kingdom of heaven" (Matt. 5:3).*

With this, Jesus opens the door to heaven wide for everyone. Rich and poor, straight and queer, young and old, educated and uneducated; Republicans, Democrats, Independents, MAGA, Black Lives Matter; the forgotten, and the marginalized. Everyone. No one is left

---

* Bolz-Weber, *Accidental Saints*.

out. And it's not just an invitation—it's a promise. The wealth and joy of this kingdom, the very joy of heaven, is ours too. Jesus spent his life on earth showing us what this kingdom looks like, revealing its treasures, offering us glimpses of the riches we were meant to receive. And all of this is available to us now.

Accept this blessing:
You are loved by God. God's love and the fullness of God's kingdom are yours to claim. The door is open. Walk through it, knowing you are deeply, profoundly, and unconditionally loved.

Jesus says, "Blessed are those who mourn, for they will be comforted" (Matt. 5:4).

It's as if Jesus is telling us, "I see you. I've been there. I know what it's like to feel the weight of loss, to hurt, to want to give up." He doesn't just acknowledge our pain, he enters into it with us. And here's the promise: You are not alone. Jesus assures us that the same Holy Spirit who carried him through his darkest moments is the same Spirit that will carry us through ours.

But Jesus doesn't stop there. He shows us what it means to be a community that puts others first. He teaches us how to give of ourselves, fully and without hesitation, knowing that in doing so, we'll find others who will give their all for us in return. In the midst of our pain, there is comfort—both from Jesus and from the loving, generous community he calls us to be.

Accept this blessing:
You are loved by God. You are not alone in your sorrow, and through Jesus, you will find the comfort and support you need.

*Jesus says, "Blessed are the meek,
for they will inherit the earth" (Matt. 5:5).*

THIS REMINDS us that we don't have to fight, manipulate, or compromise our integrity to make our way in the world. Be who God made you to be, and the world will make space for you. Jesus shows us that we are beloved children of God, heirs to divine glory, both now and forever. Stay true to yourself, because you are made for greatness, from love for love, and with grace to give grace.

Accept this blessing:
You are loved by God. Your gentleness and kindness
will be rewarded everywhere you go.

*Jesus says, "Blessed are those who hunger and thirst
for righteousness, for they will be filled" (Matt. 5:6).*

HAVE you ever been so hungry that you had to convince yourself you're full? Jesus experienced a hunger like that in the wilderness, and in that moment, he was tempted to put his physical needs over his spiritual ones. But he refused. "Man does not live by bread alone, but by every word that comes from the mouth of God" (Matt. 4:4), he said. In the same way, when we hunger for righteousness, God will fill us with what we truly need. Jesus teaches us to be the bread of life and the cup of salvation for others—helping quench the world's thirst for justice and peace.

Accept this blessing:
You are loved by God. With all of God's love pouring in and out of
you, you will have more than enough to give away.

*Jesus says, "Blessed are the merciful,
for they will receive mercy" (Matt. 5:7).*

RETALIATION HAS no place in the kingdom of God. When anger or violence comes your way, don't return it in kind. Instead, offer mercy and kindness. People might try to exploit your generosity, but stand firm. The mercy you show will be returned to you. Jesus never wavered in showing mercy. He showed us with his life that mercy is the way to justice, and through his resurrection, we see the reward of that mercy. Let us go and do the same.

Accept this blessing:
You are loved by God. Share the mercy you experience with someone so they can experience it too.

*Jesus says, "Blessed are the pure in heart,
for they will see God" (Matt. 5:8).*

YOU DON'T NEED to conform to the world's brokenness. Jesus invites you into a new way of living, where love is the source of strength and success. You can live with authenticity and purity—by focusing your life on loving God, loving others, and serving both. You are made to be clean in heart and action, and the way to do that is simply love.

Accept this blessing:
You are loved by God. When people see you living your true self, loved and adored by God, they will glimpse the divine.

*Jesus says, "Blessed are the peacemakers,
for they will be called children of God" (Matt. 5:9).*

JESUS, the Prince of Peace, brings calm to the storms of life. He shows us what true peace looks like—not just seeking peace but making it. Peace isn't passive, it's active—it's made. Start small, right where you are. Peace is a gift from God, and we are called to receive and share it. When you make peace, you will discover that you are a child of God, an heir to God's peace.

Accept this blessing:
You are loved by God. You were made from love for the purpose of love.

Jesus says, "Blessed are those who are persecuted for righteousness' sake, for theirs is the kingdom of heaven" (Matt. 5:10).

IT'S one thing to get in trouble for doing something wrong. But have you ever been persecuted for doing what's right? For standing up for what's good and just, even when it costs you? Jesus assures us that when we endure persecution for righteousness, we see heaven come to life in this world. Stand firm in love, and you will experience the kingdom of heaven here and now.

Accept this blessing:
You are loved by God. You are blessed for doing the right thing, even when it's hard.

Jesus says, "Blessed are you when people revile you and persecute you and utter all kinds of evil against you falsely on my account. Rejoice and be glad, for your reward is great in heaven, for in the same way they persecuted the prophets who were before you" (Matt. 5:11–12).

LET's count it a blessing that God sees our true worth—beyond money, beyond status, beyond any worldly measure. God focuses not on our poverty, but on the richness of our love. Blessed are you who stand up for others, who show up when a friend needs you, or who defends the one who is being mistreated. You are rich in the kingdom of heaven.

Accept this blessing:
You are loved by God. Count it a blessing that God sees
through the costumes and masks you wear to fit into this world.
God loves you just as you are—real, divine, true.

How blessed are we? Very blessed, according to Jesus, who not only reveals our future but gives us a taste of it today. His blessings are not just for us, but for us to share with others in his name.

Jesus flips the script on everything we thought we knew about the world. He doesn't just accept the status quo—he transforms it. The last become first. The hungry get fed. The persecuted inherit the kingdom. This is how God, who has loved us since the beginning of time, is changing everything for good.

Jesus shows us who God truly is—and who we are in God's eyes. He doesn't just walk through the world; he turns it upside down, revealing that wherever there's hunger, wherever there's pain, wherever injustice reigns, or tears are shed, God is there. God is there, bringing blessings in the most unexpected places.

A friend of mine is a teacher in a rough neighborhood. He's a big guy with quiet strength, never demanding respect, but earning it through his consistent kindness, willingness to listen, and calm in the face of disruption.

One day, a student who had been angry and rebellious approached him, asking, "Why are you always so calm? Don't you get angry?" My friend simply said, "The world will try to make you loud. But the strength of quiet, humble love is stronger than anything." Blessed are those who are at peace, those who realize the true strength of meekness—that it's not weakness but power under control, the power of love that changes lives.

It's easier to dismiss these beatitudes as impossible tasks meant only for saints. Only people like St. Francis, right? But if that were the case, Jesus would only be inviting the greatest among us. Let's be real, no one but God fits that bill. Thankfully, that's not what Jesus does. He invites people like you and me—ordinary folks full of faults and fears—to turn the world's assumptions upside down. He calls us to be the ones who love and bless. Jesus doesn't say "theirs will be the kingdom," he says, "theirs *is* the kingdom." That's present tense. Right now. Jesus reminds us that God blesses us so the world can know God and claim those blessings for themselves. It's up to us to pass them on as if they grew on trees!

Francis taught his followers that it's more important to be like Jesus than just worship him. We're called to mirror Christ in the world, to see him in every person and every act of love. Treat others like you're serving Jesus himself, and you'll know how blessed you truly are.

How blessed are you to cry with a friend in their loss,
to have a heart full of compassion and a handful of tissues?
God will fill you with all the love and care you need.

How blessed are you when you're content with who you are, hungry
for God's righteousness? The kitchen of God's love is always open.

How blessed are you to make peace with your enemies and still smile when
others ridicule you? The saints and angels are applauding.

How blessed are those who realize that living the gospel isn't irrational—it's
the only rational way to live.

Francis knew he had enough faith to fully surrender to God's will. Through Jesus, he experienced God's unconditional love, and with every person he served, his faith grew deeper. Francis took that mustard seed of faith and used it in simple, profound ways.

Jesus shows us that the life of faith is an act of love. When we allow God to embrace us with love, we can then embrace everyone we meet with that same love. Like Francis, we can be servants, doing what we were called to do—mirroring Jesus and practicing heaven here on earth.

8

YOU ARE THE FLAVOR OF THE WORLD

"You are the salt of the earth; but if salt has lost its taste, how can its saltiness be restored? It is no longer good for anything except to be thrown out and trampled underfoot."
—Matthew 5:13

I came across a meme once that read, "Salt on top of salt for me!" As I was about to send it to my wife, the queen of all things salty, I realized she was the one who posted it. We have, as a family, a rather "salty" reputation. And in her eyes, that's a compliment. Our pantry is a testament to that devotion. We've got your basic Morton's table salt—the classic with the little girl and her umbrella on the container. Then kosher salt, because, well, sometimes you need to keep things kosher. There're the basics like garlic salt, celery salt, onion salt, and an impressive array of sea salts from as far as Australia.

And then the real fun begins. Dozens of various sized containers holding various kinds of infused sea salts stand on top of one another. We have Thai ginger salt. "Hot Rocks," a pepper-infused salt that could probably strip paint. There's Kimchi salt. Vintage Merlot salt. Lemon salt for fish, paprika salt for pork, and dill-tomato infused salt for chicken. There's even Vidalia onion salt tucked away in a jar, a secret I sneak onto my bagels when no one's looking. As I peer into the cupboards, I see red Spanish salt, blue Persian salt, two kinds of black salt from Hawaii, and three different Peruvian salts in various shades of yellow. My wife even keeps a couple of saltshakers stashed in her purse and car—just in case. Of all the different, unique varieties of salt we have, I can say with great confidence that each one also has the distinct flavor of...salt.

Jesus says, "You are the salt of the earth" (Matt. 5:13). It may not be the weirdest thing he ever called his followers, but it's certainly one of the more profound, especially when it comes to the love he's called us to share. It's a good metaphor. His audience was mostly simple, everyday kind of people. Many, still fresh in their journey of faith, would have grasped the significance of salt. It wasn't just something you sprinkled on your meal. Salt was invaluable in the ancient world.

Back then, salt was a precious commodity—used for flavoring and preserving meats, healing wounds, as well as bartering, paying for labor and sealing covenants. For us today, salt is an essential mineral. It's the only trace mineral present in every cell of our bodies. Without it, our bodies wouldn't function. Salt maintains our hydration, balances our electrolytes, and keeps us alive. Too little salt leads to chaos in the body—heart attacks, strokes, disease. Too much and we risk high blood pressure, kidney damage, and toxicity. But in just the right measure, salt is essential for life.

In essence, Jesus tells his disciples to "Have salt in yourselves and be at peace with one another."

As a kid, whenever I had a sore throat, my dad would make me gargle saltwater. It tasted awful but worked wonders to reduce the inflammation. Salt is a healing agent for tired muscles and a balm for aching feet. In her spiritual writings, one of the church's leading female mystics named Catherine of Siena is said to have called Jesus' blood "sweet medicine" that heals and restores souls to wholeness. Just as a saltwater gargle can soothe a sore throat or a warm salt bath can alleviate muscle aches and fatigue, this saying reminds us that we play a vital role in the healing and restoration of the world.

Salt is also used to enhance the flavor of food. In some households, it's the secret weapon to enjoying your mother-in-law's cooking. But in our house, no meal is complete without a selection of salts to sprinkle on top. My wife believes in the magic of salt—different varieties elevate the flavor of specific dishes. She likes to remind me that Jesus says we too are meant to enhance the goodness in others, to bring out the best in the people we encounter. Be the salt, not the meat or potatoes. Be the thing on the table that becomes invisible when mixed with others. Be the thing that makes everything pop and gives purpose to life itself.

To paraphrase author Debie Thomas, Jesus didn't say we should become salt or try to be salt. He simply declared, "You are the salt of the earth" (Matt. 5:13). This is who we are, not a goal we are to strive for. As salt, we are not meant to preserve ourselves but to preserve what is not ourselves. We exist to enhance life, to heal, to soften, to restore.*

As a minister and a parent, I have been to my fair share of potlucks. At each one, there's always that person who brings something so fancy you wonder if they've secretly hired a chef. You know the type. They show up with a tray of sushi that looks like it belongs in an art gallery, or a salad with ingredients so exotic you start questioning if you even have the right to be eating it. And then there's the rest of us—just bringing what we know, whatever's easy, a casserole or a bag of chips. But here's the thing. When everyone's getting their plate, there's always someone who grabs the saltshaker. Doesn't matter how fancy the food is, or how exotic the quinoa salad might look—what they really want is the humble salt to make sure the flavors are just right. That's salt. It's not the centerpiece of the meal, but it *makes* the meal. It brings out what's already there, making everything better without anyone even noticing. It's not shouting for attention. It's just quietly doing the work. I think that's what Jesus is

---

* Debie Thomas, *Into the Mess and Other Jesus Stories: Reflections on the Life of Christ* (Eugene, OR: Cascade Books, 2022), 164-66.

getting at here. Just be the one who flavors the world. Bring out the good in everyone.

The wonderful American mystic Thomas Merton saw Jesus as the true salt in an otherwise bland world consumed with conformity. To briefly paraphrase his theology, Merton saw Jesus' radical love as the one true ingredient that challenges illusions and cuts through the surface, adding the right flavor to make the heavenly meal of life pop. Salt's importance to an ancient society also stemmed from its ability to preserve food. It kept meat from spoiling, allowing for transportation and storage. Jesus calls us to be like salt in the world, to prevent corruption, to preserve the good amidst the bad, to stop evil from spreading. The way I see it, Jesus is the salt that makes life's vulnerabilities sacred. He transforms our brokenness into something beautiful and beloved.

Jesus tells us to bring flavor out of life's moments, especially those marked by pain or struggle. We are sent to be his healing presence—restoring the broken, amplifying the dignity of the oppressed, and making room for everyone at God's table. And around that table, my wife would probably lean back in her chair and say to me, "You know, it's not just about passing the salt. It's about seeing the quiet truth underneath the surface of things—finding flavor in the things we think we already know." She knows being salt isn't about being loud or flashy but about seeing the sacred in the ordinary, even when everything else seems to be drowning in the noise. Salt doesn't try to be the star; it just quietly makes everything it touches a little more alive.

Dietrich Bonhoeffer, who was martyred for his stance against Nazi tyranny, saw Jesus as the ultimate embodiment of salt, through his self-giving love that resisted oppression—even to the point of death. Just as salt draws out the true flavor of food, Jesus helps us draw out the fullness of life. He teaches us to live for others and to see the world through eyes of love and compassion.

George was one of those quiet, "always there when you need him" types who lived near the church I worked at in Michigan. One icy evening, I stayed late at the office hoping the rain would let up—but it didn't. It just turned to snow. The sidewalks were a slippery mess, and I hesitated to step out, knowing the dangers of black ice. Then I saw George, quietly walking down the street with a bag of salt, spreading it without fanfare, quietly helping his neighbors stay safe. As he passed, he blessed me by tossing an extra handful my way. I watched him continue on, thinking, "There goes Jesus, in the flesh—worth his weight in salt, making everything better just by showing up."

This idea of being worth your weight in salt comes from ancient Rome when soldiers were paid in salt. Back then, salt was actually worth its weight in gold. It was a form of wealth that people fought over. It was also a weapon used in warfare. When salt lost its flavor, armies would spread it on an enemy's land, rendering it barren and unproductive. It's been described as "the 'scorched earth' tactic of warfare before Agent Orange was devised."* We see this strategy used in the book of Judges when Abimelech sowed his own capital of Shechem with salt after quelling a revolt (Judges 9:45). Jesus warns us not to lose our saltiness. When we lose our ability to enhance, to heal, and to preserve, we become useless. Or worse, we become harmful. As I think about all that salt in our cupboard, it never dawned on me that it could all stop being salty someday. And what if all their distinct flavors became indistinct? Salt is only good as long as it does what it's supposed to do.

A couple of years ago, I ate at a restaurant called Salt. As its name suggests, every dish came paired with a unique variety of salt—gathered from all over the world. There were over a hundred types, each one with a distinct purpose, meant to enhance the flavor of the food in front of you. It struck me how much that mirrors the body of Christ. There are all kinds of Christians, some more refined, others a little flakier, but we all share the same purpose: to shake out God's

---

* J. Barrington Bates, "Careful Seasoning, Proper 21 (B)," *The Episcopal Church*, September 27, 2015, https://www.episcopalchurch.org/sermon/careful-seasoning-proper-21-b-2015/.

love all over the place, giving people a taste of what Jesus can do to change them and their communities.

Dorothy Day, the 20th-century activist and cofounder of the Catholic Worker Movement, lived as the truest kind of "salt of the earth"—preserving dignity, enhancing community, and blessing people with extra handfuls of God's love all over the place. Her life was a powerful example of what it looks like to take Jesus' words to heart, using simple acts of goodness to bring out the best in the world around her.

Dorothy grew up in the heart of New York City, witnessing the deep divides between the haves and the have-nots. After a childhood marked by turbulence and years of radical atheism, Dorothy experienced a profound conversion to Catholicism. It was this conversion that moved her to live out Jesus' love and justice in the world. She saw the call to be "the salt of the earth" as an invitation to preserve dignity, hope, and love—especially in those whom society had forgotten or pushed aside. She once said, "If we share in Christ's poverty, we must also share his salt."[*]

With only a few dollars to her name, Dorothy cofounded the Catholic Worker Movement during the Great Depression. She opened her home to offer refuge to the hungry, homeless, and brokenhearted. But she wasn't just a voice of comfort; she became hands that served, feet that walked the hard road, and salt that preserved the hope of God's love in desperate places. She was a window into heaven, where light and love overcame the darkness.

Every morning, Dorothy would rise early, pray, and head into the streets, arms loaded with bread and soup. Day after day, she offered food, clothing, and a listening ear, welcoming the forgotten with kindness and acceptance. She was there when no one else was. She was there when the city turned away. The movement she started grew into a community of people—true "salt of the earth"—committed to sharing what they had, fighting for justice, and living out Christ's love

---

[*] Dorothy Day, *The Reckless Way of Love: Notes on Following Jesus*, ed. Carolyn Kurtz (Maryknoll, NY: Orbis Books, 2017), 13.

in their daily lives. When her work got hard, the authorities criticized her, and her friends scoffed at her for living in such harsh conditions, Dorothy would smile and say, "We are the salt of the earth. If we lose our flavor, we lose our purpose."[*]

Then there's the story of Father Greg Boyle and his work with Homeboy Industries, another living example of what it means to be the salt of the earth in a place the world had all but given up on. Through radical kinship, compassion, and an unshakable hope, Boyle has embodied Jesus' call to be salt, bringing transformation and healing to those left for dead on the margins of society.

In what one could easily describe as the most violent piece of real estate in the country, Boyle watched his East LA community suffer from gang violence, poverty, and cycles of incarceration. While the world condemned or feared those trapped in this life, Greg saw them differently. He saw the inherent dignity and worth in each person, recognizing that they too were the salt of the earth. So Greg took a radical leap and decided to mix his salt with theirs—bringing with him hope, healing, and new possibilities.

He founded Homeboy Industries, an organization dedicated to offering jobs, training, and support to former gang members and those looking to break free from the cycle of violence. But this wasn't about charity—it was about kinship: recognizing each person as a beloved child of God, part of his own human family. As he often says, "We don't go to the margins to make a difference. We go to the margins so that the folks at the margins make us different."[†] For Greg, being salt means creating a place where everyone can rediscover their worth, no matter their past.

Each morning, the doors of Homeboy Industries open to former rivals—men and women hardened by life on the streets—who come seeking a fresh start. Greg's presence, his willingness to listen, and his refusal to judge bring out the flavor of Christ's compassion, making

---

[*] Dorothy Day, *The Reckless Way of Love*.
[†] Gregory Boyle, *Tattoos on the Heart: The Power of Boundless Compassion* (New York: Free Press, 2010).

each person feel valued and accepted. And loved. That's the flavor of good salt.

Over time, Homeboy Industries became a model of redemption, showing that no one is beyond the reach of God's love. The transformed lives were proof that Jesus' salt could bring healing even in the most wounded places. I once heard Greg say, "Imagine a circle of compassion, and then imagine no one standing outside that circle." This radical inclusivity, inspired by Jesus' own life, was salt to a community, offering flavor, healing, and preservation to those who might otherwise be lost.

Debie Thomas writes, "Salt at its best sustains and enriches life. It pours itself out with discretion so that God's kingdom might be known on the earth—a kingdom of spice and zest, a kingdom of health and wholeness, a kingdom of varied depth, flavor, and complexity. In his Sermon on the Mount, Jesus makes concrete the work of love, compassion, healing, and justice. It's not enough to believe. It's not enough to bask in our blessedness while creation burns. To be blessed, to be salt, to be followers of Jesus, is to take seriously what our identity signifies."*

Jesus tells us, "You are the salt" (Matt. 5:13). He doesn't say that you will become salt—you already are everything the world needs to see God's love and goodness. You already carry the power to transform lives and enhance the flavor of the world. Jesus wants us to elevate the good in society, pointing others toward God through our saltiness. He showed us how—by leading with humility and compassion. For Jesus, being salt meant having a gentle, loving spirit that put others' needs before his own. He taught us to be servants, preserving faith in our communities, nourishing others with Christlike love.

For saints like Teresa of Ávila, being salt meant living in deep union with God, letting that inner life overflow into compassionate action. For her, true saltiness occurred when her relationship with God bore fruit in service and self-giving. Francis of Assisi lived out saltiness through simplicity and kinship with all creation, finding joy

---

* Thomas, *Into the Mess and Other Jesus Stories*, 166.

and authenticity in harmony with the world. Thomas à Kempis, in *The Imitation of Christ*, urged believers to live as salt by practicing humility and obedience. He reminded us that true Christian influence doesn't come from outward power but a quiet dedication to Christ. This inner transformation, he taught, is what brings out the flavor of God's presence in the world.

These saints remind us that when we detach from the pursuit of wealth, success, and social approval, we're free to live authentically for God. When life is fixated on worldly gain, it loses its saltiness and purpose. Jesus tells us to just be salt. Serve one another. Care for those in need without seeking recognition. As à Kempis urges, "Do good while you still have time." The small, unseen acts can have lasting impact. The power of salt lies in its hidden presence—it dissolves, purifies, heals, and brings out the best in whatever it touches. God blesses you with giant handfuls of love to enhance your life so you can enhance the lives of others. You are the flavor of the world.

Someone once came up to me after a sermon and said, "While we can't lose our soul, we can lose our savor." We all risk becoming unsavory—doing more harm than good. We see this in our politics and churches, when Christians fail to stand for what's right, turning a blind eye to the corruption around them. Such people are not worth their salt. If there's no Christ in your Christianity, you have no value in God's kingdom.

Jesus says, "You are salt." If you lose your saltiness, how will others taste God's goodness? To be his disciple is to never lose the capacity to love and value those who are brought into our lives, especially those folks who have been pushed aside or kicked to the curb. Jesus calls us to seek justice, show mercy, have integrity, and speak up for what's right—even if it costs us.

We are salt. We are valuable to God. It's through how we live Christ's love in the world that others see their worth in God's kingdom. Whether you're regular table salt, smoky sea salt, or salt of a different color, you are salt. I am salt. It's up to us to season the world with the Good News of Jesus Christ, who sustains us—spiritually and physically—so we can heal and enhance our communities, right here, right now, in God's kingdom. Good salt does what it's supposed to do—flavor the world with God's love and grace.

9

SHINE ON, YOU CRAZY DIAMOND

"You are the light of the world... Let your light shine brightly before others that they may see all the good you are doing and give glory to your God."
—Matthew 5:14, 16

I am of that age now. I'm afraid to admit it, but I have become that old man who walks around the house readjusting the thermostat and turning off lights that no one will own up to leaving on. I have come to accept our house is haunted by a few mischievous gremlins. They love to mess with me. I'm convinced that these little creatures are the ones cranking up the heat and flipping on lights in the middle of the day, just to drive me crazy.

Then again, I might be the gremlin. My vision's not what it used to be—though let's face it, it wasn't great in the first place. I'm forgetting things, like turning off lights. Maybe I'm the one inadvertently causing all this trouble. But I do know one thing for sure: light is essential to all of us. It's how we navigate, how we find our way.

I was taught about light from Mr. Dempsey, my high school biology teacher. He was a very chubby man who sweated a lot. But there was a kindness to him and a welcoming grace that made each student feel that they were important. Even someone like me, who was nearly impossible to teach. Mr. Dempsey would help me with issues I was having outside of the classroom. He was, I guess you could say, a light in my life.

Light is the source of energy for everything living. Trees need it. Birds need it. Even the ocean needs it. And the guy across the street—he needs light as much as my lawn does. Light is life. We see this in the miracle of photosynthesis where plants take sunlight and turn it into energy. Whether we're eating the plants directly or eating the animals that eat those plants, light is essential to living. Without it, we're nothing.

When my son was little, he had to have every light on. The brighter the better. I swear the amount of lumens emitted in his room were bright enough to land a plane. I used to think he needed every light on because he was scared of the dark. Turns out he couldn't see very well and needed glasses. All those lights helped him navigate a blurry world. Jesus says, "Be the light." Help others see the world more clearly.

But what good is a lamp if it's not plugged in? If it's not turned on? A light's purpose is to shine. And just like a flashlight or a lamp is turned on when we need it most, our light is meant to be a beacon. But we're not supposed to hoard that light. We're called to share it. Jesus didn't mean we should be walking around like biological flashlights with a spotlight on us all the time. He wasn't talking about the sun or the artificial lights we rely on for comfort and safety. He was talking about the light that lives inside us all—the kind of light that only comes from God. The light that flickers and burns and sometimes shines more brightly in some of us than in others. But it's there in all of us, whether we see it or not. And that light? It's not for us to hide away. It's meant to be shared. It's meant to give light to those stumbling in the dark, to offer clarity where there is confusion, and to remind others of the goodness of God's love. When we let our light shine—not for the praise of others, but so that God might be glorified—we become a part of a greater purpose.

That's the light Jesus is talking about. A small burning ember of

God's glory that we all possess. While some of us might flicker a little brighter than others, the truth is we all have this light. Not because we've earned it, but because God knew we would need it. It's a spiritual light that helps us see and understand the difference between good and bad, the metaphorical bright and dark side of our inner being. And when we tap into its power, this little light can begin to radiate peace, hope, and love in ways that can pierce the darkest of places—especially when everything around us feels chaotic or hopeless.

I remember staying at a friend's place one night. His room was built into the center space of a giant warehouse. This meant no windows and no outside light creeping in. When the lights were off, it felt like I was drowning in total darkness. It was suffocating, and I even had trouble breathing. But way over in the corner I spotted a tiny green light glowing from his laptop charger. It was my lifesaver. The longer I focused my eyes on it, the brighter it grew, putting my soul to ease. That's the power of light. The smallest glow can bring a glimmer of hope.

Jesus says, "You are the light of the world" (Matt. 5:14). You. Are. Light. When life feels overwhelmingly dark, there is still a light within us—illuminating, even when we can't perceive it. This light is Christ. Barbara Brown Taylor guides us through the darkness with this advice. "When we allow ourselves to be the light of Christ, we do not need to seek it out; it already shines in us. To live as children of the light is not to be something we have to become, but to be something we already are."* You are light. Shine brightly.

You might think your light is weak or barely noticeable, but in a world stumbling through the dark, even the smallest glow matters. The thing is, light doesn't just exist for itself. It exists to illuminate, to guide, to reveal. Light exposes truth, it casts out fear, it leads people home. Thus, we are called to radiate God's love in our relationships, our communities, and the broken places where we think light and love can't reach.

---

* Barbara Brown Taylor, *Learning to Walk in the Dark* (New York: HarperOne, 2014).

Jesus doesn't want us to hide our light, but to be the light. Not just reflect it or bask in it. Be it. We *are* light. This is who we are. It's our identity. Our purpose is to live as children of the light shining through the cracks of our own brokenness. This divine light has the power to bring healing and hope to a world that might have trouble seeing it.

The Bible speaks clearly about this light. Jesus is called the light of the world, and John reminds us that "in Him, there is no darkness at all" (1 John 1:5). Jesus goes on to say, "If we walk in the light as he himself is in the light, we have fellowship with one another" (1 John 1:7). That's the thing. When we walk in that light, we are called to bring others along with us. The world might be dark, but we are called to shine that light into it, just as Christ did. This spiritual light is the same light that was there at the very beginning, when God spoke light into existence and interrupted the chaos of darkness. And just like that original light, the light of Christ cannot be overcome by darkness. Ever. When we walk in the light of Christ, we see glimpses of God's glory, even in those dark and cavernous places we sometimes stumble into.

We are the light of the world. The light we possess is Christ in us. This is the light of God's love that breaks through the darkness, allowing others to see their inherent worth in God's heart. As St. John of the Cross wrote, "In the evening of life, we will be judged on love alone. It is love that transforms us and others into vessels of divine light."* When we walk in the light, we can see the goodness in others, the Christ in them.

There is a Sanskrit greeting that has become a part of the pop culture vernacular these days. *Namaste*. It means, "I greet the holy one in you." To say that to someone is to acknowledge the fullness of God in the goodness of every soul. It says, I unite my divine light with your light. While so many of us love to say it, I'm afraid we don't do it very well. I think most of the problems stem from our inability to

---

* John of the Cross, *Sayings of Light and Love*, trans. Kieran Kavanaugh and Otilio Rodriguez (Washington, D.C.: ICS Publications, 1991), Saying 64.

recognize the divine light in each other. As a result, we are missing out on really understanding God and ourselves.

This is exactly what Jesus did when he was approached by a man possessed with a legion of demons. He looked beyond this man's darkness to his divine light. By uniting his light with the man's light, healing happened. All that is good, right, and true became whole again. Jesus did the same when he embraced the leper. And forgave the woman caught in adultery. In fact, this is what Jesus did with everyone he met. He said, "Namaste. I see your light, and I give you mine."

This is precisely why Jesus tells us not to hide this light or even tuck it away in a corner. He calls us to shine—to let our light be seen by others so that God can be seen through us. Jesus invites us to illuminate God's love, exposing the truth of God's reality that heaven has come to us. This can be hard to see if everyone is walking around with baskets covering their heads.

Just as our physical eyes need light to see clearly, we need spiritual light to guide us through life—especially during challenging times when everything feels dark. I look at all the crazy shit Jesus says as beams of spiritual light that, when put together, become like a divine flashlight—bringing clarity, hope, and direction, even when I'm not sure where the next step will take me.

Jesus says, "I am the light of the world. Whoever follows me will never walk in darkness, but will have the light of life" (John 8:12). This isn't just a metaphor about physical light. It's about spiritual clarity. When we follow Jesus, we have a guiding light that helps us navigate life—one that shows us how to live with love, kindness, and grace. It helps us make sense of what's right and wrong, what's important and what's fleeting. When that light is covered or dimmed, we feel like we're stumbling around in the dark, unsure of where we're going. But unlike animals with night vision, we don't need to rely on our own abilities to see in the dark. We have God's light in us. This light isn't bound by physical conditions. It's always available, bringing hope, comfort, and clarity even in the darkest moments.

Now, on a side note, I do think we tend to give darkness a bad rap.

We've made it the punching bag of metaphors—the go-to villain. Darkness is where bad things lurk, where lost people wander, where hope goes to die. Or so we tell ourselves. But if light and dark coexist in the same space, then maybe God also lives in both. Maybe darkness has a holiness we've been too scared to name. I mean, why else would every single seed get shoved deep into the soil, buried in the dark? If darkness were a mistake, wouldn't seeds just sprout in the light, skipping the whole underground ordeal? But they don't. No, the whole thing starts in a hidden place.

When my kids were in preschool, they did a science experiment with lima bean seeds—you know the one. They'd press them inside a plastic baggie with a wet paper towel and tape them to the window. And lo and behold, those little suckers would sprout. Then our kids would bring them home for their parents to kill.

But that's the exception. Most seeds get shoved deep into the dirt, where the tiniest sliver of light manages to sneak through. And what happens? The shell cracks open. But get this—the seed's first instinct isn't to reach for the sky. It doesn't panic, thinking, gotta get outta here! Gotta find the sun! No. It does the exact opposite. It embraces the darkness. It pushes its roots down. It establishes a foundation in the depths. It feeds on everything buried in that hidden place—the rich, unseen, forgotten things. And only after it has rooted itself in the dark does it push upwards, break the surface, and reach for the sun.

That's how life works. That's how transformation works. We keep thinking we have to escape the darkness to be whole. But maybe the dark isn't what breaks us—it's what makes us. But we also need light. We can't survive in total darkness.

Jesus says, "Let your light shine so others can see your good works and give God glory" (Matt. 5:16). We are called to be children of the light—which exposes the darkness and reveals all that is good, right, and true. This is our divine birthright. Our purpose in life. Our calling. It's who we were made to be—beacons of love. People, created in God's image, who amplify the light in others. Or...I guess we could also be people who dim it. We can call out love, justice, and mercy. Or we can choose bitterness, resentment, and fear. One of those choices leads to life. The other? Darkness. Be the light.

The Apostle John wrote, "This is the message we have heard from him and declare to you: God is light; in him there is no darkness at all" (1 John 1:5). John encourages us to walk in the light just as Jesus did and to live with the same love and truth illuminating through us. And he reassures us that when we do, we are made whole. We are able to shine that little heavenly light into the lives of others. Again, Barbara Brown Taylor writes, "The light that comes from God does not cast shadows. It calls us to step out of the darkness, to see one another as we are, to see each person as beloved, as worthy of God's care, as a vessel for God's light to shine through."*

But even in the face of this despair, we cling to this unshakable truth: "God is light, and in God, there is no darkness at all" (1 John 1:5). That light? It's always there. It's in us, and it's for us. When we walk in that light—together, with God, and with one another—we find joy. Not a fleeting joy, but a joy that comes from walking in truth, a joy that can't be shaken, even when the world around us feels like it's crumbling.

I was walking my dog on one of those rare winter days in Los Angeles when thick black storm clouds loomed overhead. Then right in the middle of that gloomy canopy, a crack opened up. A single beam of sunlight pierced through the storm clouds and struck the earth. That heavenly ray of light, cutting through the storm, brought peace to my heart. It reminded me that no matter how dark the clouds may get, God's light is always trying to break through.

The goal of internalizing the shit Jesus says is simply to let the light in, and to let it shine out. You're called to be the light of the world, to shine in the darkness, to bring warmth, hope, and love to those who need it most. Jesus says even the smallest light, when placed in the right spot, can illuminate an entire room. If your light is hidden, it does no good to anyone. But if you let it shine, it can brighten someone's life, even if it feels like your light is small. Jesus

---

* Taylor, *Learning to Walk in the Dark*.

knew that the world can sometimes feel dark and divided, but he asks you to reflect God's love. To stoke the flame of love in others, so that the light of God can shine through us all.

You were made to shine. And as you shine, others will see that light and be drawn to it. Through each act of love, mercy, and justice, God's light will shine brighter and brighter in the world. Jesus says you are that light. Go, illuminate the world with your love. Eugene Peterson said it so well in *The Message*: "Giving, not getting, is the way. Generosity begets generosity" (Mark 4:25). And to paraphrase Richard Rohr, anything exposed by the light will be illuminated, and anything illuminated turns into light.[*] The more you give away your light, the more light you will receive in return. Why hide it?

Paul writes, "For once you were darkness, but now in the Lord, you are light. Live as children of the light" (Eph. 5:8-9). When you walk in the light, you reflect God's glory. You become a beacon of hope, radiating love, mercy, and grace so God can be, as Augustine wrote, "more truly imagined than expressed, and exists more truly than He is imagined."[†]

Jesus calls you to throw off the baskets, pull the lamps out from under the bed, and light up the world with God's glory. As a child of the light, you are meant to shine brightly before others so that they "may see your good works and give glory to God" (Matt. 5:14–16).

Martin Luther King Jr. said it best: "Darkness cannot drive out darkness. Only light can do that. Hate cannot drive out hate, only love can do that."[‡] You shine brightest through acts of generous compassion and mercy. When you guide others through storms into the safe harbor that is Christ, you reflect His light and bring others back to the warmth of God's love. Every time you offer love or listen without judgment, you radiate Christ's light further and fill the space with God's glory.

---

[*] Richard Rohr, *Everything Belongs: The Gift of Contemplative Prayer* (Cincinnati: Franciscan Media, 2003).
[†] Augustine. *Confessions*, trans. Maria Boulding (Hyde Park, NY: New City Press, 1997) book 10, chap. 16.
[‡] Martin Luther King Jr., *Strength to Love* (Boston: Beacon Press, 2010), 37.

So don't hold back from shining brightly. Plug yourself into Christ. And illuminate with such brightness that the sun and moon are no longer needed. Stand in the spotlight of God's unwavering love, and let your goodness be seen, until heaven and earth are one again—a holy city where God's light will shine over all of us.

10

RIGHTEOUSNESS STRAIGHT UP OFF THE CHARTS

> *"Whoever breaks one of the least of these commandments and teaches others to do the same will be called least in the kingdom of heaven, but whoever does them and teaches them will be called great in the kingdom of heaven. For I tell you, unless your righteousness exceeds that of the scribes and Pharisees, you will never enter the kingdom of heaven."*
> —Matthew 5:19–20

Jesus isn't in the business of making things easier. He speaks hard truths. But he always speaks truth. And the truth he speaks isn't about building walls or putting up barriers—it's about breaking down walls that separate us from God, from each other, and from the truth of who we really are. While he rarely minces his words, some of the things Jesus says can sound harsh, strange, or cryptic. So when he says, "Unless your righteousness exceeds that of the Pharisees and the teachers of the law, you will certainly not enter the kingdom of heaven" (Matt. 5:20), he's not just laying down a rule—he's inviting us into a radical rethinking of what righteousness really is. According to him, it's the key to unlocking heaven.

Jesus' goal is to awaken our hearts, realigning them with God's heart. Sure, sometimes that sounds a little subversive, maybe even countercultural, and I think that's why many of us find Jesus and his message to be such a challenge, or even a threat, to our normal way of thinking and living. But if we're going to take Jesus seriously, sometimes that will mean breaking a few rules or upsetting the apple cart. That doesn't mean we're in the wrong. The goal isn't to tear down what God has given us, but to build something better—God's kingdom here on earth.

As Jesus moves through his Sermon on the Mount, he's speaking to a crowd, not just his twelve disciples. Folks from all walks of life have followed him up the mountain to hear what he has to say. Some might be there to judge or criticize, but they're listening, nonetheless. And right after he tells them to be the salt of the earth and the light of the world, he says to the doubters, "I didn't come to abolish the law, but to fulfill it." If this were a movie, this would be the time the director would shout, "And, cut!"

So here we have it in black and white. Jesus was a rule-follower. But he was also a rule-breaker. And that's part of the reason so many good people struggle to live up to what he says. We like to pick sides—and we always want to be on the winning side. In this kingdom of heaven that Jesus is ushering in, we're all on the right side. Most of us just don't know it yet.

When someone asks me if my church is "Bible-based," I always pause. What does that even mean? And why is that the first question people ask? Are they suggesting there's another book I should be reading? A secret guide to life? It makes me wonder if we've done a disservice and made the Bible into some kind of litmus test for what constitutes as a real church or a fake one.

The truth is, Christians don't own the Bible. We just rent space in it. Every word on those pages was written by a Jewish person. Yet, ever since the fourth century, Christianity has essentially hijacked this book as though we've superseded Judaism. But that's not the full story. Christianity didn't replace Judaism—Jesus didn't come to start a new religion. He clearly came to fulfill the old one. At least, that's what the Bible says.

And while Christianity has been gracious enough to give Judaism a small space in the Bible, we've often reduced their sacred texts to a rule book—a list of dos and don'ts. If that's not offensive enough, we've also weaponized those texts, using them to shame and exclude people from growing closer to God. If there's one thing I learned from my fundamentalist upbringing, it's that the Bible doesn't work as a rule book any more than it works as a litmus test. But if we need to know the rules, Jesus is kind enough to boil all six-hundred-plus rules down to two: Love God. Love everyone. "On these two commandments hang all the laws and prophets" (Matt. 22:40).

Instead of dividing the Bible into two parts, we'd be better off embracing it as one collection of sacred stories that guide us in our relationship with God and with one another. If we don't take these stories seriously, we might never really know God, our neighbors, or even ourselves.

So yes, my church is a Bible-based church in the sense that we use scripture to strengthen our faith. But we don't just accept it blindly as a rule book to follow. I struggle with its words, and I'm not ashamed to admit that. But the struggling helps me grow closer to God and build stronger communities. I don't take every word literally; I take them seriously. Because this isn't just a historical document—it's a living, breathing map for life. A guide that leads me to become more righteous, not more religious. And I think that's exactly the point Jesus is making. "Unless your righteousness exceeds the righteousness of the religious elites, you will never see the kingdom of heaven" (Matt. 5:20).

This is what it's all about. This is why Jesus calls us to repent. Why he blesses those who haven't been blessed yet. This is salt-and-light stuff, right here, right now. Jesus gets us to rethink our ways of doing things so that the only shit we're capable of doing is all the good stuff.

A few years back, while Stephen was still a teenager, he was kicked out of his mom's house. He did what he could to get by, but that often meant making choices that hurt others. One night, while "getting by," Stephen beat a young kid within an inch of his life—someone's son in the wrong place at the wrong time. Most of the time, Stephen felt nothing by these actions. But this kid was different. Something about him, crying and bleeding, brought back old memories of being kicked by his stepfather who had been taught the way to show love was with violence. Overcome by the shame and pain he'd caused this boy, Stephen ran off into the night. But you can never run fast enough or far enough away for your past to get lost.

I met him later that evening outside the church. He'd been drinking and had just about hit rock bottom. He said he wanted to repent. When I asked, "Do you mean, confess?" he was quick to correct me. "No, I want to repent." I would quickly learn that meant he "just wanted to sit in his sin and feel like shit."

Jesus calls us to repent, but he doesn't want us to sit in our shit and feel bad. He wants us to change—actually change. To rethink our whole way of doing life so this shit we do doesn't get done anymore. Repentance isn't about guilt. It's about turning things around and choosing a different path. Through it, we become transformed by God's love and aligned with God's righteousness.

For some, the Bible can be a book of shame and guilt that points out all our failures. It condemns and doesn't offer very good news. For others, it's a book about second chances. When we tune into what Jesus really has to say, we find a new way to do shit. We find ourselves not just "getting by" but thriving in our new transformed hearts.

Jesus says, if you want to see heaven in real time, change your perspective. See the Bible not as a rule book, but as a story that reveals God's heart and will for us. This takes commitment. It requires a willingness to change—to rethink everything. Our minds, our hearts, our actions—all of it must be so focused on what God is doing in the world that people might confuse us for one of the religious elites. But it's not about keeping rules; it's about having a transformed heart that seeks justice, mercy, and God's covenant faithfulness. And that's not just for a select few. It's for all of us.

A few verses later Jesus says, "You must be perfect as your heavenly Father is perfect" (Matt. 5:48). That's a big ask, isn't it? But here's Jesus, taking that challenge and putting it front and center, calling us to pursue a standard of holiness and righteousness that the world has, frankly, long since abandoned. It's a high bar. And he sets it by comparing his followers to the best of the best—the scribes and the Pharisees.

Scribes are the scholars we see on college campuses. The Ph.D.s in tweed coats, enjoying tenure at the best universities. Those writing books on theology that only a handful of their peers could even begin to understand. The guardians of God's Word—literally. The scribes copied the ancient scrolls, preserved them, and interpreted their meaning. They were meticulous, studious, maybe even a little pretentious. But while they played an important role in keeping God's word alive, Jesus had a bone to pick with them. They were so focused on the letter of the law, on the technicalities, that they often missed the heart of the law—and the spirit behind it. They got lost in the details, but the details didn't lead them to greater compassion, mercy, or justice. Jesus called them out for it, pointing out how they preserved the word of God without living it.

And then there were the Pharisees—priests juiced up on holy steroids. They were the religious leaders, striving to live in a way that preserved holiness and purity in every part of life. On the surface, that's not a bad thing. In fact, it's something everyone should strive for. But here's the catch: the Pharisees, for all their zeal, sometimes took things too far. I'm sure their intentions were good, but Jesus didn't hold back in his critique—he accused them of hypocrisy. While they meticulously followed the law, they missed its deeper purpose. Jesus called them whitewashed tombs. They looked good on the outside, but inside, they were filled with rot and death. Their focus on legalistic obedience blinded them as well from the very things scripture says are at the heart of God's righteousness: compassion, mercy, and justice.

The scribes and Pharisees were so dedicated to the Law that their names became synonymous with righteousness. For many of us, this conjures up images of people who are proud, self-congratulatory, and quick to judge those they deem sinners. And they still exist today. Maybe they don't wear the same robes or titles, but I'd venture to say that there isn't a church or synagogue in the world that doesn't have at least one person sitting in the pew, quietly judging, proof-texting what's being taught, and scrutinizing who tithes and who doesn't, who keeps their Sabbath and who doesn't. They know the rituals, but not how to show compassion to someone who has fallen. They're really good at keeping up the act, of wearing a mask of piety while missing the heart of what Jesus was about. And that's dangerous. When we focus so much on following the rules, we forget the very thing that makes us righteous: compassion, mercy, and justice. These are the things that show the world who we really are, not how well we keep up appearances.

Now, here's where I think it gets interesting. The Pharisees were the good ones. They really were. They dedicated their entire lives to bringing their communities back in line with the ways of God. They were the reformers of their time, passionate about getting the Jewish people to honor their covenant with God. And they did this by upholding the laws and prophets. Jesus calls us to do the same, but with love as the greatest of the laws.

Jesus says, "Anyone who breaks one of these laws and teaches others to do the same, will be called least in the kingdom of heaven" (Matt. 5:19). That's a tough pill to swallow, especially for those whose piety has earned them high esteem. But Jesus is calling them out—pointing out that their rigid adherence to rules has gotten in the way of practicing what they preach. He continues, "But whoever practices and teaches these commands will be called great in the kingdom of heaven" (Matt. 5:20). And here's the heart of it: Jesus isn't interested in rule-following for the sake of rules. He's about right living, right relationships, mercy, justice, and grace. He's talking about a righteousness that transcends the legalism of the Pharisees. This heaven that Jesus awakens us to see, is wherever and whenever we do what God desires most. When we practice love, mercy, justice, and grace we start to see the divine at work all around us.

More than blindly following a set of rules or engaging in empty religious rituals, Jesus is calling us to go deeper, beyond the rules. He's asking us to expand our understanding of righteousness, to deepen our relationships with God and with each other. God's righteousness, according to the prophets, isn't about dogma or ritual; it's about caring for the oppressed, advocating for the marginalized, living with integrity, and practicing peace and forgiveness. It's the way of love. "What does the Lord require of you," the prophet Micah asks, "to do justice, love kindness, and walk humbly with your God?" (Mic. 6:8). This is the way of Jesus, and everything he says points to this truth. Love equals right living with God. It's the key to seeing heaven in real time.

Jesus always pushes us beyond the superficial to a life of radical love. This means loving without judgment, without condemnation. It means going beyond the ritualistic performance of religion to live with deep, heartfelt obedience to God's will. And that obedience has room for everyone, even those we might think are beyond grace. This will often require us to move beyond rule-following to a life where love is the highest law. And sometimes, that means breaking the rules to get there.

We see it clearly when Jesus meets the Samaritan woman at the well (John 4:7–31). He breaks all kinds of social and religious taboos just by speaking with her. She wasn't just a Samaritan—a group that Jews traditionally despised—but she was also a woman. She wasn't just any woman, but a woman whose lifestyle was deemed unacceptable. In that culture, she wasn't allowed to speak to a man who wasn't her husband—especially a religious man like Jesus. Yet Jesus disregarded all those social and religious boundaries. He doesn't see her through the lens of gender, ethnicity, or past mistakes. All he sees is a beloved child of God. Moved by compassion, he offers her living water—a symbol of spiritual renewal and inclusion. In doing so, Jesus transcends the boundaries of the law to fulfill its deeper purpose: transforming and reconciling humanity.

A similar thing happens when Jesus visits Zacchaeus, the tax collector (Luke 19:1–10). Zacchaeus was despised by his community because he worked for the Romans and had swindled many people out of their money. When Zacchaeus, eager to see Jesus, climbs a tree to get a better view, Jesus could have easily passed him by. He could have paid attention to anyone else. But that's not what happens.

Instead, Jesus stops, looks up, and calls Zacchaeus to climb down. He's so moved with compassion that he accepts Zacchaeus' invitation to share a meal in his home. Of course, the Pharisees are always lurking nearby, watching Jesus closely, waiting to accuse him of spending time with people like Zacchaeus—those who are corrupt, hated, and shunned by society. But Jesus shows us what true righteousness looks like by accepting the invitation.

Conventional wisdom would say, "Ignore him. Shun him." Jesus says, "Love him." And in doing so, Jesus teaches us that our pursuit of righteousness isn't about following the rules or staying within the lines. It's about embracing those whom society has rejected. It's about extending compassion and love to those who are marginalized, even when it's uncomfortable or unpopular. Because of Jesus' willingness to exceed the righteousness of the religious elites, Zacchaeus's life is changed forever. He repents and promises to make restitution, vowing to give half his wealth to the poor and to pay back four times what he took from others. Jesus responds by saying, "Today, salvation has come to this house." Salvation isn't a ticket into heaven; it's heaven itself shining through Jesus.

God's righteousness starts with love, the kind of love that is moved with compassion, mercy, and grace. A love that leads to personal and social restoration. A love that inspires repentance and reparative restitution. This is the love Jesus calls us to—a love that goes beyond the boundaries, the rules, and the norms to embrace the very ones society often casts aside. Righteous love is about feeding the physically hungry rather than starving the spiritually stuffed. It is about caring for the sick rather than shaming them for their condition. It's about welcoming children, going the extra mile, and giving to everyone who begs from you without asking for anything in return. It's about welcoming the Stephens and sitting with them in their shit. This is how righteousness is defined and lived out in the kingdom of heaven. Being the salt and light in ways that exceed your wildest dreams.

Jesus says, "A tree is known by its fruit...and on the day of judgment, you will have to account for every careless word you utter"

(Matt. 12:33, 36). Still, how many of his followers continue to prioritize gun rights over human rights? How many churches are content to exclude certain groups instead of extending the embrace of welcome? How many preachers wear pins that say, "Jesus loves you," while holding up signs that say, "God hates you"? Jesus will send his disciples out as "sheep among wolves" (Matt.10:16) with one mission: "Go and proclaim the good news that the kingdom of heaven has come near" (Matt. 10:7). He told them, "Cure the sick, raise the dead, cleanse the lepers, cast out demons" (Matt.10:8). He never said, "Hate," "take up arms," or "deny people access to God." Change the way you think, and you will see the kingdom of heaven.

Anthony Clavier writes, "The road to holiness is the path of love, compassion, of caring and sympathy, of helping each other along that journey, stopping to assist those who have become tired, have fallen on the way, or who have given up in despair."* For St. Teresa of Calcutta, this meant seeing the face of Christ in the poor, the rejected, and the forgotten and loving them as though she were serving Jesus himself. Following Jesus isn't about legalism—it's a call to transcend rules and embody a higher spiritual standard, a standard that recognizes the inherent dignity and worth of every person as made in God's image.

When we welcome and honor others as God has welcomed us, the words of scripture—laws, prophets, gospels—begin to take on flesh. When we live a life that mirrors Christ's, we reveal the way of Jesus: a way of love and righteousness, manifest in him and through him. "Love one another as I have loved you" (John 13:34). Love is the greatest commandment, the foundation of "all the Law and the Prophets" (Matt.22:40). Love is the window to our understanding as well as the key to right living. Love is how we bear the fruit of the kingdom of heaven. It is the light that cannot be hidden. And it's how we do better than the scribes and the Pharisees until the space between heaven and earth is no more.

---

* Anthony Clavier, *Path to Holiness: Discovering God in Catholic Devotionals and Spiritual Practices* (Harrisburg, PA: Morehouse Publishing, 2000), 4.

11

THE DUDE ABIDES

"Abide in me, and I will abide in you..."
—John 15:4

There's this game my family loves on road trips—*Would You Rather...?* It's a simple way to pass time and start conversations that sometimes go off the rails. I've used it in team-building exercises, too, because it's a great equalizer. Each card begins with, *"Would you rather..."* and then offers two impossible choices. Would you rather lose all the money you made this year in a Ponzi scheme or forget every memory you made? Would you rather always hit red lights or suffer through eternal slow internet? Some are easy—puppy or kitten? Others make you squirm, like: *would you rather have Jesus as your roommate or Donald Trump as president?*

You might think that last one's a slam dunk. But the thing about roommates is they're temporary. Presidents too. They show up, stay for a while, and eventually, the lease is up. Some seem like a great idea at first, but then you learn the hard way that shared space and shared life are two different things.

Good things about having a roommate:

- Split rent and utilities
- Someone to cover for you when you're not home
- Built-in company

Bad things about having a roommate:

- They eat your food
- They borrow your stuff
- They snoop
- They make *unusual* noises
- They're always there

This list can go on and on, but I would bet that more often than not, the bad side of having a roommate would be a lot longer than the good. Now, imagine *Jesus* as your roommate.

Pros:

- Unlimited wine
- No judgment
- House plants never die (unless it was a particular fig tree)
- He always has your back

Cons:

- He *knows* your business
- You *can't* lie to him
- He lets *everyone* in
- Someone is *always* getting their feet washed in the kitchen

I really think Jesus would make a great roommate. But like picking a president, I'm not sure I'd actually choose it. And yet—he chooses us. He says, "Abide in me, and I will abide in you" (John 15:4).

Thanks to a great film, *The Big Lebowski*, the world now has the phrase, *"The Dude abides."** It's part Jedi wisdom, part biblical reference, and fully the mantra of a man either profoundly at peace or profoundly high. The Dude is the kind of roommate who eats your last slice of pizza and shrugs, saying, *"That's just, like, your opinion, man."*

What seems like a throwaway line at the end of the movie—*"The Dude abides"*—is now shorthand for a whole way of being. In the last scene, the Dude is at a bowling alley bar when the narrator asks how the tournament is going. They exchange pleasantries. As they part, the narrator tells him, *"Take it easy, Dude."* And with his signature chill, the Dude replies, *"Yeah, well, the Dude abides."*

Jesus also uses the word *"abide"* at the end of a long walk with his disciples, as they head toward the garden where he'll soon be arrested. It's hardly the same relaxed, let-it-slide attitude of the Dude. And yet, they both live fully in the moment. If anyone truly lived by this *abide* mentality, they'd probably get through life with a whole lot less fear of the future and regret over the past.

For the Dude, *abiding* means rolling with life's absurdities. For Jesus, *abiding* means trusting so completely in love that nothing—not betrayal, suffering, or even death—can shake it. Different approaches, same unshakable presence. Then, of course, there's *the other Jesus* in *The Big Lebowski*—the Latino bowling champion with the unforgettable line: *"No one fucks with the Jesus."* Maybe the church could use a little of that confidence.

The Hebrew Jesus and the Dude share a way of abiding. But while one abides in the Spirit of God, the other abides in vodka—the spirit of his beloved White Russian. And, as far as we know, Jesus wasn't medicating himself with marijuana. *But they both abide.*

Jesus knows what abiding with him means for his disciples, especially in this moment. He knows that following him isn't easy. He has already warned them that one will betray him and the rest will

---

* *The Big Lebowski*, directed by Joel and Ethan Coen (Universal City, CA: Universal Pictures, 1998), film.

abandon him. He sees fear creeping in. And yet, he has prepared them for this. He shows them how to live in such faith that nothing is impossible. Like the Dude's wisdom, Jesus's words are simple: "Don't worry. Be present. Be ready. Abide in me. And my Spirit will abide in you."

In the Christian tradition, *abiding* isn't just about location—it's about presence, like the in-dwelling presences of God. It's relational. The Greek word for "abide," *meno*, means "to remain, stay, or continue." It's not a weekend retreat; it's a permanent dwelling, a mutual and faithful relationship where believers live in the constant reality of God's presence. This isn't some new idea Jesus is springing on his disciples. They've been steeped in it their whole lives. Their Jewish roots are anchored in the understanding that God abides with his people—in both a physical and a spiritual sense.

In the Jewish tradition, the Hebrew word *Shekhinah* describes God's manifest presence—it's a way of saying, *God moves into the neighborhood.* This is the presence that dwelled in the Tabernacle and later in the Temple, the holy nearness of a God who refuses to remain distant. In Exodus 25:8, God tells Moses, "Let them make me a sanctuary, that I may dwell among them." Not hover over them. Not check in every once in a while. *Dwell.*

And now Jesus is saying the same thing in a new way. "God is here. God remains. Even when I am gone, God is still abiding with you." It's as if Jesus is saying, "Stay with me, even when you can't see me. You do that by embracing and sharing all that I have taught you."

This echoes ancient rabbinic wisdom, which taught that God's presence isn't confined to a building. It moves, it speaks, it breathes through the words of Torah and is made visible through acts of loving-kindness.

It's not just *in* the Temple—it's *in us.* We become God's dwelling place every time we love, every time we keep the commandments, every time we reflect the God who is love. Jesus makes it plain: "I give you a new commandment, that you love one another. Just as I have loved you, you should also love one another. By this, everyone will know you are my disciples, if you have love for one another" (John 13:34–35).

To abide in Jesus is to abide in love. And when your life is spent dwelling in God's love, you live without fear of the future or shame of the past.

Jesus speaks of this mystical union like this:

"I am the true vine, and my Father is the vine grower. He removes every branch in me that bears no fruit. Every branch that bears fruit he prunes to make it bear more fruit...Just as the branch cannot bear fruit by itself unless it abides in the vine, neither can you unless you abide in me. I am the vine; you are the branches...Whoever does not abide in me is thrown away like a branch and withers; such branches are gathered, thrown into the fire, and burned...My Father is glorified by this, that you bear much fruit and become my disciples. As the Father has loved me, so I have loved you; abide in my love. If you keep my commandments, you will abide in my love...so that my joy may be in you and that your joy may be complete" (John 15:1–2, 4–6, 8–11).

Looking at the world around him, Jesus makes God's truth tangible. Among the leafy vines, heavy with grapes, and the fires burning in the vineyards of Kedron, Jesus reimagines a passage from Isaiah. The prophet had used the vineyard as a metaphor for Israel, writing of how God had expected good fruit but found wild, bitter grapes instead (Isaiah 5:1–7). Jesus paints a picture of their belonging to a single, living organism, rooted in God's heart. Whether you're a leaf, a branch, or even a tendril, everything attached to this vine is nourished by God's love and grown for the sole purpose of bearing good fruit. And any part that refuses to grow? It *gets a haircut*, like my daughter so profoundly stated while watching me prune back the tree in our front yard.

Jesus describes God as a loving, attentive gardener—one who carefully prunes, not to punish, but to prepare us for something greater. This is why he tells his disciples, *"Abide in me" (John 15:4)*. Stay with me. Let God take up residence in you, so that together we can share God's faithful heart forever. To abide is not just to exist—it's to flourish. This relationship emphasizes dependence, life, and fruitfulness that result from a close, abiding connection with God.

Picture a wisteria vine spilling over a garden arbor. Its branches stretch in every direction, covered with potential blooms. But over time, some drift too far from the main vine. They pale, wither, and stop blooming. So the gardener steps in—pruning whatever doesn't help the plant grow. And soon, the vine is thriving again, bursting with life. Jesus looks at his disciples the same way, reminding them: "Just as these branches depend on the vine, you depend on the love and presence of God. Remain in that love, and you'll bloom in ways you never imagined."

As a novice gardener, I've learned that proper pruning yields better fruit. I've experimented on my apple and avocado trees and noticed that each branch, when pruned correctly, produces more. Jesus says God does the same with us—cutting away what doesn't serve us so we can bear more fruit. We are free to wander. Free to stretch along the trellises of life, sometimes without direction. But no matter where we go, the gardener remains—pruning, shaping, tending the vine. "I abide in you" (John 15:4).

While the pruning process can be painful, the sharp pinch of the shears is necessary for our spiritual growth. The same could be said about the searing heat of the fire. We will all experience both at least once in our lives. But we don't need to be afraid. Fire, contrary to popular imagination, isn't always about destruction. Jesus isn't talking about some eternal pit of torment here. He's looking at the literal fires burning in the valley. They provide light along the pathway. Create energy for cooking. Provide heat to keep people warm. But fires do more than that. They take dead branches and transform them into ash. An avid gardener knows that wood ash is an excellent source of the nutrients that plants need to thrive.

If God can take two rough-hewn wooden branches—the very cross of Christ—and turn them into an instrument of salvation, then surely God can take our worst and turn it into something good as well. When we reduce fire to punishment, we miss a powerful message that is truly transformational. God is always at work, pruning and refining—not to destroy, but to restore. To bring life, not death. This is what love does. It changes and transforms us from the inside out.

Everything God does is to increase the yield of love.

That's the essence of Jesus' ministry—transformation. His words and actions don't just invite us to believe in him; they invite us to change the way we see ourselves, God, and one another. And that transformation always starts with love.

Now, Jesus doesn't just say, "Abide in me," he says, "Abide in me as I abide in you" (John 15:4). It's a partnership. A relationship. But it's more than that. It's a reminder that God has already made the first move, already chosen to abide with us. Now we're invited to respond. To attach our life to his and draw from God's abundant love that will shape the fruit we produce—love, joy, patience, kindness, goodness, faithfulness, gentleness, and self-control (Gal. 5:22–23).

To *abide* means to *stay*, to *remain*, and to *be nourished* by the source of life itself. Jesus says, "I am the vine; you are the branches" (John 15:5). Whether we like it or not, we are already a part of God. The only choice we have is how close we're willing to stay.

Years ago, I visited a winery in Sonoma Valley and learned something fascinating—grapevines thrive under stress. The soil, the climate, the tension of growth—all of it adds to the character of the grape. The most unique flavors come from the fruit's proximity to the central vine, where the nutrients are most concentrated. The lateral branches, which naturally wander, are carefully guided so they don't lose their strength or grow sour. If a branch gets too far from the vine, it stops producing fruit. It's like that with humans too. If we wander too far from Jesus, we stop producing the fruit of love. "Apart from me, you can do nothing" (John 15:5).

And we really can't. We can't nourish ourselves. We can't prune ourselves. And we certainly can't bear the fruit of God's kingdom if we aren't drawing from a healthy source. But when we abide—when we stay close to Jesus, to love itself—something happens. That love starts bearing fruit. With roots deeply embedded in God's heart, Jesus' love feeds us, heals us, and empowers us to make love blossom everywhere we go.

While the world points inward—*take care of yourself first, look out for number one*—Jesus points outward, reminding us to love one another and telling us, the more you give, the more you will receive. To abide in Jesus is to *become like Jesus* who doesn't just *tell* us about love—he *embodies* it. He abides always and closely in God's love—the same love that also flows through us, changing the way we see the world. This is how we produce the kind of fruit that lasts.

Debie Thomas sees a dichotomy to abiding, describing it as both *passive* and *active*. She says it like this, "To abide is to stay rooted in place. But it is also to grow and change." * If we abide, we get pruned. If we abide, we bear fruit that others will see and taste. If we abide, we accept nourishment that isn't of our own making. And if we abide, we have to live in community with other branches, messy as it is. But this is the oneness God calls us into—not to lose our identity, but to be united in love. A love that transforms. A love that changes *everything*.

> *Heaven happens when the whole world*
> *is tangled up in the vines of God's love.*

Abiding in Jesus isn't just about hanging out with him. It's about *showing up* for him—by living out his love and making a difference in the world. Jesus says, "The harvest is plentiful, but the workers are few" (Matt. 9:37). There is work to be done—in ourselves, and in the world.

---

* Thomas, *Into the Mess and Other Jesus Stories*, 144–146.

12

SERIOUSLY? DON'T BE ANXIOUS

"So do not worry about tomorrow, for tomorrow will bring worries of its own. Today's trouble is enough for today."
—Matthew 6:34

The Sunday before people rush out to cast their votes for the next President of the United States, I offer my congregation a word of comfort. The nation is divided, as it always seems to be, and anxiety is thick in the air. Who will fill the most important seat in the world? I remind them not to worry. God's kingdom doesn't hinge on any election. The Church has survived world wars, civil wars, corruption, division, famines, and fires. It will continue to survive, just as it has for 2,000 years—although that's debatable.

I tell them what I need to hear myself: God loves every Republican, every Democrat, and everyone in between—equally, unconditionally. Their votes do not matter to God, though their actions matter in heaven—this new world Jesus has ushered in. If, in this kingdom, God's love transcends politics, so can we. A strong community will always rise above the messiness and pettiness of party differences. I say this with my whole heart—but the truth is, even I feel the anxiety. I wonder what this election means for my family and for our growing church. Then God disrupts my fear.

I should be used to this by now. God has a way of shaking things up, of dispelling my anxieties in ways I never see coming. Leaving a well-paying career for ministry? That was one. Someone once described my new vocation as "a lifetime of wiping a poor man's ass." Turns out, that poor man's ass is my own.

One of my favorite divine disruptions happened just weeks after I got into the master's program at Fuller Seminary. I woke up before dawn with a crushing pain in my chest. Sweating. Struggling to breathe. My gut told me it wasn't a heart attack, but it sure felt like one. And the whole time, a voice repeated in my head, *How will I put shoes on their feet? How will I put shoes on their feet?* My kids. Three of them. And now, a minister's salary. Jesus says, "Don't worry about tomorrow. Today will give you enough shit to worry about" (Matt. 6:34, my interpretation). Not what one wants to hear in the middle of a cardiac arrest.

Instead of waking my wife to take me to the ER, I decided this was the perfect time to pick a fight with God—using language more suited for a sailor than a seminarian. Have you ever been so angry with God that you just unleashed a torrent of rage and profanity? This was my moment. I let God have it. No matter what I yelled, no matter how I cursed, that inner voice just kept on repeating, "How will I put shoes on their feet?" It's amazing what we worry about, especially in dire situations.

Maybe it was fears about money. Maybe I didn't truly believe I was doing the right thing. I'd been fighting this call to ministry for decades, fighting God for just as long. But in that moment, I needed proof. I needed to know that I wasn't delusional, that I wasn't about to wreck my family's security for nothing. I needed God to prove that this was real.

I've known my call to ministry was real since I was thirteen. That realization paralyzed me. *Prove it*, I demanded. Show me this isn't all in my head. I knew the only way God could prove it to me was to put the onus back on God because only he could answer, "How will I put shoes on their feet?"

Now, theologians have a formal name for what I did next. It's called Bible Roulette. It's where a desperate, terrified seminarian—mid-panic attack—demands proof from God, flips open the Bible, and stabs a finger at a random verse. That verse—obviously—is supposed to be the answer. I didn't know this game had a name when I first played it. My ego assumed I invented it, but in my desperation to get that voice in my head to stop talking, I grabbed the Bible next to my bed, opened it at random, slammed my finger down, then looked. Matthew 6:28: "And why do you worry about clothing?"

I was done. God had won.
And I knew I was officially, completely screwed.

It was both the most terrifying and the most relieving moment of my life. Like all the words of Jesus, this passage surged through me like an electric charge. I sobbed into my pillow, unable to fight anymore. And the second I surrendered, the grip on my chest released. I could breathe again. The stress I'd carried for decades melted away.

Then, in that moment, I heard God whisper, *"I've got you. You are mine."*

What was I so worried about? That's easy. We all have a list, locked and loaded. We worry about our health, our jobs, our security. About our country and who's in charge. About whether we'll have enough food, enough money, enough safety. There's a Jewish saying: If you have food on your table, you have enough. Do not worry. If you have a table to eat that food off of, you have more than enough. Do not worry. If you have food left over, then you have enough to share. If you have more than one shirt in your closet, you have no reason to worry about what to wear.

One of the most repeated phrases in all of scripture is *"Do not be afraid."* Or *"Do not fear."* Or *"Do not worry."* Jesus says it four times in just these few verses (Matt. 6:23–34). It is both familiar and foreign, because the world is always giving us more to worry about. Wars. Civil unrest. Pandemics. Fires in the west, hurricanes in the east. Climate collapse. Yet Jesus has the audacity to say, "Don't worry about tomorrow. Tomorrow will worry about itself" (Matt. 6:34).

Jesus ushers in the kingdom of heaven, and it's here. It's all around us. It's within reach. He says to trust in God's provision, to seek God's kingdom first (Matt. 6:33). Keep your focus on God. Trust in God's faithfulness and care. Look around. The birds do not plant or harvest, and yet they have enough (Matt. 6:26). The lilies do not toil or spin, and yet they are clothed in beauty (Matt. 6:28-29). If God takes care of them, why do I worry about the future, when I could be spending time with God in the present?

Jesus always invites us into heaven to be with God *now*. He's not against planning for the future, not saying don't have a savings account or a retirement fund. He's warning us about the anxiety that robs us from living fully *in* the present moment. Jesus challenges his followers to live shaped by faith, trusting that God sees our needs and is more than able to provide. Henri Nouwen once said, *"We can only be where we are. When we are fully present to the moment, we live life to its fullest."*[*]

When Jesus says, *"Don't worry,"* I know it can sound like a cliché, like something you say when you don't think someone's problem is worth getting worked up over. When my oldest daughter had to move herself into college her freshman year—because of the COVID pandemic—her mother and I told her, *"Don't worry, you've got this."* Maybe it sounded like a throwaway phrase, but we knew she knew it herself: she didn't need to worry, because God has been with her always.

We said the same thing to our other daughter when she was anxious about going back to school after a year and a half of learning at home. *"Don't worry, you know where things are. You know what to expect."* And when our son started his freshman year at a prestigious

---

[*] Henri J. M. Nouwen, *Here and Now: Living in the Spirit* (New York: Crossroad Publishing, 1994), 35.

Catholic high school—the one he'd worked so hard to get into—you know what I told him? *"Don't get yourself kicked out. They don't give refunds."* It was my way of reminding *myself* not to worry for him.

I say it all the time: *"Don't worry."* But sometimes, saying it does more harm than good. How do you tell a woman fleeing the Taliban not to worry? Or tell a friend on the edge of divorce, *"Don't worry"*? It's hard to speak those words into such difficult situations and not sound tone-deaf to their pain.

Between wars and rumors of wars, a fragile economy and political unrest, it's hard not to have some worry rattling around inside your head. Maybe you don't have to worry about food or clothing, but you worry what others think about you or say behind your back. Parents worry about their kids. Kids worry about their parents. Someone worries about getting a promotion. Someone else fears losing their job. Not long ago, people were even worried about something as simple as finding enough toilet paper.

Jesus tells us this kind of worry won't add another second to our lives. It won't help us sleep. It won't erase our gray hairs. Maybe that's why I love Alfred E. Neuman, the mascot of Mad Magazine, with his goofy grin and famous line: *"What, me worry?"* His advice was always the opposite of what my teachers told me in school. They wanted us to worry. Worry about grades. Worry about our future. Worry about what God would think of us. They seemed more interested in filling us with fear than with faith.

Jesus calls us into an alternative way of living. A way that's focused on God's righteousness and provision. He says, *"You can't serve two masters. It's either God or money"* (Matt. 6:24). But how many of us actually believe that, much less live like we do? Jesus knows that if our hearts are set on wealth, we will *always* worry—about how much we have, about how to get more. But that's the world's way. Jesus is the antidote. If our hearts are set on God, then no matter what happens—good times or bad times—we have no reason to worry. Sounds easy. Unless you're a single mom choosing between rent and groceries. But this passage isn't about what money can buy. It's about what God can provide.

Some of the most faithful hearts in the Church get this. They remind us to stay focused on God, knowing God's presence is enough for the moment we are in. St. Teresa of Ávila teaches us, "Do not let your thoughts wander to what you cannot control. God alone suffices."* She echoes Jesus' words: Don't waste energy worrying about what's outside your grasp. Meister Eckhart says, "Do not worry about tomorrow. God is the God of today." † And Thomas Merton found peace in releasing his worry to Christ. He writes, *Worry is a form of attachment. True peace comes when we surrender all our anxious thoughts into God's hands and dwell in the moment he has given us.*‡

The real question isn't, "Will God show up and provide for me?" It's, "Do I actually believe God is intimate, caring, and trustworthy?" Jesus looks at the birds and the wildflowers, noting how everything is held in God's delicate, loving care. "Why do you worry about what you will eat or wear?" he asks (Matt. 6:31). If this good God takes care of the least of these, surely God will take care of you.

I know what you're thinking: *This is a little out of touch with reality.* Doesn't Jesus know how the world works? That everything runs on money and consumerism? I get it. I have the credit card bills to prove it. I also have kids who need to eat. I need to eat. I have to put shoes on their feet and mine. I need a car and gas to actually live into this calling. I need a place to gather with people for worship. And all of that takes money. It takes planning. It takes making things happen on time. If I'm not careful, it can all spiral into fear, worry, and anxiety. I have to trust that what I have is enough to get me where I need to be. I have to trust that God is faithful—to a fault.

Jesus also gets it. He knows what it's like to be human and to face the problems of his day the way we face ours. He knows we need food and clothing. He knows we need air, water, gravity, and sunshine. And where do those things come from? Not the government. Not the

---

* Teresa of Ávila, *The Collected Works of St. Teresa of Ávila,* vol. 1, trans. Kieran Kavanaugh and Otilio Rodriguez (Washington, D.C.: ICS Publications, 1987), 294.
† Meister Eckhart, *Selected Writings,* trans. Oliver Davies (London: Penguin Classics, 1994), 218.
‡ Thomas Merton, *New Seeds of Contemplation* (New York: New Directions, 1961), 88.

stock market. They come from the Creator of all—the one who made you, me, and everything else. That's why Jesus points to the birds and flowers. They don't toil. They don't stockpile. They don't live in fear of the future. They rely on God's provision.

If I've learned anything, it's that worry always pulls me out of the present. It makes me obsess over what's next, or dwell on what I did wrong—instead of showing up, *right here, right now,* where God's presence can actually shine through me. Jesus calls us to live fully in the present, in the space between heaven and earth, between us and them, me and you—because *this* is where God meets us—disrupting our worry with compassion and love.

When I worry about the past or stress about what tomorrow might bring, I'm not focusing on Christ—the one who ushers in God's kingdom. And that kingdom? It's *happening* all around me. Jesus reminds us, "*Don't worry, because where you are is where you need to be.*" He invites us to open our eyes, to see God in *everything*—in the birds, the trees, in babies...and even in our enemies. Once you get that, what's left to worry about?

I know if my heart is set on God, I'll see how I'm under God's loving care. God won't leave me without support, just as God hasn't abandoned the forests or the oceans we keep destroying at a reckless pace. If Jesus' life, death, and resurrection mean anything, it's that *God is in control.* Out of death, God brings new life. That's good news. It means I can face life with all its uncertainties and unknowns with the same confidence that comes from staring into an empty tomb. It means God not only *sees* and *cares* about my situation but *moves* to help alleviate the stress it causes.

After my first quarter of seminary, I tested God one more time. It happened when I was signing up for classes for the next quarter. More classes meant more money. The severance from my old job was gone. My unemployment had run out. I needed $4,000 for tuition. This time, I didn't yell. I didn't curse. I just prayed. *God, you promised me.* Then I put the tuition on my credit card. *Do not worry.*

I hadn't even received the confirmation email before the doorbell rang. It was Rick, our mailman. Now, if you ever run into Rick, you might as well settle in. The guy loves to talk. Usually, it was about sports or family or, sometimes, God. That day, we went back and forth about who was winning the Lakers-Spurs game that night. We argued for a good fifteen minutes before he finally handed me a thick stack of mail. I shuffled through it, distracted, until I realized something—there were envelopes from churches all over the country. And inside those envelopes, there were checks. Scholarship money. Gifts from people I'd never met, who had been moved to help pay my tuition. By the time I opened the last envelope, I was holding $3,750 in my hands. And like the idiot I was, I had the audacity to tell God, "*Thanks, but you're $250 short.*" Then I smirked, "*But don't worry, dude. I got it.*"

Of course, I should have known better. Later that day, my pastor called. He needed someone to fill in for him on Sunday. My ego jumped at the chance. I said yes before he even finished the sentence. That Sunday, when I stepped up to the pulpit, there was an envelope waiting for me. Inside? A check for $250. Divine provision. Now, I wish I could say this happens all the time. It doesn't. But it's happened just often enough to remind me where to keep my heart focused—on the one who puts shoes on my children's feet.

Jesus calls us to imagine the world differently—to see life through God's eyes, to value what Jesus values, and somehow, that always includes you and me. He knows we'll face challenges. That life will overwhelm us. That we'll panic. That we'll have nights when fear grips us so tightly we can't breathe. And so, he tells us—again and again—to keep our eyes and hearts on God, the one who tends to the fleeting life of grass with such beauty and care. If God watches over the least of these, how much more does God watch over us? Be here. Now. With God.

God sees us. God provides. God holds us. Why let fear steal the joy of *now*? God's heart is big enough to hold every living thing ever created. God's table is wide enough for all of us—where we gather as one, strengthened by Christ's love, ready to face whatever comes with courage and hope. So, why waste another second worrying?

Jesus calls us to step into the kingdom of heaven, where there is *always* enough—enough love, enough grace, enough of God's abundance to go around. So, loosen your grip. Breathe. Let go of fear. Trust that the one who feeds the birds and clothes the lilies has *got you*. And that is more than enough.

13

DON'T GIVE ME THAT OLD WINE, I WANT SOMETHING NEW

*"No one puts new wine in old wineskins.
The new wine will burst the skins
and be spilled, and destroyed."*
—Luke 5:37

In my lifetime, I've witnessed all kinds of history being made—astronauts landing on the moon, all five of Kobe Bryant's championships, and the births of my children. But more recently, something happened that changed how we view reality itself: the world watched as Moroccan influencer Kenza Layli became the first Miss AI—a title earned by a digital creation, not a real person. And here's the kicker: no human mind or hand designed her. She is 100% artificial. This AI marvel—and the other nine contestants like her—emerged from data, algorithms, and code.

In her acceptance speech, Miss Layli echoed the power of AI: "AI is a transformative force that can disrupt industries, challenge norms, and create opportunities where none existed before." It hit me like a ton of bricks: humanity has created something that no longer needs our input. Whether we embrace it or fear it, AI is here. And it's shifting the world and shaping a future that runs without the need for human control.

AI is the new frontier. And just like any major shift—telegraph, printing press, electricity—there are those who embrace it and those who fear it. The same could be said for Jesus and his message. When he speaks, the world doesn't always know what to do with the shit he tells us. His call for change shakes up the status quo, it threatens the comfortable structures of society—much like AI. Jesus doesn't just offer a new way of doing things; he calls us to see the world in a completely new way. His radical love pushes against the old ways of thinking. And it's this radical love we must keep our focus on.

"No one puts new wine into old wineskins; otherwise, the new wine will burst the skins and will spill out, and the skins will be ruined. But new wine must be put into fresh wineskins. And no one after drinking old wine desires new wine but says, 'The old is good'" (Luke 5:37–39).

This simple metaphor speaks to the heart of what Jesus is about. The old wineskin—representing old ways, old structures, old patterns—is too rigid to contain the new wine of God's kingdom. The Pharisees, with their rules and rituals, can't contain the boundless love Jesus offers. Their hearts, like old wineskins, are too rigid to embrace this new way of being. New wine—the love and grace Jesus brings—needs a fresh vessel to hold it.

I have this vivid childhood recollection of stomping grapes with my mom in the bathtub. I can't recall why, but I remember our laughter as we squished grapes between our toes. It was a messy, imperfect experiment in making wine. The bottles didn't quite work —some exploded from the fermentation process, while others brewed up a beautiful bouquet of biohazard mess. But there was joy in the attempt. And kudos to my mom for stepping out of her comfort zone to try something new. Now that I think about it, I'm sure it was my mom who taught me not to be afraid to break from tradition, even if it meant stepping into the unknown. Or a bathtub of gooey mess.

Jesus isn't afraid to break traditions either. He isn't shy to do things in a new way. He and his disciples break countless social taboos. They eat with outcasts, disregard the laws about ritual washing, and even defy the religious elites who hold tightly to the old wineskins. Jesus knows the law—and he also knows the hearts of those who wield it. When they criticize him for not adhering to their strict rules, Jesus doesn't just challenge their actions; he challenges their hearts.

When the Pharisees question why his disciples don't pray and fast like they do, Jesus answers, "No one puts new wine into old wineskins." It's not that Jesus disregards the law—he puts love and grace at its center, showing that external actions are meaningless without the internal transformation of the heart. That's his yoke—his way of interpreting and teaching the scripture: deepening its meaning to make it personal and within everyone's reach. He says things the way he does because he wants us to have a new understanding of ourselves and our relationship with God.

The Pharisees are stuck in their old ways, unable to embrace the new wine of God's kingdom. They are always accusing Jesus of breaking laws and traditions, but he constantly shows them how to actually fulfill these very laws they care so much about. By putting love at the core of everything. Love is what the law has always pointed to, but it had become lost in their rigid observances. The kingdom of heaven Jesus proclaims isn't about external compliance; it's about an internal transformation of the heart—one that expands and stretches to love in radical, inclusive ways.

In the movie, *The Jerk*, there's this hilarious scene where Navin Johnson, played by Steve Martin, is dining at a fancy restaurant with his new girlfriend. The waiter brings them their food, but when Navin spots snails on his plate, he's horrified. He calls the waiter over in a panic, exclaiming, "Waiter, there's snails on my plate!" The waiter, trying to keep his composure, assures him it's a delicacy, but Navin won't have it. Then he takes the bottle of wine, hands it to the waiter, and says, "I don't want any of this old stuff. Bring me something new. Something from this week!"[*]

---

[*] *The Jerk*, directed by Carl Reiner (Universal City, CA: Universal Pictures, 1979), film.

Just like Navin demands a fresh plate, Jesus demands a fresh heart—a heart willing to let love and grace transform you from the inside out. Jesus calls us to a new life, a new way of seeing, and a new way of loving. "I don't want any of that old stuff," Jesus says. "Bring me new wine!"

Anyone used to drinking wine from a bottle aged in oak barrels should remember that in the first century, wine was produced in vessels made from animal hides. They used this method because the skins could stretch and expand as gas was produced during the fermentation process. Old wineskins were already stretched to their limit. They couldn't handle the new wine without exploding—damaging both the wine and the vessels.

The old wineskins of law, tradition, and ritual are incapable of holding this love Jesus speaks of, the kind of love that can't be confined by the old structures of *us versus them* or *I'm better than you* kind of thinking. It demands a new kind of heart—a heart that can love without boundaries, without conditions. That's why Jesus says the kingdom of heaven is not something we possess but something we live out, a kingdom defined by love not by law.

Jesus knows that the Pharisees aren't bad people. They know the law inside and out—but they always seem to miss the point: God's law is never about external compliance. It's always meant to draw us into a deeper, more loving relationship with God and with one another. God is always coming to us, to play and stomp on grapes with us. Jesus constantly calls them—and us—back to the heart of the matter, back to where God is waiting for us to jump in the tub to laugh and dance. It's not about being perfect. It's about allowing God's love to break open our hearts and flow freely through us into the world.

Like new wine in new wineskins, the kingdom of God is about expansion. It's about growing, evolving, and stretching in love. To embrace the kingdom is to be willing to change, to let go of old structures and mindsets that prevent us from loving fully and freely. It's about becoming pliable vessels, willing to let God's love grow and transform us from the inside out.

Jesus doesn't dismiss the power of the law; he embraces it fully, with his entire life. When asked about the greatest commandment, Jesus answers, "Love God with all your heart, and love others as you would want to be loved." Then he goes further, saying that all the laws and prophets hang on this love (Matt. 22:35–40). Jesus knows the scriptures and the law, but he also understands that while some, like the Pharisees, focus on outward appearances, God looks at the heart. As Jesus and his disciples live out this new wine of love, they know they're being watched, and when the religious elites try to shame them, Jesus responds by showing them the true heart of the law.

Greg Boyle tells a story of some homies who, after speaking to a large crowd of people, were surprised that everyone was listening to them. They were more used to being watched than being seen. People who cling to old wineskins have trouble, like the Pharisees, seeing others differently. If you break the law, you are a criminal for life. That's the old wineskin. It's good for some. But it's not what they are serving at God's party.

When the Pharisees criticize Jesus' disciples for not washing their hands before eating, Jesus reminds them, "It's not what goes into the mouth that defiles a person, but what comes out" (Matt. 15:11). This is the new wine—shifting the focus from external rules to internal transformation. Yes, cleanliness has its place, but true purification begins within, in the promises we make to God and each other.

Jesus knows that hatred, judgment, and violence all spring from the heart. He challenges us to look beyond the surface and examine the love we show to others, especially those we judge. The way we love reveals the condition of our hearts, and this love is where our relationship with God begins. It's where God comes to dwell in us. Jesus is essentially asking his accusers, "Look at your heart. Look at your love. Where is God in it?"

Old wineskins can't contain this new wine without being destroyed. And that's the point. If our actions aren't grounded in our love for God and others, they serve no true purpose. And if our old ways are preventing us from growing in this love, God will find a way to tear them down. The way of Jesus is a radical shift from the old. It transforms us from the inside out, inviting us into a new way of being that overflows with love and grace.

Jesus calls us to repent—to change the way we think, act, and live. This requires a new mindset, a fresh framework for living and being. The old way simply can't contain it, and if we try, both will be destroyed. Richard Rohr puts it this way: "God keeps creating things from the inside out, so they are forever yearning, developing, growing, and changing for the good. To fight transformative and evolutionary thinking is to fight the very core concept of faith."* Jesus isn't just telling us to "fix your own stuff before judging others" but to look deeper into the core of our faith. If your faith hasn't evolved, it hasn't transformed you.

You've probably heard the saying, "Wine gets better with age." Even when it's sitting still in a barrel, it continues to evolve—softening, mellowing, and harmonizing into something richer and deeper. As it matures, new flavors emerge, and the impurities settle out. This is a beautiful metaphor for faith. Just as wine transforms over time, becoming fuller and more complex, our faith should mature when it dwells in the new wineskins of Jesus' love. Our old ways—bitterness, pride, and rigidity—are softened by grace, making us gentler and more approachable. Our raw zeal is refined through life's trials and God's patience, adding depth to love, joy, peace, and wisdom.

Throughout this process, the Holy Spirit integrates our joys, sorrows, strengths, and weaknesses into a unified testimony of God's goodness. Like aging wine, our faith deepens in color and complexity, growing richer with the golden hues of hope and the deep reds of sacrificial love.

But this transformation can only happen in new wineskins—hearts willing to shed old structures, habits, and mindsets that prevent our spiritual growth. Just as new wineskins are pliable, so must we be open to the radical call of Jesus. When we embrace this call, we become like fine wine—living, breathing testaments to God's

---

* Richard Rohr, *Jesus' Alternative Plan: The Sermon on the Mount* (Cincinnati: Franciscan Media, 2022).

glory. Our evolving faith reflects the Creator, drawing others to taste and see that the Lord is good.

To follow Jesus is to change. In fact, it's impossible to stay the same person—something has to give. Fear, anger, judgment, pride, hatred, ignorance, bitterness, divisiveness—none of these can stay in God's kingdom. There's no room for politics, nationalism, racism, or sexism. Jesus' new wine won't mix with these old wineskins. His love and grace just can't be contained by "us versus them" thinking.

I know this from experience. In 2017, I reluctantly started a new church in my backyard. For two long years, I struggled, clinging to old traditions, feeling like a failure, questioning my faith, and doubting my calling. The more I tried to prove I was doing church "right," the more frustrated I became. But in 2019, a wise Kenyan missionary gently said to me, "New wine belongs in new wineskins. Jesus was very clear about that." That was my turning point. What I once saw as a curse became one of the greatest gifts—a blank slate to live out the gospel in new and meaningful ways.

Rohr is right: faith isn't stagnant. It's always growing and evolving, because God is alive in us. We must keep seeking new ways to reveal God's love—meeting today's needs with grace and embracing tomorrow's challenges with joy. Just like new wine ferments and changes, our faith must deepen and expand. We must be flexible, alive, and open to the Spirit's transformative work—becoming a creative laboratory of God's inclusive love.

Just as AI is reshaping industries, Jesus is challenging us to transform our hearts and communities with the new wine of God's love. The Pharisees knew the law, but as Jesus says, "They don't take it in their hearts and live it out in their behavior" (Matt. 23:5–6, *The Message*). Jesus invites us to open our hearts so God's love can pour out, not as obedience to the law but as love that compels us to live in harmony with everyone. As Jesus says, "Love one another as I have loved you" (John 13:34).

Love is the new wine we are meant to serve. It's the wine that gets us all intoxicated—not with taking, but with giving. It's in the way we love that we reveal the true spirit of the law. And that love is what the world desperately needs.

Despite constant criticism and resistance, Jesus always stands on the side of love. Love is the new wine, and your heart is the new wineskin. We are all vessels of his love. And we're serving his wine—not ours. He doesn't store it in us for safekeeping; he gives it to us to pour out liberally.

We have many good friends who collect wine from all over the world. On special occasions, if we're lucky, they will uncork a bottle or two for us to enjoy together. For Jesus, every day is an occasion worthy of uncorking God's love. He calls us to share it not only with our friends but with those who despise us. The world is thirsty for what he offers. And Jesus sends us out to pour God's love generously, so no one is left without.

Every interaction and every relationship is an opportunity to pour someone a glass of this love. Every day, we are given the wine to live the gospel in new ways, so everyone we meet can become intoxicated with Christ—the one who took a cup of wine and said, "This is the blood of the new covenant poured out for all, for the forgiveness of sins. Every time you drink of this cup, do so in remembrance of me" (Matt. 26:28).

14

LIVING WATER

"Give me something to drink."
—John 4:7

In a church I served in Michigan, one of our members, a man by the name of Scott, would come into my office every Sunday, just minutes before I had to process with choir. He always walked in without knocking, filled with great excitement. If it were to ask for prayer or even a handout, I'd have no problem, but that was never the reason. He came because he wanted to tell me a joke. The dirtier the better. I never put a stop to it because I think we both knew the only reason he showed up at all was to see how I would respond.

Of all the jokes he told me, this is the only one I can share. It's a story about a country boy named Little Willy. I could already see where this was going. Anyway, Little Willy's grandma sends him to fetch a bucket of water for Sunday supper, and knowing it was the Lord's Day and all, Little Willy took the job with a little extra reverence. He grabbed the old bucket from its nail by the back door and ran down to the well at the edge of the property.

When he dipped the bucket in, two big, mean, glowing eyes

stared back at him. He dropped the bucket and bolted back to his grandma.

She just nodded. "Oh, that's Huckleberry. That old gator's been living down there since I was your age. Ain't never hurt nobody. He's probably more scared of you than you are of him."

Little Willy thought about that for a second. "Well, Grandma," he said, "if he's more scared of me than I am of him, I reckon that water ain't fit to drink no more."

Just a few months later, I repeated the joke at Scott's funeral, where many in town who had never set foot inside a church had gathered to say their final goodbyes. There was something sacred about that moment when we all groaned together. By sharing his joke with his friends, a bridge was built between two seemingly opposing camps on either side of the river. Jesus might call this living water.

Clean, fresh water is getting harder and harder to find these days. But we all need it. Without it, all of us would die within a few days. In fact, water is so important that our bodies actually have a specific drought management system in place to ensure our survival. A mere 2 percent drop in our body's water supply can throw us off balance, mess with our focus, and weaken our muscles. Go longer, and things start shutting down—our heart races, blood pressure tanks, and organs fail.

Just as a car cannot run without gas and oil, the body cannot work without water. It serves as a lubricant in digestion, regulates body temperature, and flushes harmful toxins from the body. Water is life. Fly over the Great Plains, and the story's written right there on the land: where there's water, there's green; where there's none, dust.

The Bible knows this too. Water shows up 770 times in scripture. On the first page—the Spirit of God is hovering over the waters. That's how the whole thing starts. Creation, destruction, renewal—it all flows through water. A few chapters later, God cleanses the world with water in Noah's time. Then God parts the Red Sea—water—to set people free. And God pours water into the desert when all hope seems lost.

*Blessing. Judgment. Deliverance. Salvation.
That's living water.*

In the Jordan, Jesus steps into the water, fully human, to be baptized with the rest of us. Then, just to make sure we don't miss it, he walks on it, stills it, turns it into wine. Water reveals who he is. And in the end, it's the water and blood flowing from his side that tell us everything.

Where there's water, there's life. And in him—the living water, poured out for all—there's life that never runs dry.

In what might sound like the beginning of a joke, Jesus walks up to this invalid who's been stuck —thirty-eight years—waiting by the pool of Bethesda. The story goes that when the water churns, miracles happen (John 5:1–9). But no one ever helps the guy into the water. He just sits there, waiting. Jesus doesn't bother with the pool. He just heals him—no water necessary. Turns out, Jesus *is* the water. Restoration, healing, mercy—it's all right there in him.

All throughout scripture, water symbolizes more than life and vitality. It's also more than hydration. It's purification, cleansing, blessing, judgment, renewal. It demonstrates faith when Jesus calms the storms at sea. Every drop whispers the same truth: God offers living water to a world that's parched. Jesus knows this. That's why he sits by a well one day and flips the script.

He takes an ordinary, everyday situation to make a spiritual point: Where there is living water, there is everlasting life.

I know dry seasons. I've spent too much of my life spiritually dehydrated, chasing things that never filled me. Maybe you know the feeling. Maybe you're there right now—bone-dry, running on empty. That's when God invites you to sit at the well. To drop your empty bucket into the deep unknown. And to draw up living water—the kind that actually satisfies. No need to worry about Huckleberry. God is there with you, offering refreshment.

We see this in a story about Jesus who meets a Samaritan woman as she comes to draw water. He's tired and thirsty. In the scorching mid-day heat Jesus says, "Give me a drink" (John 4:7). It seems his disciples are out buying food and apparently had all the cups with them. The Samaritan is shocked by his audacity. "How is it that you, a Jew, ask a drink of me, a woman of Samaria?" (John 4:9). It's like the Hatfields and McCoys—Jews and Samaritans don't mix. But Jesus doesn't care about the rules. He just tells her, "If you knew who I was, you'd be asking me for water. The kind that never runs dry" (John 4:10, 13).

Now, do yourself a favor—put yourself in this story. You're the one walking to the well, same as you do every day. Same dusty road. Same bucket. Same routine. You might have something weighing on you, or maybe you're just zoning out, enjoying the momentary escape. Nothing about this day feels different.

Except for him. A stranger sits there. A Jewish man. And not just any Jewish man—one who is tired and thirsty and asking for help. You're the one holding the bucket. You have what he needs.

Now, let's skip over the part where we say Jesus is divine—meaning, technically, he shouldn't get tired or thirsty like we do. Just for now, let's sit with his humanity. The part of him that's like you and me. The part that gets worn out, hungry, thirsty. It's strange to think of Jesus needing something from me. Isn't it supposed to be the other way around?

But here he is. He's thirsty. And he can't get a drink on his own. No bucket. No cup. No 7-Eleven where he can stick his head under the soda fountain. He needs help. From a stranger. And not just any stranger—a Samaritan woman. By this humble act, we learn how to care for the simple needs of one another. Even those we are taught to avoid.

That's the first shock. The second? She helps him. This story isn't just about water. It's about breaking barriers. Jesus, a Jewish man and a spiritual teacher, isn't supposed to even talk to her. A Samaritan. A woman. Someone his people see as unclean, impure, other.

But Jesus doesn't care about the invisible lines people draw between each other. He doesn't see an enemy. He sees a person—with a past, a heart, and a bucket that can quench his thirst. And this whole conversation? It's layered.

Because here's the thing about Jews and Samaritans. They're family. Just the kind of family that stopped talking to each other long ago. Their beef started centuries earlier, back when Israel split into two kingdoms—north and south. Then came exile, intermarriage, theological disputes, a whole lot of resentment. The Jews built their temple in Jerusalem. The Samaritans built theirs on Mount Gerizim. Both claimed to worship the God of Abraham, but they couldn't agree on how to do it. That doesn't seem like a reason to squabble, but as anyone with family can attest, it does not take much for cousins and siblings to stop talking to each other.

By Jesus' time, the division was cemented. Jews saw Samaritans as heretics. Samaritans saw Jews as arrogant and exclusionary. Sound familiar? One group blaming the other; each side convinced they have it right. It's no different than today—Democrats versus Republicans, each side pointing fingers at the other. Despite these divisions, biblical stories about the two groups are frequently used to emphasize themes of unity and compassion, the most famous being the story of the Good Samaritan. And right here at this well, Jesus blows past centuries of history and dysfunction. This woman knows the rules. She knows she and Jesus are supposed to stay in their separate lanes. But she keeps talking. And so does he.

Now, remember—you're in this story. How do you respond when someone you've been taught to hate asks you for water? Maybe like this woman: "Who do you think you are? I owe you nothing." Why would she help someone whose people see her as less than a dog?

But Jesus? He knows what's behind her resistance. He doesn't need to be divine to get it. The family feud between Jews and Samaritans runs deep. So instead of picking at old wounds, he reaches back to a time before they were divided. He says, "If you knew the gift of God, if you knew who was asking you for a drink, you'd be asking me for water. The kind that never runs dry" (John 4:10, 13). It's a subtle hint, to say the least. A small crack in the wall between them. But does she get it? Probably not.

She fires back. "With what? You don't have a bucket, a cup, nothing." She's probably wondering if she should pour it in his hands or throw it in his face. And then, as if she's setting him up, she asks: "Where do you get this 'living water'? Are you greater than our ancestor Jacob, who gave us this well?" (John 4:11–12).

Jesus answers, "Everyone who drinks this water will be thirsty again. But the water I give? They'll never thirst" (John 4:13–14). See, this isn't just about quenching thirst. It's about seeing the Messiah in the face of a stranger—and responding. God's love spills into the world through small, unnoticed moments. It trickles into us, but when we respond, it bursts out like a broken fire hydrant. It's newsworthy. It's exciting enough for someone to burst into their cousin's office and shout, "I have found the one our grandparents told us about!" This is the kind of shit Jesus says that gets people to notice.

And because this woman stops to help a thirsty stranger, her life changes. So does her community.

John's Gospel makes this clear: one small act of kindness done with selfless love can begin a ripple of renewal. This isn't just about going to the well to find faith. It's about what we do with our faith bucket once we have it. A well full of water is only useful if someone draws from it. If left untouched, it becomes stagnant.

Some of the things Jesus says and does might seem innocuous or even humorous. But his words are always profound and life-changing. His words remind us that we are vessels of God's love. Vessels that hold living water. Vessels that nourish souls, restore hope, and replenish joy when the world runs dry.

One day, I told my friend Scott to meet me later that night back at the church, around the same time there was an Alcoholics Anonymous meeting happening. He looked at me with his big, worried look. I told him, "God has a drinking problem. And he needs your help." We're the ones holding the buckets by the well of life. Is it empty? Or is it full?

Through Christ, God gives us a way to tap into the source of life itself even when we feel empty or parched. But will we draw from it? Will we share what we've been given? Because every act of love quenches our desire righteousness. Every act of mercy fills the deepest wells.

Jesus says it like this, "Blessed are those who hunger and thirst for righteousness, for they will be filled."

God is blessed when we are filled. And we are blessed when God is filled. Living water flows both ways. Sip by sip, gulp by gulp, God drinks us in. Mixing us into the great, eternal, living water. And where there is living water, there is everlasting life.

15

THE SMALLEST ACT OF COMPASSION IS THE BEST KIND OF WELCOME

> *"Whoever welcomes you welcomes me, and whoever welcomes me welcomes the one who sent me. Whoever welcomes a prophet in the name of a prophet will receive a prophet's reward, and whoever welcomes a righteous person in the name of a righteous person will receive the reward of the righteous, and whoever gives even a cup of cold water to one of these little ones in the name of a disciple—truly I tell you, none of these will lose their reward."*
> —Matthew 10:40–42

Some years ago, I was part of a leadership team at a conference in Milwaukee, Wisconsin. As you might imagine, the responsibilities included running between meetings and lectures. In the space between these obligations, I bumped into a woman who, like me, was rushing to catch the elevator. She looked exactly as frazzled as I did. The badge around her neck told me she was part of our group, and that she was a first timer. Or what I call a fish out of water.

Instead of listening to the voice in my head—the one that was craving a few seconds alone in a quiet elevator—I listened to the voice of my heart. I turned and welcomed her. The conversation was nothing profound by any standard, but the presence of Christ was undeniably there. For a moment, his peace settled between us, calming us in our shared busyness. Truly, "where two or three gather in my name," he says, "I'm right there with you" (Matt. 18:20).

Later that evening, I ran into the woman again. We sat next to each other and talked, two strangers connecting over dried-out salmon and mushy green beans. I learned that she had arrived a day late because her flight from Boston was delayed by storms battering the East Coast. After enduring a twenty-hour travel nightmare, she said that one simple, kind gesture from a smiling stranger had made her stress disappear for a moment—enough time to feel welcomed.

That's what happens, right? One act of kindness, both people are touched, the kingdom of heaven comes near. Whether big or small, any act of compassionate welcome is a form of serving Christ—and welcoming him into whatever space we're in. Jesus invites us to see what a life anchored in acts of compassion could be like—whether that's God's compassion for us or our compassion for others. You might want to flip back to chapter one and remind yourself of what you should have memorized by now.

In one of his daily blog posts, alternative business guru Seth Godin wrote, "It's natural to believe that everyone else is as confident, assured, long-term thinking, and generous as you are on your very best day. But that's unlikely. Because everyone else is probably not having their best day at the same time. Once we realize that the world around us is filled with people who are each wrestling with what we're wrestling with (and more), compassion is a lot easier to find."*

If you're like me, I suspect your compassion is running a little lean these days. We find ourselves picking who gets a piece of our heart, knowing someone will miss out. No matter who we choose—and hopefully, it's everyone—there's no way we can do this without

---

* Seth Godin, "Everybody Else," *Seth's Blog*, June 25, 2020, https://seths.blog/2020/06/everybody-else/.

God's grace. Welcoming and giving—this is the way of Jesus, the way we transform ourselves, the way we interact with the world, and the way we show the world who we belong to. But Jesus also reminds us that we're not just called to give, we're called to receive too. He says, "Whoever welcomes you welcomes me, and whoever welcomes me welcomes the one who sent me" (Matt. 10:40).

Jesus says these words after he sends the twelve out into the world on their first mission trip. They go out like sheep among wolves to proclaim the good news and to perform the healing works he's been doing. They are to share in his ministry, and they're to share in his poverty, carrying no money or extra clothes. They must rely completely on the hospitality of others for shelter and sustenance (Matt. 10).

Jesus is all about compassionate welcome. It's no surprise why. In these three short but powerful verses (Matt. 10:40–42), he uses the word "welcome" six times, pointing us to the importance of hospitality in furthering God's kingdom of love and grace. One of the most sacred things a religious institution can practice is radical hospitality. Sadly, most churches have forgotten this.

In his set of monastic Rules, Benedict emphasized that hospitality isn't just about offering material comforts but seeing the face of Christ in each person who came to them. He wrote, "All guests who arrive should be welcomed as Christ, for He is going to say: 'I was a stranger and you took me in.'"* By welcoming others with the same love and care we'd show Jesus, we're living out a transformative faith.

This is how it worked in the ancient world: showing hospitality to an individual didn't just welcome the individual but the entire community that had sent them—all those the individual represented. Welcoming a disciple of Jesus meant receiving the very presence of Jesus himself, as well as the one who sent him. Teresa of Calcutta often told people the only reason she was able to do the work she did —caring for the poorest of the poor who were dying on the streets—

---

* St. Benedict of Nursia, *The Rule of St. Benedict, Chapter 53*, translated by Timothy Fry (Collegeville, MN: Liturgical Press, 1981), 90.

was because she saw the image of God in others. She looked at others with the eyes of Jesus. And welcomed them with the heart of Jesus. When Jesus is all we see, our brothers and sisters, friends and enemies, neighbors and strangers alike, all become him. When we welcome them, we welcome Jesus, and the one who sent him.

It shouldn't surprise you to hear me say compassion is always felt first in the heart. This is where God plants Christ, the divine image, in us. To bear the image and likeness of God is to be like little Christs, proclaiming God's glory in our relationships with God and others. Paul reminds us that we share the same mind that was in Christ Jesus (Phil. 2:5). But do we have the same will to welcome and serve others in love as he did? When we pass by people, do we see strangers, or do we see the divine image of God?

I would argue that most of the shit Jesus says points us to live the kind of life that brings this kingdom of heaven closer and closer. Jesus is always pointing our hearts toward the other, to see and approach every situation with a God-filled heart. This is where real and genuine relationships begin and thrive. Whether the relationships are close and loving or distant and occasional, when God is at the center of our welcome, we'll find rich rewards.

I remember a moment during the COVID pandemic when I failed miserably at this. I had everything lined up, ready to refinance our house. But when the lender began processing the paperwork, we discovered the bank holding our mortgage had put a forbearance against our house as a precautionary measure at the start of the pandemic. This was a big stumbling block for me to say the least, in that it blocked us from taking advantage of the historically low lending rates that would have saved us a lot of money each month. After being on hold for an hour with the bank, Kathleen and I decided to go there in person.

The young man who greeted us was eager to help; honestly, I wasn't eager to accept it. I was angry, frustrated, and had little compassion in my heart for him or what he had to say. Sensing this, my wife took the lead. She's the best diplomat in these kinds of situations. She always has the ability to see the divine in others when I can't.

Kathleen knew it wasn't this man's fault. He didn't mess up our refinancing—someone in the corporate office did. By understanding that small truth, she entered the conversation with what Richard Rohr would call *a Christ-soaked heart*, a heart where God is at the center. Despite his best efforts to fix the situation, Kathleen and I left—me still angry and frustrated, her calm and at peace. By placing God at the center of this ordinary—albeit unwelcome—situation, Kathleen trusted God would work it out. And by the next morning, everything had worked out. The forbearance had been removed. No matter how big or small the situation seems, if God is at the center, so too are God's compassion and power. That's our reward.

It might not be the easiest thing for us to do, but we have to practice compassionate welcome all the time, no matter what. I'm not saying we need to perform grand, heroic acts of mercy or put ourselves in harm's way. All God asks is that we act, that we do something that helps another. Jesus says it's as simple as offering someone a drink of cold water. As Kathleen proves to me time and time again, a God-centered life of faith consists of many small gestures of love. And according to Jesus, every single gesture is significant—eternally so.

When our middle child was around ten, she took our dog out for a walk. As he was heading down the sidewalk, she noticed a man digging up the hard, dry dirt in our neighbor's yard. It was a hot summer day, and he was sweating profusely. I can't speak to how or why my daughter noticed him, but she did. More importantly, she saw him with the eyes of a compassionate heart. In seeing him, she felt his distress. And more than that, she was moved to help. She came home and grabbed two water bottles and a plastic cup filled with ice to give to this tired laborer. I can only imagine how surprised the man must have been to receive such a thoughtful and unexpected gift from such a small child.

The Christmas story is about the most unexpected gift ever given to the world: a small, vulnerable baby. Through the eyes of this child,

God saw our pain and suffering with a compassionate heart and was moved to do something about it. Through human beings like you and me, or my daughter and Jesus, the kingdom of heaven comes near—bringing salvation, mercy, and grace to all of God's children. Whoever welcomes anyone, welcomes the one who sent him (Matt. 10:40).

Whether or not Colleen saw this man as made in the same divine image as her isn't really the point. She saw him with the eyes of a compassionate heart and allowed God to move through her to act. Jesus tells us that a cup of cold water is one of the smallest of gifts—something almost anyone could give. Yet, it's precious—life-giving—to the person who is truly thirsty.

Community activist Shane Claiborne shows us that real transformative change often begins with simple acts of kindness. He states, "We are not called to change the world all at once, but to practice resurrection one small act of kindness at a time."*

It doesn't take much to usher in the kingdom of heaven. A simple text message to check in with a friend who is going through a difficult time. A random act of kindness to a stranger without expecting anything in return. When we notice God in the other, and move to honor God in that person, the kingdom of heaven is ushered in. And our reward is full.

I remember my first real meal in the hospital after throat surgery. I was told to take small bites, but my hunger got the best of me. I started shoveling food into my mouth, and before long, I was choking. It was too much, all at once. I think Jesus is telling us something similar: There's work to be done, but don't bite off more than you can chew.

Maybe your plate feels full right now—responsibilities stacking up, emotions piling on. If you're not careful, it can overwhelm you and paralyze you from getting anything done. But this is where Jesus meets us, offering words of encouragement.

It's in all of our small gestures that people start to see the gigantic

---

* Shane Claiborne, *The Irresistible Revolution: Living as an Ordinary Radical* (Grand Rapids, MI: Zondervan, 2006), 115.

love of God in their midst. Maybe you don't even realize it, but the little things you do—the meal you make for your kids, the time you spend talking to a grumpy neighbor—these are the things that show the world what a Christ-soaked heart can do. This is radical hospitality. "Whoever welcomes you welcomes me, and whoever welcomes me welcomes the one who sent me" (Matt. 10:40).

Saying good morning to a neighbor who lives alone might not seem like much. But for that person—the one who's being noticed, the one who's receiving that simple gift from you—it can be both powerful and life-giving. Jesus teaches us that everything we do can be a holy act when we take the love and compassion we have for someone we care about and offer it to someone we don't particularly like.

Our job isn't to save others in the sense that we're their saviors. It's not our job to make them like us or believe what we believe because, in truth, they're already one of us. They're already one of God's own, whether they realize it or not. Jesus sends us out into the world with one job: Love. More specifically, "Love one another as I have loved you" (John 13:34). When we love the other, we're loving the Christ within them.

Jesus makes this crystal clear in his final parable in Matthew's Gospel—the parable of the Sheep and the Goats. He tells us that, in the end, the way we treat one another is a reflection of the way we're treating him. "Just as you did to the least of these your brothers and sisters, you did it to me" (Matt. 25:40). Giving water to the thirsty, food to the hungry, justice to the oppressed and imprisoned—these are the greatest acts of worship we can offer God because, in doing them for others, we're doing them directly for God. This is the same idea when Jesus says, "Whoever welcomes you, welcomes me, and the one who sent me" (Matt. 10:40).

Basil the Great understood hospitality as more than just a warm welcome—it was about building community and serving Christ by serving others. He put it simply, but profoundly: "The bread you store up belongs to the hungry; the cloak you treasure up belongs to the naked; the shoes you keep back belong to the one who is barefoot."[*] For Basil, hospitality wasn't just about opening your door to guests—it was about how you shared what you had with those in need. It was about recognizing that everything you hold onto could be used to serve Christ in the person standing before you. It's in this exchange—offering what you have, no matter how small—that the kingdom of heaven breaks in.

Jesus says this to remind us to live into his way of righteousness. The way of a Christ-soaked heart of compassion is giving water to the thirsty, food to the hungry, and justice to the oppressed and imprisoned. This requires us to trust God, to be vulnerable, and to share what we have with each other. As Marcea Paul writes, "Our efforts to welcome and love others are important because Jesus sees it and receives it as worship."[†]

Why do so many churches forget this? Instead of opening doors to welcome people who look different or love differently, they push them out. Instead of being inclusive with their love, too many are becoming exclusive and determining who is worthy enough to join. God says you are worthy. End of story. That's all. You are worthy in God's heart. And so is everyone. What's so hard to understand about that? Welcoming one another with a compassionate heart is not only healing and life-giving—it's salvation! By that, I'm not saying you should show love only to get into heaven. You show it so heaven can get into you.

All it takes is the smallest amount of faith in God's love for us and a willingness to love, so we can give that love away in everything we do. The real gift they are welcoming isn't you or me. They are welcoming Christ himself and the One who sent him.

---

[*] St. Basil the Great, *Homily on the Gospel of Luke, Homily 6*, in *On Social Justice*, trans. C. Paul Schroeder (Crestwood, NY: St. Vladimir's Seminary Press, 2009), 33.

[†] Marcea Paul, "Even One Cup (Pentecost 4, June 28, 2020)," *The Episcopal Church*, June 22, 2020. https://www.episcopalchurch.org/sermon/even-one-cup-pentecost-4-a-june-28-2020, accessed June 26, 2020.

16

RECONCILE NOW, DAMN IT!

> *"When you are offering your gift at the altar, if you remember that your brother or sister has something against you, leave your gift ...and go; first be reconciled...then come and offer your gift."*
> —Matthew 5:23–24

Sibling rivalry runs deep—and I know it well. My brother and I were pros, each day a new round in the ring. Who was right, who was wrong, who was stronger, faster, or had the last word. It was chaos—complete with yelling and pushing. The only time I can remember my mom stepping in to stop a fight was when I finally got the upper hand on my brother. I was thirty.

Now, my wife's family was a different story. She's one of nine kids—six girls and three boys. The battlefield might have looked uneven, but it wasn't. Each kid had to defend their turf, and it was a dog-eat-dog world. I have no idea how loud or vicious it got, but the way my wife tells it, if they got caught fighting, the punishment was always the same. They would have to hold hands and sing, *"Let there be peace on earth, and let it begin with me."* By the end of the song, they had forgotten what they were fighting about. Apologies weren't required, but reconciliation was nonnegotiable.

When my wife tells that story, I realize what her parents were teaching them. Reconciliation isn't just about smoothing things over—it's about loving each other when it's hardest. It isn't about getting along in the good times; it's about making things right in the messy, broken moments. This was a lesson on peacemaking, showing up for each other, choosing peace, and not letting pride or anger define us.

We've carried this approach into raising our kids. Through it, they've learned to love each other when it wasn't easy and everything in them wanted to hold on to the fight. Reconciliation is love in action. Even when we don't feel like it, it has to be the first thing we do to live a life of peace. This is how we show up. This is how we choose love, no matter what.

Jesus says, if you've got a beef with someone, don't even think about stepping into a place of worship until you've sorted it out. Sounds about right. But if we really took this shit seriously, it might be the death knell for every church out there. The pews would be empty. The priests and pastors gone. I'm pretty sure my brother and I wouldn't have even made it past the church parking lot.

But Jesus isn't just talking about the big blow-ups, fistfights between brothers or sisters, or screaming matches between parents and kids. Jesus is pointing us to something deeper, something we don't always want to face—the grudges we hold. Those little unresolved hurts, the quiet resentments we nurse in the shadows of our hearts. Jesus understands that these, too, matter to God. The secret jealousy we feel, the quiet judgment we cast on others, all that shade we throw without saying a word—those things matter. Because we matter to God.

If we don't take the time to take inventory of our actions, they'll fester and turn toxic. And, boy, toxic is what we humans do best, isn't it? Ridding these things from our lives could also jeopardize divorce lawyers and put therapists out of business. But what happens when we hold onto anger, bitterness, or even pride? Healing doesn't happen when we keep a scorecard of offenses. I've been guilty of this—holding onto petty anger for years, just so the person knows I'm still mad about whatever they did. It's a silent way of keeping them small.

And that's as harmful as any physical or mental harm because it diminishes someone else, makes them less than us.

Jesus calls us to something different, something harder but ultimately more freeing. He calls us to step out of our comfort zones, to make the first move, to seek peace with those we've hurt and those who've hurt us. This shouldn't be hard—it should come naturally to us, as natural as breathing. A life lived in peace, free from those grudges, should be the goal. But, as we know all too well, it's never that simple. Healing old wounds takes time. And our pride so often gets in the way. Too often, we hold onto anger like it's a hot coal, hoping the other person gets burned, but in the end, it's only us who suffer. So, before you do anything, reconcile.

St. Augustine wrote, "For the man who knows how to forgive a wrong done to him is greater than the man who knows how to perform many mighty deeds."* It's a simple yet profound truth: true strength is found in the ability to forgive, to make peace, and to reconcile.

The Bible is full of people who have learned this the hard way. Take Jacob and Esau—two brothers whose rivalry nearly destroyed their relationship. Jacob tricked Esau, stealing his birthright, and yet somehow they found a way to make peace. Joseph, sold into slavery by his jealous brothers, eventually reconciled with them, offering grace where there could have been bitterness. Even Jonah, the reluctant prophet, ran from God's calling but found his way back into reconciliation with God. In every one of these stories, the act of reconciliation not only healed relationships but brought about something greater for the whole community. Their willingness to mend what was broken became the very thing that transformed them—and the world around them.

Rumi, who often spoke of love as the force that heals and unites, wrote, "Out beyond ideas of wrongdoing and rightdoing, there is a

---

* *The Works of Saint Augustine: A Translation for the 21st Century*, ed. John E. Rotelle and trans. Edmund Hill (Hyde Park, NY: New City Press, 1990s–2000s).

field. I'll meet you there."* Reconciliation moves us beyond the need to be right or justified and toward a space of love; to a field where all can meet in peace.

The Jewish celebration of Yom Kippur is a powerful reminder of how reconciliation transforms not just individuals but communities. Through fasting, prayer, and introspection, individuals seek forgiveness and strive to make peace with God and one another. It's not about avoiding our sins; it's about confronting them and choosing to repair what's been fractured. Yom Kippur teaches us that even our worst mistakes can be forgiven—that true reconciliation is always possible.

John had been estranged from his brother for years because of a business dispute. John found some discrepancies in the books and, feeling betrayed, accused his brother of cheating. Unable to prove it, they stopped talking. Years went by, and his anger continued to fester. John knew his brother was a good man, a man who cared for his family, a man he had once trusted. "It's eating me up inside," he told me. "I don't know what to do." I told him what Jesus would tell him to do—reconcile before it's too late.

John reached out. He apologized. And his brother responded with grace. It wasn't just reconciliation—it was spiritual healing, a renewed connection not just with each other but with God. Jesus reminds us that our relationships with others are inseparable from our relationship with God. If you have beef with a brother, make fixing it your top priority.

Jesus knew this because he *is* one of us. He sits in the synagogue, watching people come to worship God, all while their hearts are weighed down with anger and bitterness. He sees them approaching the altar, more focused on revenge than reverence. Why else would he say these things, if not to heal and transform us?

That's what the kingdom of heaven is about—transformation. Jesus holds up a mirror to our hearts and makes us face the anger we

---

* Jalāl al-Dīnn Rūmī, *The Essential Rumi*, translated by Coleman Barks (San Francisco: HarperOne, 1995), 36.

bury deep inside. He asks, "What good is your love for God if it's nothing more than an obligation?" He forces us to wrestle with our hearts, to ask ourselves if we're truly offering love or just going through the motions. There's a Hebrew proverb that tells us, "No one who conceals transgressions will prosper, but one who confesses and forsakes them will obtain mercy" (Prov. 28:13). We can't hide from our wrongs. But we can own them and fix what is broken.

Jesus connects personal forgiveness with divine forgiveness: "And when you stand praying, if you hold anything against anyone, forgive them, so that your Father in heaven may forgive you your sins" (Mark 11:25). Our willingness to forgive and seek reconciliation reflects our understanding of God's forgiveness for us. As John Chrysostom stated, "Let us be ashamed, who, while we ask forgiveness, do not ourselves forgive."* Don't bother seeking forgiveness from God while withholding it from others. Leave your gift and reconcile first.

Jesus knows that the greatest gift we can give God is our heart. He calls us to move beyond religious rituals into a deeper transformation, one that changes how we see ourselves, God, and others. For Jesus, reconciliation is not just an act—it's a sacred rite, a divine movement of the heart that transcends outward appearances. He says things like, "Blessed are the pure of heart, for they will see God" (Matt. 5:8), and, "A good person produces good things from the treasury of a good heart, and an evil person produces evil things from the treasury of an evil heart" (Luke 6:45).

God knows our hearts. We were made in God's image, divinely stamped with God's love—a sacred imprint etched into us, the very epicenter of the divine. This is where God meets us, in the raw truth of who we are. Remember how Jesus reminds us, "It is not what goes into the mouth that defiles someone, but what comes out; for what comes out of the mouth proceeds from the heart" (Matt. 15:11).

So Jesus calls us to love God with our whole heart—and then to love our neighbors as ourselves (Matt. 22:37). This isn't just about

---

* John Chrysostom, *Homily on Matthew 6:12*, in *Nicene and Post Nicene Fathers, First Series*, vol. 10, ed. Philip Schaff (Peabody, MA: Hendrickson Publishers, 1994), 193.

feeling a surface-level affection. This is about loving with your entire being—your heart, your soul, your mind. But here's the catch: if our hearts aren't good with others, they probably aren't good with God either. This is why Jesus is relentless about reconciling our anger, our wounds, and our hurts. True reconciliation means speaking from the heart—and to the hearts we've wounded.

Years ago, I hurt someone I care deeply about. It wasn't intentional. It came from a place of exhaustion and frustration. But she became an easy target because of unresolved issues I'd been carrying for years. She said something that cracked open the door I'd been keeping shut on all those buried emotions. And I snapped—letting out everything I'd been holding back for far too long. It wasn't fair, it wasn't kind, and it certainly wasn't Christlike. But once those words were spoken, there was no taking them back. I couldn't put them back in that dark place. Instead, I crawled into it.

Embarrassed by what I said, I apologized. But deep down, I knew I was just trying to avoid people's anger...and trying to save face. Over the following weeks, a dark weight hung over me. My soul felt heavy, almost suffocating. Then I realized I wasn't really angry with her anymore—I was angry with myself. And I discovered that forgiveness is the hardest when you have to forgive yourself. That weight started to take its toll on me—mentally, emotionally, spiritually. I knew the only way out was to swallow my pride and make amends—not just with her, but with myself. Like Jesus says, "If you hold anything against anyone, forgive them, so that your Father in heaven may forgive you" (Mark 11:25).

In AA, there's a saying, "Clean up your side of the street," which really gets to the heart of what it means to take responsibility for the harm we've caused. It's about owning up to our part, no excuses, and doing the hard, honest work of repairing what's been broken. I'm so grateful that the person I hurt was willing to meet me in that place, to receive my amends, and walk through the tough road of reconciliation with me. And as we did that, our relationship grew, not just healed—it became stronger than it had ever been before. Because I was the one to initiate the reconciliation—and did so from a place of sincerity and humility—I wasn't just making things right with them; I was making things right within myself. And in that process, I was transformed.

Jesus knows this will happen when you approach the work of reconciliation with an open heart: not only is the other person healed, but so are you. It's a kind of grace that changes you from the inside out.

Anyone who has walked the Twelve Steps path understands how crucial this work is to one's healing and recovery. It's about more than just saying "sorry." It's about taking responsibility and allowing that accountability to transform our hearts. Jesus' mission was all about this transformation—challenging our usual ways of thinking and acting, not from a place of shame or force, but with peace, love, and a willingness to be made new.

Jesus knew that true healing comes through forgiveness—whether we are the ones seeking it or the ones offering it. And the beauty is, science affirms this truth. Unresolved conflict, left to fester, can bring physical illness—from chronic stress to weakened immune systems. Time and time again, forgiveness was at the center of the healing miracles Jesus performed. It is in our willingness to forgive and reconcile that we truly understand the depth of God's forgiveness toward us. As Paul says, "Bear with each other and forgive one another if any of you has a grievance against someone. Forgive as the Lord forgave you" (Col. 3:13).

For me, forgiveness begins with God, but it doesn't end there. It flows through us into every relationship. We can live this out by following Jesus' lead. He teaches us, "Do not judge, and you will not be judged. Do not condemn, and you will not be condemned. Forgive, and you will be forgiven" (Matt. 7:1). Or put another way, "The measure we give others is the measure that will be given to us" (Matt. 7:2). If we truly believe Jesus' words, then why would we choose anger over love? Why hold a grudge when we could let God's grace shine through us instead? To call ourselves Christians is to strive to be like Christ—who made sharing God's love, mercy, and grace his greatest mission, and who invites us to do the same.

Reconciliation isn't a one-time act; it's a posture, a radical love that opens our hearts wide, making room for both joy and sorrow. It requires letting go of the divisions we've created, crossing the boundaries we've set, and inviting those we've cast aside into the fold of grace.

This kind of love isn't just a lofty idea—it's something we live. We show up in each other's lives, bringing all of ourselves—the broken parts as well as the beautiful—and offering them as a gift, no matter how messy or complicated they may seem. It's not about fixing everything or having all the answers. It's about being present with one another in the most vulnerable and intimate ways, knowing that by doing so, we are part of a healing process that creates a more just and compassionate world.

Such love tears down the walls that divide us and allows each person to be seen with the dignity and respect they deserve. As we live reconciliation—not as something we *do* but as something we *embody*—we become living signs of hope for a world that desperately needs it. In loving one another—despite the past and despite the pain—we rewrite the story of the world and make it whole again. John of the Cross wrote, "Where there is no love, put love—and you will find love."*

Jesus simply says, "Love one another." For those of us who choose to take his words to heart, remember that he also says, "Blessed are the peacemakers, for they will be called children of God" *(Matt. 5:9)*. Seeking peace with those we've hurt, or who have hurt us, is the most powerful way we can love and be loved. By living with a forgiving heart and a loving awareness, we reveal to the world what God's love and reconciliation look like in real time. And Jesus reminds us that this is more important than any other form of worship.

---

* John of the Cross, *The Collected Works of St. John of the Cross*, trans. Kieran Kavanaugh, and Otilio Rodriguez (Washington D.C.: ICS Publications, 1991).

17

YES, YOU HAVE TO LOVE ALL THE ASSHOLES, TOO

"Love your enemies; do good to those who hate you;
bless those who curse you; pray for those who mistreat you.
If anyone strikes you on the cheek, offer the other also, and from
anyone who takes away your coat do not withhold even your shirt.
Give to everyone who asks of you, and if anyone
takes away what is yours, do not ask for it back again.
Do to others as you would have them do to you."
—Luke 6:27–31

One night, sitting around the dinner table, my kids were talking about a woman they admired. They discussed her the way my son and I might dissect the stats of a basketball player, comparing her qualities and achievements. Then Colleen, my younger daughter, mentioned something that stopped me in my tracks: "Yeah, but did you know she's a PK?"

In case you're unfamiliar with the term, a PK is a pastor's kid. It's not an easy role. For one, you're living in a glass house, and the world is always standing outside, holding rocks. Those rock holders believe a PK is supposed to be different. They're not allowed to swear, lie, cheat, or steal—and heaven forbid they pig out at a church potluck.

But the pressure doesn't stop there. They expect you to have all the right answers to all the big questions about faith. And no matter who asks—whether it's a fellow congregant, a stranger, or a skeptical cousin—you're supposed to be able to answer with the certainty of a seasoned theologian. And then, there are the unspoken rules from the ministers of such children. Watch what you say and do or it will eventually wind up in a sermon.

I remember catching my youngest as he was about to throw a punch at one of his siblings. I yelled, "What the heck do you think you're doing?" It was one of those knee-jerk, parental responses we all have. But instead of looking guilty, he quickly fired back with, "She wants me to hit her." Before I could ask, "What the heck are you talking about?" he confidently added, "Jesus said it's okay!" There was my seasoned theologian.

"And where does Jesus say it's okay to hit someone?" He shot back without hesitation, "Do to others what you want them to do to you." He spoke the words with such conviction, I almost bought it. But my curiosity still needed more explaining.

"She hit me, so I guess she wants me to hit her back."

There you have it. Checkmate. Mic drop. Sometimes, the most profound truths show up in the most unexpected ways. Yet what really surprised me was how well a five-year-old PK had been paying attention in church.

Neither Jesus nor my son pulled this out of thin air. This ancient call to empathy and compassion has been shared across time and cultures. In the *Babylonian Talmud*, it's written: "What is hateful to you, do not do to your fellow" (Shabbat 31a). For Prophet Muhammad, the *Hadith* is clear: "None of you truly believes until he loves for his brother what he loves for himself" (Sahih al-Bukhari, Hadith 13). Empathy, then, is the very measure of faith.

In Hinduism, the *Mahabharata* teaches, "This is the sum of duty: Do not do to others what would cause pain if done to you" (*Mahabharata* 5.1517). Buddhism echoes this sentiment with: "Hurt not others in ways that you yourself would find hurtful" (*Udanavarga* 5.18). And Confucianism, with its focus on social harmony, offers the simple yet profound teaching: "Do not impose on others what you do not wish for yourself" (*Analects* 15.23).

The *Tao Te Ching* speaks to our interconnectedness, urging us to "regard your neighbor's gain as your own gain, and your neighbor's loss as your own loss."* The theme is echoed in Sikhism, when the *Guru Granth Sahib* says, "I am a stranger to no one, and no one is a stranger to me. Indeed, I am a friend to all" (*Guru Granth Sahib*, Ang 1299).

Of all the different ways the Golden Rule is expressed, Marcus Aurelius put it in a way even a preschooler can understand—if they're paying attention. "What you do not wish to endure yourself, do not make others endure" (*Meditations* 10.14).

This call to compassion—which transcends religion, culture, and time—has been passed on to us. And yet, somehow, it often takes a child to remind us of the power of practicing this simple, ancient truth. You'd think it would have evolved a little further by now. Instead, as my son taught me, we've just reinterpreted its meaning to fit our narrative.

Rumi wrote: "When you see someone else's pain and sorrow, be tender as if you were suffering the same...Be a lamp, or a lifeboat, or a ladder. Help someone's soul heal. Walk out of your house like a shepherd."†

This is Jesus' ministry in a nutshell: Be the kind of person that makes the kingdom of heaven come alive for others. That includes all the people you'd rather not be kind to. Yes, the shit Jesus says turns the world as we know it on its head, and he's inviting us to do the work of salvation that transforms our world into God's kingdom.

In a world so quick to return violence for violence, Jesus calls us to heal rather than harm, bless rather than curse. This is the kingdom of God—where the meek inherit the earth and love breaks down

---

* Lao, Tzu, *Tao Te Ching*, trans. D.C. Lau (New York: Penguin Books, 1963), Chapter 49.
† Rumi, *The Essential Rumi*, trans. Coleman Barks (San Francisco: HarperOne, 1995), 207.

every barrier. Live like the shepherd, lead with tenderness, and be the healing light in a broken world.

Jesus teaches us that love and mercy are the only measures that matter. Love your enemy. Do good to those who hate you. Pray for those who hurt you. Give without expecting anything in return—not even a thank you (Luke 6:27–30). And just when we're about to tune him out, he hits us with the punchline: "This is what God has done for you, so go out and do the same for others" (Luke 6:36). If God has shown you love, then show it to others. If God has shown you mercy and grace, what's stopping you from offering that same mercy to someone who's hurt you? And if God forgives you, then forgive. Are you starting to see the picture?

Vaughn Crowe-Tipton humorously but rightfully notes, "Congregations respond to this text the same way my children respond to seeing cooked spinach on their plate. No matter how much I explain the nutritional value, no one around the table really wants to dig in."* Jesus' words can be hard to swallow. Even when I crave the spiritual nourishment they offer, it's tough to take that first bite. But if we ignore them, we'll miss out on something much bigger.

Jesus is always pointing us to an alternative life—grounded in God's way. He says, "I am the way, the truth, and the life. No one comes to the Father except through me. If you know me, you know my Father. And from now on you do know him and have seen him" (John 14:6–7). I point this out because Jesus' whole ministry was about revealing who God is. God is not a religion—or a doctrine like some have made this passage out to be. Jesus is simply saying, if you want to know the way to God and if you want to understand God's truth, then look at what he does—and do it. That's how you'll discover what life is all about.

If love is the religion of God, then practicing this religion faithfully might mean stepping into spaces where people disagree with

---

* Vaughn Crowe-Tipton, "Pastoral Perspective on Luke 6:27-38," in *Feasting on the Word: Preaching the Revised Common Lectionary, Year C, Volume 1*, ed. David L. Bartlett and Barbara Brown Taylor (Louisville: Westminster John Knox Press, 2009), 384.

you, despise you, or even hate you. When you enter those spaces, ask yourself, "What do I want people to do for me; and how can I take the initiative and do it for them first?" The effort you make may inspire others to do the same. What Jesus asks might seem radical, even insane. But if we take the initiative to be like him—loving, helping, blessing, and giving—then we begin to understand the kingdom of God in a clearer, more profound way. Dare I say, we even make heaven come alive.

I used to work in an office where, in the lunchroom, someone had hung one of those inspirational posters that read, "You get out what you put in." It always struck me as out of place—especially in a room where the whole point is putting food into your mouth. But the truth that Jesus inspires is similar. And if you take what he says to heart, you'll get more than you could ever imagine.

If you want to live in a world filled with peace, then bring peace into the world, and more peace will follow. If you pick on someone, expect to be picked on. If you judge, you'll be judged. If someone harms you or steals from you, Jesus says not to retaliate, because retaliation only creates more of the same. But just as violence begets more violence, generosity begets more generosity.

Jesus invites us to participate in ushering in the kingdom of heaven where God's will is done. We have a choice. We can love our enemies, or we can hate them. We know which choice Jesus made.

Given the state of our world today, it's hard not to feel like Jesus is setting us up to fail. Love your enemies. Do good to those who hate you. Bless those who curse you. Pray for those who abuse you. Everything about these invitations seems to go against the grain. The world tells us to reject this kind of thinking, because it makes us look weak and vulnerable. The world likes power. It even killed Jesus for daring to ask us to live this way. But Jesus wants us to do something radical. He's not giving us nice, moral guidelines. No, he's calling us to break the very foundations of the world we've built and rebuild them on the foundation of God's will: love, mercy, and compassion, not hate, power, and greed. Jesus is ushering in God's kingdom, and he shows us the way to make heaven come to life before our very eyes.

I have a friend who loves to pick up trash as we walk our dogs. "It's the one act of kindness I'm able to do," she tells me. Even if that was accurate, her actions are noticed by others. I've seen people mirror her willingness to make our park a little less messy. Imagine what we could do to the mess we've created in this world, if we all just picked up the mess around us and loved it like we'd want to be loved.

Desmond Tutu once said, "We are each a God-carrier, a tabernacle of the Holy Spirit, indwelt by God the holy and most blessed Trinity. To treat one such as less than this is not just wrong, it is veritably blasphemous and sacrilegious."[*] The world doesn't need more religion; it needs more people who will carry and birth love. Love is God's religion we share through kindness.

Mark Twain once said, "Kindness is the language which the deaf can hear and the blind can see."[†] And you know what? If we choose it, we can do it. We've all seen how human kindness works in times of disaster—when a hurricane strikes, or in moments of crisis like September 11, 2001. In those moments, strangers don't hesitate to help strangers. We act like family. But the truth is, as long as homelessness exists, as long as children sleep on our streets, we are in a constant state of crisis.

The homeless are the lepers of today. The drug addicts are the possessed. The immigrants are the aliens. And let's not forget the widows, orphans, and incarcerated. God knows that when we see someone suffering—whether they're lonely, thirsty, hungry, poor, or in need of any care—we have a choice. We can choose to ignore them, or we can choose to be like Jesus, who said, "The least you do to one of these, my brother or sister, you do also to me" (Matt. 25:40).

Again—I can't stress this enough—Jesus' words and sayings always invite us to participate in the redemption and transformation of our lives, communities, and world. He takes the simple idea of loving and showing kindness—treating people the way we want to be

---

[*] Desmond Tutu, *God Has a Dream: A Vision of Hope for Our Time* (New York: Doubleday, 2004), 33.
[†] Mark Twain, quoted in William George Jordan, *The Power of Truth: Individual Problems and Possibilities* (New York: Fleming H. Revell Company, 1902), 47.

treated—and flips it on its head. He's asking us to do the same with those whose political views, morals, or language are different from ours.

I recently saw these words scrawled on the wall in the men's room: "Being vulnerable is the only way to allow your heart to feel true pleasure." Apparently, Bob Marley said it. But it sounds a lot like Jesus.

Love, real love, is a risky business. Jesus knew that. He calls us to face our enemies head on—not with retaliation or harm, but with kindness and compassion. That means being willing to expose our weaknesses—to be ridiculed, to be mocked. Jesus says when we turn the other cheek, the kingdom of heaven comes alive. When we treat others with kindness instead of retaliation, the kingdom of heaven comes alive. By showing people who we truly are—the messy, flawed, bumbling us—we open ourselves to love and acceptance. And people begin to get a foretaste of heaven in their midst.

In her TED Talk, "*The Power of Vulnerability*," Brené Brown famously said, "What makes us vulnerable is what makes us beautiful." * She reminds us that vulnerability is simply "allowing ourselves to be seen"—even in our imperfections. My wife often reminds me that we are perfect with all our imperfections. Jesus isn't asking us to be flawless; he's asking us to be faithful. In that faith, we find strength, not our own, but the strength of the one who dwells in us.

That's the whole point of ushering in a new kingdom. Jesus wants to bring down the walls of the world so that God's kingdom can rise up through us. His way of life, his radical love, cracks open the foundations of this world, revealing the true reign of God! Every time we rise above hatred, let go of anger, and surrender our egos to embrace God's love, a part of our world crumbles away. It's as if Jesus is punching holes in our defenses so others can see what God's love really looks like. To live the way of Jesus—loving with such faith that nothing, not even death, can cause us to tremble—is to love with

---

* Brené Brown, "*The Power of Vulnerability*," *TEDxHouston*, June 2010, https://www.ted.com/talks/brene_brown_the_power_of_vulnerability.

such intensity that others can't help but see the world God is creating. This is the beauty of vulnerability and the joy of faith in Jesus. But let's be real—it's not easy. Faith, like love or kindness, takes practice.

Jesus says, anyone can love their spouse or kids, or those who love them back. What takes faith is to love those who hate you, despise you, and wish you harm. With all the anger and rage in the world today, there are plenty of opportunities to put Jesus' words into practice. Who knows what our love and kindness might spark? If we let our hearts break open and punch a hole in our walls, God's love can pour in and do what it does best. If we do what Jesus calls us to do, how many clenched fists and angry stares will be left? How many people will still be afraid?

Loving. Caring. Blessing. Giving. These are the footsteps of Christ. And he's calling us to walk in them. It might sound tough, but the reason is simple: one day, you might be the one who needs those things. The measure we give will be given back in ways only God can provide. Jesus calls us to a new community, where God's unconditional love is the standard for everything. This is true in the space between you and me, just as it's true between us and them. Jesus said, "Your reward will be great, and you will be children of the Most High."

As Rob Bell likes to ask, "What if Jesus meant what he said?" If we're going to follow him, if we're going to walk in his footsteps toward God's heart of love, our answer has to be a resounding "Yes!"

God is kind, so be kind. God is merciful, so be merciful. God is love, and you—made in God's image—are also love. Did Jesus mean it when he said, "Be easy on people and life will be easier"? Yes. Is it true that if you give your life away, you'll receive it back with bonus blessings? Yes. But only if we make ourselves vulnerable and willing to do the work. If we only listen to Jesus but never live his words, what's the point? If we accept God's grace but don't offer it to others, where's the joy in that gift? Faith isn't just something we proclaim—it's a way of life that goes against our natural inclinations.

"Love, do good, offer, give..." Jesus means it.

Mr. Rogers certainly got it. As he so beautifully stated, "All we are ever asked to do in this life is to treat our neighbors—especially the ones in need—exactly how we would hope to be treated ourselves. This is our ultimate responsibility." * When we allow our anger to be transformed into compassion, we no longer fear those who seem different from us. *Mr. Rogers' Neighborhood* broke down walls of racism, sexism, and all the other *isms* that divide us. He took Jesus at his word and said, "Yes."

Gandhi also believed Jesus meant what he said. When Gandhi said, "Love is the force that can liberate,"† he meant that to truly be free, we must love our enemies—even the cruel, terrorizing, and unjust. Love must be the standard by which all life is measured. In the kingdom of God, righteousness is born from love, not anger. And that love grows when we share it with each other.

Love is the religion of God. Love is our goal. Despite our failures, God still loves us. Even when we struggle to forgive, God still forgives us. God looks at us and always says, "Yes."

It doesn't matter if you're a pastor's kid or anyone else's kid, let even your enemy bring out the best in you, not the worst. When we manifest understanding, compassion, kindness, and generosity as Jesus did, then Christ is present, and his words become the truth, the light, and the way that leads all life into God's heart and home. You. Me. And yes, even our enemies.

---

* Fred Rogers, *Life's Journey According to Mister Rogers: Things to Remember Along the Way* (New York: Hyperion, 2005), 91.
† Mahatma Gandhi, quoted in Thomas Merton, *Gandhi on Non-Violence: Select Texts from Mohandas K. Gandhi's Non-Violence in Peace and War*, ed. Thomas Merton (New York: New Directions, 1965), 18.

18

THE KINGDOM OF HEAVEN IS A CONDIMENT

"The kingdom of heaven is like a grain of mustard seed that a man took and sowed in his field. It is the smallest of all seeds, but when it has grown it is larger than all the garden plants and becomes a tree, so that the birds of the air come and make nests in its branches."
—Matthew 13:31–32

There's a good chance you have a bottle of mustard in your kitchen. It's a common condiment most of us keep on hand and yet we barely know anything about it. I think it's safe to say that mustard takes up less space in one's head than it does in one's refrigerator. Just to prove my point, did you know that mustard is made with distilled vinegar, water, number one grade mustard seed, salt, turmeric, paprika, spice, natural flavor, and garlic powder? Probably not. Did you know French's Yellow Mustard brand claims zero calories, no artificial colors or flavors, and is gluten-free. Don't worry. Neither did I.

I believe there are two things in life that mustard complements perfectly: hot dogs and hot pretzels. Rarely do I eat either, but when I do, there had better be a bright yellow squeezable bottle of mustard within reach. I can't say if Jesus ever had a warm, giant pretzel battered in salt, but I'm pretty positive he never ate a hot dog, at least not one made from pork. Which might explain why he uses this condiment to describe the kingdom of heaven.

Jesus says, "The kingdom of heaven is like a mustard seed" (Matt. 13:31).

When I think of mustard, I'm reminded of a trip I took with two friends during spring break. Like most starving college students, we barely had enough gas money—and hardly enough for beer. Food was typically an afterthought. Our bellies were empty, and we knew we'd have to eat at some point on this trip, so we hit up the local grocery story and grabbed whatever was cheap. As I was standing in line with my meager provisions, my friend Gordon showed up. He was balancing a jar of mustard and a loaf of bread on top of three cases of beer. No cheese. No meat. No fancy extras. Just mustard, bread, and beer. It was as simple as it gets. But for Gordon, there was nothing better than a mustard sandwich with a cold beer. Who would have thought that something so simple, made from a humble, scrubby weed, could bring so much joy? Looking back now, decades later, I see both Gordon and the mustard seed in a new light.

The ancient mystics say, "God is nothing." Not that God is absent, but that God is not confined to any one thing. God is in everything—everything!—even the simplest things. Even mustard. Even bread. Even a humble sandwich. So that's where the kingdom of heaven is as well. It's in the ordinary, the overlooked, the seemingly insignificant items and people we discover in life. If God dwells in heaven and if God is in all things, then that must mean all things reveal a part of heaven.

The Gospel of Matthew introduces us to the kingdom of heaven when John the Baptist cries out in the wilderness, "Repent, for the kingdom of heaven has come near" (Matt. 3:2). Then Jesus echoes this same message as he begins his ministry (Matt. 4:17). As I've mentioned, the word *metanoia*, while often translated "repent," means something much bigger. In the original Greek, *meta* means "beyond" and *noia* means "mind or thinking." This roughly translates to go beyond your mind. Basically, think differently. Jesus is inviting us to change our perspectives. Change the way we see. Understand that

God is not just *one thing*—God is in every living thing. Change the way you think for the kingdom of heaven is here!

Jesus isn't revealing some distant, ethereal realm, but a radical reorientation of how we see the world. It's not about waiting for some far-off place to be revealed; it's about recognizing that God is here, now—in everything. The kingdom of heaven is not a faraway dream or an abstract concept. We can see it with our eyes, touch it with our hands, and taste and savor its goodness on a hotdog bun. It's as close as the earth beneath our feet, as present as the air we breathe, and as real as a mustard sandwich.

All of Jesus' parables point us to this truth, using metaphors of things that grow—seeds, plants, faith, weeds—as signs that the kingdom is alive in the world. And it's not just alive but growing and transforming, surprising us with how something so small, humble, and hidden can grow to reveal a deeper truth. The mustard seed—so tiny, so easily overlooked—grows into a plant that provides shelter and nurture. In the same way, the kingdom of heaven starts small, in overlooked places, but grows and unfolds in ways that surprise us. It's in the little things, the moments we might dismiss, where God is at work, revealing heaven on earth.

As we open our eyes to see this kingdom, we realize it's not out there in the clouds but here, in the gritty, everyday reality of life. It's in the simple things: a conversation, a gesture of kindness, a loaf of bread, a jar of mustard. In these moments, the kingdom of heaven is something that grows within and among us. It's already here, and it's waiting for us to pay attention, to let that mustard seed of love, kindness, and justice take root and grow. And just like that, the kingdom of heaven, so close and so real, will unfold right before our eyes.

Jesus uses parables to help us see that God is not hidden away in some far-off place. God's divine presence isn't a distant dream; it's here, right in the midst of our everyday lives. We might not always recognize it, but that's exactly what Jesus came to reveal—to open our eyes to the kingdom that's already at hand. Every time Jesus healed the sick, forgave sins, or extended compassion to the marginalized, he was making the kingdom of heaven visible. Each act of love and moment of care revealed God's realm breaking through into the here and now.

The kingdom isn't a far-off event that only began when Jesus said it did. No, the kingdom has been here since the beginning. Jesus himself tells us that heaven has been hidden—not absent but hidden in plain sight. It's been right in front of us all along, quietly waiting for us to recognize it. Jesus used parables to help us know what to look for and where to find it. He shows us how God's kingdom can be discovered in the most ordinary places—like a mustard seed, like yeast in dough, like a small treasure buried in a field. It's in the little things, in the seemingly insignificant moments of our lives, that the kingdom takes root and grows.

When Jesus says, "Repent, for the kingdom of heaven is near" (Matt. 4:17), it's not just about opening our eyes to see it. It's about engaging with it—participating in it. Jesus doesn't want us to be passive observers. He wants us to step into the kingdom and be part of it. He calls us mustard seeds—small, seemingly insignificant, but capable of growing into something powerful and transformative. We are each called to take our small, humble faith and let it grow into a force that reveals heaven to the world. It would do us all good to read ourselves into these metaphors, because they are about us—you and me—and how we are to take our small mustard seed of faith and bring the kingdom of heaven to life.

You might feel small, like a mustard seed, but you are just as essential to the kingdom as the towering redwoods that stretch high into the skies. Those mighty trees started as tiny seeds, just like you and me started out as a little fertilized egg. Dropped by the wind or carried by a bird, these seeds landed in a small patch of soil and began to grow. If you know anything about the California Redwoods, growing is what they do best. In the same way, our faith, no matter how small, has the potential to grow and stretch into something that transforms the world around us.

Jesus invites us to be active participants in the kingdom, to grow into what we were always meant to be: people who love one another. It's through loving that we do our best growing. It's in giving of ourselves that others grow too. And the kingdom flourishes as a result. And it's not just us growing—when we love, we help others grow alongside us. The kingdom of heaven isn't some abstract, far-off dream; it's right here, right now, in the ways we show up for each other, in small acts of kindness and care.

If Jesus were telling these parables today, I can imagine him saying, "The kingdom of heaven is like a sandwich artist at Panera who gives you a little extra meat, because they notice you look really, really hungry." The kingdom of heaven is in the everyday acts of grace and mercy, in the way we treat one another, in the simplest acts of love. God's realm isn't something far away or reserved for the holy or the mighty. It's found in everyday people doing everyday things. Which tells me that what we do in this kingdom matters. Every act of love, every moment of compassion, every small seed we plant—it's all part of the kingdom growing, expanding, and revealing heaven on earth. Whether you know it or not, what you do in this kingdom is actually pretty important work.

In her beautiful book, *Liturgy of the Ordinary*, Tish Harrison Warren reveals this simple, yet profound insight: "In the overlooked moments and routines, we can become aware of God's presence in surprising ways."* She invites us to recognize that the ordinary—those small, seemingly mundane tasks—can be extraordinary avenues for worship. We have the ability to turn the everyday into something sacred. It's a choice we must make: to see the holy in the ordinary, allowing every moment to be infused with God's presence.

St. Bonaventure, a Franciscan friar, understood something simple yet profound—everything can be holy work if we approach it with the right heart. Whether he was washing dishes or cooking meals for his brothers in the monastery, he knew that it wasn't the task itself, but the love and intention behind it, that made it sacred. Bonaventure saw even the smallest acts of service—those that often went unnoticed—as opportunities to be deeply connected with God. He under-

---

* Tish Harrison Warren, *Liturgy of the Ordinary: Sacred Practices in Everyday Life* (Downers Grove, IL: InterVarsity Press, 2016), 27.

stood that time spent in the kitchen, preparing food for others, was just as holy as time spent in prayer at church. It wasn't about the task; it was about how you did it. With humility. With love. With devotion. In those simple acts, Bonaventure found God, and the kingdom of heaven came alive!

You might already be doing this—living fully present in this kingdom—and helping people open their eyes. Some may be reflecting God's glory without realizing it, simply by being who they are in the world. A friend of mine once posted pictures from a trip to the redwoods, describing the towering trees as "majestic," "wondrous," and even "heavenly." The ancient poets used these same words to describe God's glory. My friend doesn't believe in God, yet in that moment—without realizing it—she was connecting with the divine. The kingdom was right there in the very beauty she was seeing, even though she didn't have the words to name it.

Eugene Peterson once wrote, "Everything that is made is a clue that leads us back to God."* Everything—the smallest seed, the tallest sequoia, the cry of a hungry child, even the hollow gaze of a dope-sick junkie. All of it, if we only open our eyes, is pointing us back to God. Peterson reminds us, "Our ability to see anything and understand it is because of God. Even our questions about God are evidence of God. Our enlightened minds, which we may use to deny God, are a gift from God who gives us life."† The fact that we are even capable of recognizing beauty, of feeling awe in the face of the redwoods, is itself a gift from God.

Jesus knows this. He understands that the kingdom of heaven isn't just some place we wait to enter—it's here, in the things we often overlook. His life—his entire ministry—demonstrates that the divine is not confined to temples or sacred rituals but found in everyday acts of love and compassion. Jesus uses parables to help us see what is already in front of us, revealing the kingdom in our midst. Thanks to

---

* Eugene Peterson, *A Year with Jesus: Daily Readings and Meditations*, (San Francisco: HarperCollins, 2006), 93.
† Peterson, *A Year with Jesus*.

Jesus, we can also have the ability to see the world as he did, to recognize that God is as close as the breath in our lungs, as near as the person sitting next to us.

But Jesus doesn't just want us to see the kingdom. He wants us to be the kingdom. He calls us to open our hearts and hands as well. He's inviting us to be the vessels through which God's love and righteousness flow into the world, through the mundane and majestic alike. The kingdom isn't just something we observe—it's something we participate in. It's in the simple act of showing up for someone, the kindness we offer to a stranger, the way we love our neighbor. These are the everyday ways we reveal heaven on earth.

I know there are times when you might doubt your worth in this kingdom. You might even laugh at the idea that anything divine could be in your ordinary daily interactions. I've been there—wondering what difference I could possibly make. You might think that because you don't have formal education, or because you don't know the Bible by heart, or because you aren't in church every Sunday, you have nothing to offer. But Jesus says, "Think differently. See differently. Act differently. The kingdom of heaven has been revealed to you."

It's right here, right now. It's in the small things—in the way we show up for one another, in the way we love with open hearts. In our willingness to give what little we have and trust that God will take it and make it something greater. Like that mustard seed, small and seemingly insignificant, we are called to grow and bloom into something that reveals the beauty of the kingdom. The kingdom of heaven is here, in your life, in the way you live, in the way you love. What will you do with it? How will you bring heaven to earth, in your ordinary, extraordinary life?

Remember, the tallest redwood began as a small seed. A beach started with a single grain of sand. The ocean, one raindrop at a time. The kingdom of heaven is hidden in the smallest moments, waiting to grow into something powerful. And you, in your everyday life, are the seed, a small grain of sand, one of a billion raindrops. Yet, you are the one God is calling to open your heart and hands and reveal the kingdom of heaven to the world. God is in the details. And you, my friend, are part of the divine story being written—right here, right now.

19

A FEW MORE THOUGHTS ON SEEDS AND GOD

"A sower went out to sow. And as he sowed, some seeds fell along the path, and the birds came and devoured them. Other seeds fell on rocky ground, where they did not have much soil, and immediately they sprang up, since they had no depth of soil, but when the sun rose they were scorched. And since they had no root, they withered away. Other seeds fell among thorns, and the thorns grew up and choked them. Other seeds fell on good soil and produced grain, some a hundredfold, some sixty, some thirty.
He who has ears, let him hear."
—Matthew 13:3–9

One of my favorite childhood shows was *Green Acres*.* It followed the story of Mr. Douglas, a big-city lawyer who—for reasons known only to him—decides to leave the hustle of the city behind and become a farmer. His wife, though not exactly thrilled by the idea, reluctantly joins him in this rural adventure. And sure enough, Mr. Douglas, with all his big-city charm, has a hard time fitting in. And farming? Well, that proves to be far more difficult than he ever imagined.

But here's the thing: he keeps at it. He perseveres, despite crops

---

* *Green Acres*, created by Jay Sommers, CBS, 1965–1971, television series.

failing, animals misbehaving, and an endless string of things that go wrong. And in the midst of it all, his wife—smiling quietly behind the scenes—convinces him to stay just a little longer before returning to the city where they belong.

I remember one episode vividly. Mr. Douglas is standing in a failing field of dying corn stalks, looking at the evidence of all his hard work going to waste. The crows, as it turns out, are the least of his worries. His dreams are falling apart before his eyes. And yet, just when he's ready to give up, his wife finds a solitary ear of corn, untouched, standing tall amidst the wreckage. She pulls it from the stalk and hands it to her husband—this tiny, perfect symbol of hope. It's a moment of tenderness, of grace amidst the absurdity.*

That's what Jesus does in his parable of the seeds and the soils—he shows us that even in the places where things seem hopeless, where dreams appear to die, a flicker of grace can always take root. Sometimes, it's in the last place you'd expect to find it. And—perhaps more importantly—those small, quiet moments remind us that the soil of our hearts can always be tilled again, no matter how barren it may seem.

Jesus tells us about a farmer who just starts tossing seeds everywhere. Now, I spent some time in rural Michigan, and I can tell you that when you're planting seeds, it's not as carefree as all that. You've got to till the soil, break up the dry surface, remove the rocks, and make sure the soil's ready to welcome the seeds. You water, you fertilize, you prepare—it's work. And it's all essential to giving the seeds a fighting chance.

But not in Jesus' parable. This farmer doesn't bother with any of that. He's got a sack of seeds, and he's flinging them every which way—without rhyme or reason. He strolls along, tossing seeds into the wind with a grin, like he's got a pocketful of magic and doesn't mind where it lands. To most people, this would seem like a waste of good and expensive seeds. But not to this guy. Apparently, he's got more

---

* *Green Acres*, season 3, episode 30, "Oliver and the Cornstalk," aired April 17, 1968, on CBS.

than he knows what to do with, so he's going to cover literally everything in the hope that something takes root. Some seeds fall on the road, where the birds swoop down and grab them. Others land on rocky ground, where their roots can't take hold and they wither in no time. Then there's the soil that's full of weeds, where the seeds get tangled up and choked out. But, of course, some make it to the rich, good soil, and those seeds grow into a harvest that's more than anyone could have hoped for.

For the farmers I know, this might seem wasteful—reckless, even. Seeds are valuable, after all. But God, like that farmer, doesn't seem to mind the mess. God's grace isn't concerned with where the seeds fall or how well-prepared the soil is. God's love is generous, extravagant, and free. It's scattered far and wide, without calculation, because God believes that every place—and every heart—has the potential to receive it. And when it does, the result is always an abundant, bountiful harvest, a glimpse of the kingdom of heaven, right here, right now.

Most scholars agree that this parable is a metaphor about faith. We are the soil, and God is the sower. Now if we think about it for a minute, we probably all know someone who fits each of these different soil types that Jesus describes, and of course, we see ourselves as the good soil. But if we're being honest, we know that we're not always the good soil—at least not all the time. Most of us shift between one soil type and another, sometimes in the span of a single day. Or a single hour. Which is why I think it's not enough to focus just on the soil. The sower and the seed, in my humble opinion, are the real heroes of this story.

Everyone knows seeds are fruit-bearing, life-giving, tough little things. They're resilient—even defiant at times. But they're also fragile, susceptible to all kinds of harm. Each seed, strong or weak, carries within it the potential for something great. Even the tiniest seed can grow into a mighty tree in a surprisingly short time. And what's even more amazing is that a seed can actually move through death to bring new life. That sounds like God work to me. Which brings us to the sower.

God is clearly the sower here. Our response to God, that's the soil. God is the one scattering the seeds everywhere. And what kind of seeds is this farmer sowing? What's so valuable in the kingdom of heaven that it's worth scattering so freely? I believe the answer is love —God's love. Love is the first and final word of the kingdom of God.

Here's the wild thing: the sower doesn't seem to care where the seed lands. Whether it's the footpath, the rocks, or the weedy soil, every patch gets a shot. And so do we. God doesn't hesitate to scatter love—flinging it out far and wide, unconcerned with where it lands or whether it takes root. God desires to see what kind of love each seed will yield. And we all get a shot—no one is overlooked.

God isn't content just sowing into the good soil. Though a farmer might want to preserve their seeds for the field, God is far more generous. God, in fact, prefers to cast the seed everywhere—especially where it seems least likely to grow. Even to those who may not care, or who might not respond the way God hopes. This parable shows us that the kingdom of heaven is sown with love—love poured out with grace upon grace.

This should be good news because most of us aren't great soil to begin with. Our hearts are hard, dry, rocky, or filled with weeds. It takes time to cultivate our hearts into good soil. But God doesn't mind. God is patient and generous, always scattering love, mercy, and grace, even when it feels like we're not ready for it. Grace, mercy, forgiveness—these are the fruits that grow out of God's love for us. Love is the good news, the Word made flesh in Jesus Christ, the very seed of everlasting life.

The Burren National Park in County Clare, Ireland, is a beautiful example of this kind of place. The word *burren* comes from the Gaelic word for "rocky place." The park is made up mostly of exposed limestone pavement with a little soil cover. At first glance, it appears barren. But here's the thing: it's also been called "fertile rock" because, amid the rugged landscape, you'll find a remarkable mix of nutrient-rich herbs and flowers.

The Burren's scattered pockets of wet, peaty soil nestled among cracks in the limestone are home to twenty-three of Ireland's twenty-seven unique orchid species, not to mention a variety of other plants and wildlife that thrive in those hidden crevices. It's easy to imagine how much we'd miss if we only focused on the soil that looks good on the surface—or for that matter, if God only sowed love where we thought it would take root easily. Thankfully, God doesn't do that. God doesn't overlook anyone. God loves us all and wants to be with us all. We all get seeds.

Henri Nouwen wrote, "The greatest gift we have is the gift of being loved by God. We are loved not because we are good, but because God is good. We are the soil that God wants to transform into something new and beautiful."*

Jesus reminds us that the sower throws seeds into all kinds of soil—the rocky, the barren, the broken—because God's vision for the world often shows up in the strangest and most broken places. Much like a dandelion seed, God's love floats through creation, finding its way into nooks and crannies we'd never expect. It's up to us, the soil, to let that love take root.

Jesus calls us to be participants in this heavenly kingdom. But the reality is, God is in control of what we sow. According to Jesus, our call is to bear the fruit of love, regardless of the state of our soil or the circumstances we find ourselves in. If we love, God can build us up, strengthen us, and make us capable of holding the world in our branches. But will you allow God's love to take root in you, and let it grow, and produce the fruits of the Spirit: love, joy, peace, patience, kindness, goodness, faithfulness, gentleness, and self-control? (Gal. 5:22–23).

Every botanist knows that seed-bearing plants always produce more seeds. And it's the same with love. Love produces more love. Kindness produces more kindness. Generosity and gentleness—they all multiply, just like seeds. So the question isn't whether God will sow that love, but whether we will let it take root and grow into something that, in turn, gives life to the world around us.

---

* Henri J. M. Nouwen, *The Return of the Prodigal Son: A Story of Homecoming* (New York: Doubleday, 1992), 43.

But here's the thing: we are not just the soil—we are also the seed and the sower. Jesus invites us to receive God's love, grow it, and scatter it without ever worrying about running out. He knows some will reject that love with hardened hearts, but even the hardest of hearts can reflect God's truth and beauty. Jesus also understands the abundance of God's ways. Some will embrace God's love and thrive, but when the struggles hit, we might be tempted to turn away. We often forget that the seed has already been planted. God's word has already been written on our hearts. Where there's a seed, there's always the chance for new life, even if it's been dormant for a while. Think about Amaryllis bulbs—they sit buried or frozen for most of the year, but when the time comes, they blossom into something beautiful.

Jesus also points out that some of us will work hard to grow stronger in faith, but we have to be cautious. We're vulnerable too. The lure of greed, the need to control, the lust for power, and the like can pull us away from trusting God's abundance. But if we focus on building the kingdom of heaven right here, right now, in our hearts and minds, we'll thrive. We'll bear the fruit of God's love a hundredfold. These sprouts give us hope, showing us how God's love can turn barren ground into something life-giving.

Someone once told me that God isn't concerned about which soil the seed falls on because God believes in the power of the seed. God's focus is on the harvest—the spiritual food that will feed the world. Love has the power to take root in the harshest places. Will you let it grow and bear justice, mercy, and grace even in the toughest terrain?

God is patient, sowing seeds of love everywhere because God's redemptive story can reach anywhere. God sows seeds of love, deals with the wheat and the weeds, and transforms shrubland into a thriving sanctuary. This is how it works in the kingdom of heaven: our hearts are transformed into fertile ground.

Jesus uses the most ordinary things to show us what God can do. I think it's because God works through ordinary people like you and me, continuing what Jesus began. As St. Teresa of Ávila famously said, "God has no hands, no feet, no voice except ours; through these,

God works."* God works with the everyday—ordinary bread, ordinary wine, an ordinary table, an ordinary grave. And God works through everyday saints like you and me—imperfect as we are—to bring about the kingdom of heaven. Seeds producing more seeds. Love producing more love.

Jesus makes it clear: we're not just spectators in the kingdom, we're participants. If we're going to follow him, then we have to walk the way he walked, live the way he lived. It's not just about loving God and loving others—it's about serving both, about being the hands and feet of God in this broken world. This is how we become the visible presence of God's love to a world that is crying out for it.

We may never have the chance to heal someone with a touch, but we can be there when they're suffering. Just by holding space, by being vessels of God's compassion, we bring the kingdom of heaven close. We may never feed thousands with a few loaves and fish, but with every meal we share, every dish we bring to a lonely neighbor, the kingdom of heaven draws near. Every smile we give someone, every flower we plant, every wrong we right, no matter how small—these are little pieces of heaven made visible to those who might never see it otherwise.

As John the Apostle wrote, "No one has ever seen God; but if we love one another, God lives in us, and his love is made complete in us" (1 John 4:12). And so it is. Each time we love, we show the world that God is here, in the middle of it all, working through us.

Love is the way Jesus invites us to usher in the kingdom of heaven. Love is the way we carry on his ministry throughout the ages. In all his teachings and parables, Jesus reminds us that this kingdom is everywhere we intermingle and grow together. It is here we join Jesus in sowing good seeds—in the way we love, forgive, care for and tend to the needs of others, in the way we serve even our enemies instead of demanding to be served ourselves.

Whenever and wherever we show love through acts of compas-

---

* Teresa of Ávila, quoted in Rebecca Laird, *Power of Prayer* (Nashville: Upper Room Books, 1997), 43.

sion, kindness, hospitality, humility, justice, and peacemaking, God is made manifest in us, and the kingdom of heaven is brought within reach of everyone. Paul reminds us, "It's God who works in you to will and to act in order to fulfill God's good purpose" (Phil. 2:13). And what is that purpose? To spread the glory of God's love across all of creation. This isn't just the work of saints; it's the way of becoming one. And it's the way of Jesus, who invites us to follow him.

As ordinary as you may feel, you are made a little extra-ordinary through the power of God's love. Just as a tiny seed can grow into a tree of life, even the smallest amount of faith can "cause the mountains to quiver and jump into the ocean" (Luke 17:6). It may be hard to wrap your head around, but that's okay. The disciples had trouble with it too. That's why Jesus often taught in metaphors—why he looked past the faces of his listeners and revealed the kingdom of heaven in ways they could understand.

Through Jesus, you not only see the nearness of God, but you also become the nearness of God. So embrace every moment as sacred, every human encounter as divine. This is what it means to be a part of the body of Christ—living life as he lived it: loving, forgiving, praying, healing, and caring for those in need. Just like he did.

Through Christ, God has opened our eyes to see the world as God sees it—holy and sacred. A place where people of all colors, classes, and conditions can live together in peace. Jesus has called you to step into those desecrated places and reclaim their sacredness. You are God's abundance, the visible presence of the kingdom on earth as it is in heaven. And through every act of charity, every meal shared, every smile offered, every wrong forgiven—that kingdom multiplies. Seeds producing more seeds. Love producing more love.

20

YOU'RE RIGHT, IT'S NOT FAIR THANKS TO GOD

"For the kingdom of heaven is like a landowner who went out early in the morning to hire laborers for his vineyard. After agreeing with the laborers for a denarius for the day, he sent them into his vineyard... 'I choose to give to this last the same as I give to you. Am I not allowed to do what I choose with what belongs to me? Or are you envious because I am generous?' So the last will be first, and the first will be last."
—Matthew 20:1–2, 14–16

Fairness. It's one of those words we toss around a lot, but what does it really mean? I grew up as the youngest of four kids, and though none of us would ever doubt we were loved equally by our parents, we each felt the reality of being treated unequally. My siblings believe I got away with so much more than them. As a parent now, I can see what they mean. Our firstborn still has so many expectations placed on her. Without her knowing it, or us knowing what we were doing, we made her our bar of achievement. I'm afraid to admit it but she still has all the pressure on her to get it right. Our second kid got a little more leeway, freedom, and grace. By the time the last one came along, well, we'd kind of lost our edge and threw up the white flag. His siblings, like my own, like to tell me, "It isn't fair."

But here's the thing about fairness: all things are not equal. Some get more, some get less. It's just the way it is. Some people are lucky enough to be born in a place where there's running water and high-speed internet. Some are just happy that the soldiers are staying out of their village. Life isn't fair. For some, the imbalance makes things feel okay, but for others, not so much.

I know Jesus knew this. His hometown was occupied by outsiders who took whatever they wanted. We don't know anything about what Jesus had to endure. But he was the oldest in his family, so I suspect the bar was set a little higher for him than the others. I suspect he also knew that, because he's constantly making this point about the kingdom of heaven: it doesn't work the same way as Wall Street.

Someone once said, "Fairness is a jewel that is rare enough to be worth the search, but no one ever finds it." I don't know who to attribute that quote to, but I suspect that person is still looking. And if they find it here, they might want to be compensated by me for referencing their words. I guess that would be a good time to shrug my shoulders and say, "Life isn't fair."

Carolyn is an elderly woman who lives at an adult living facility that I visit weekly. Every time I mention the idea that God loves everyone, she tells me the same story about a "gangbanger with Nazi tattoos all over his body." She says she watched him get fatally hit by a car. And as he was dying, "he had the nerve to pray to God for forgiveness." Each time I respond, "It's so unfair that anyone has to pray that prayer at all." I'm sticking with that. The kingdom of heaven isn't about who's first or who's last. It's not limited to just a select lucky few. This kingdom is for all people. Either we're all in, or it isn't real.

It should go without saying that Jesus' teachings and parables always present an alternative point of view. He wants us to see and think different. He doesn't want us to take all this shit he says at face value. He wants us to think and argue and push back. It really is the only way we can begin to fully understand a kingdom where God reigns. It doesn't run on us. Not our money. And not our power. It runs on God's rules. Only. You might think there are things in this world that are so unfair. And that's the point Jesus is always making.

Consider the parable Jesus tells about a bunch of workers who are hired to pick grapes in a vineyard (Matt. 20:1-16). It's harvest time, and there's too much work for the regular employees to handle on their own. So the manager goes out and hires more people to help out. Some workers are hired early in the morning, others are hired throughout the day, and yet, when paychecks are handed out, they all get the same wage. You're probably thinking the same thing. It's unfair, right? I can picture Jesus smiling, and saying, "Yes! Exactly!"

God is unfair because humans are unfair. And in case you haven't been paying attention, God's economy isn't about fairness the way we think of fairness. It's about love. It's about grace. And that means it has to be unfair in the best way possible.

Fairness isn't about giving everyone the same. But giving everyone what they need. That's how it seems to work in the kingdom of heaven. The place Jesus is always going on about.

My kids learned, at a very early age, that life isn't fair. Grown-ups get to say bad words. Older siblings stay up later than the younger children. And Dad always gets the biggest slice of cake and the largest bowl of ice cream. But at the end of the day, it's not about who's the biggest or the smallest, it's about who's the kindest, the most compassionate. Life isn't fair. Anyone who has ever done a group project knows, the one who does the least amount of work gets the same grade as the one who does all the work.

At first glance, Jesus' parable about the vineyard workers seems to reinforce this idea: Life isn't fair. But it begs the question, who exactly is it unfair to? The ones who started out early or the ones who had to sit around wondering if they were going to get any work that day. Unlike our modern perception of welfare, no work always means no pay. That's a truth in any kingdom. Anyone but God's.

But here's the hard reality of this parable. The workers hired first get the amount they agreed on. So did the ones hired last. Everyone who makes the deal is content with what was being offered. That is, until payroll comes around. Those who had worked all day in the hot blazing sun are a little more miffed when they find out those who barely broke a sweat get the same sweet deal. It's easy for us to understand their frustration, right? We all have that sense of what's fair. It's more than basic mathematics or incompetent bookkeeping—something in our gut says this is wrong. But it's not. Again, everyone gets paid according to the deal they made with the landowner.

This parable contrasts two groups: the wealthy landowner and those struggling to get by. But most of us are somewhere between the two extremes. We know what it's like to work hard, and we know the stress of barely getting it. But we live in a capitalist world where the reward goes to the ones who earn it. In heaven, Jesus does something completely unexpected. And the only way we will truly understand it is if we look at the world through God's eyes and not our own. Why? Because God's economy doesn't work like ours—and thank God for that.

Carolyn sees the world as most of us do. She saw the man hit by a car and thought, *He got what was coming to him.* She couldn't see beyond his inked skin and all that it stood for. When she sees him, she doesn't see redemption or a beloved child of God. She sees a thug. A cancer. A menace to society. Because she sees through human eyes instead of God's eyes, Carolyn assumes this man was only praying because he was dying.

We don't know if that was true. But we do know his go-to response in his suffering was to turn to God. While she sat in her car watching him bleed out, he cried out to the only one he knew who could truly rescue him. God is there for the good, the bad, and every one of us who lives somewhere in the space between the two.

God's economy is not about who works the hardest or has earned the most. God doesn't care if you've been praying all your life or just started at the end of life. God cares about grace, love, and generosity. In the same way, the landowner isn't being unfair to the early workers. In fact, he's being incredibly generous—especially with those who came last. That's the point. Life isn't fair. Some people get a head start; others have to struggle to make ends meet. God gives freely and generously to all.

That's what grace is. A love so abundant, it doesn't care about keeping score. There's enough for everyone to cash in on.

Cuban born theologian Justo González invites us to see this story through a different lens. Imagine viewing the story not from the perspective of a rich landowner, but through the eyes of an immigrant worker—the kind of person Jesus' original audience could relate to, the kind of people whose stories still play out every day.*

Many men and women come to California, where I live, searching for a chance to earn a living. My own father-in-law was one of those people—he left Ireland looking for work so he could send money back home to help care for his younger siblings. For him and his family, it wasn't about fairness; it was a matter of survival.

The same was true for the workers in Jesus' parable. There was work to be had, and the laborers had willing hands. And for their willingness, they were paid an honest day's wage—one *denarii*. Like the day laborers in the Home Depot parking lot, most are being hired to do the kind of labor that's backbreaking. They show up early in the morning so they can earn their daily bread, pay their bills, and support their families. These are not desk jobs or cushy office positions. These are the jobs no one else wants for the wages being offered.

I know this kind of work. After I lost my job, I struggled to get anyone to notice me, much less hire me. My friend Earl was contracted to do a bathroom remodel and needed a couple of day laborers to demo the place, so he hired me to tear the place down to the studs. I showed up early, rolled up my sleeves, and got to work—tearing down walls, ripping up floors. It was backbreaking, sweaty work, and it didn't take long for me to realize how much harder this was than sitting in an air-conditioned office all day. When the job was finished, Earl lined us up and paid us. We each received a one-hundred-dollar bill. To the other workers, that was fair for a full day's labor. But for me? It didn't feel right. I was used to making more

---

* Justo L. González, *Santa Biblia: The Bible Through Hispanic Eyes* (Nashville: Abington, 1996), 62–63.

money for a lot less effort. I couldn't help but think, *How do people live on this?*

This is what's happening in the vineyard parable. The landowner needs workers to harvest the grapes, so he goes out and hires some folks early in the morning, agreeing on the wage for the day. Then, he goes back a few more times—at the third hour, the sixth hour, the ninth hour—and he keeps hiring more workers, offering them the same wage. At the end of the day, the workers line up to get paid. No matter how long they worked, or how many pounds of grapes they picked, they all get the same paycheck. In other words, they all get treated the same. This is what the kingdom of heaven is about—the outpouring of God's love given to all the same—abundance.

In the kingdom of heaven, fairness isn't about giving everyone the same thing. It's about giving everyone what they need, regardless of how much they've earned or how long they've worked. This might be hard for us to fully see or understand. But to the one who is hired last, those laborers who have been waving to cars hoping to get picked for a job, this is an undeserved blessing to say the least.

It's not the American way. But it's God's way—a way that doesn't calculate the value of people based on what they've done or how hard they've worked. Everyone gets paid the same. The kingdom of heaven turns all our ideas about fairness upside down. And that's what makes it both beautiful and uncomfortable. Jesus tells us stuff that gets under our skin, challenging our assumptions and ideas. This particular story is about grace and God's love being lavished on all people, regardless of when they come to the table or how much work they've put in. This kind of love doesn't care about the hours we worked—only our willingness to show up and receive the goodness of God's kingdom matters. This is a love that doesn't measure, doesn't calculate, and certainly doesn't keep score. If only all businesses worked this way.

During the 2009 recession, as the economy was tanking, I was working at my last ad agency job before going into vocational ministry. Like us, everyone I knew was scrambling to stay afloat. At one point I worked three straight months without a day off. These were all-hands-on-deck times. Had I been making an hourly wage, it wouldn't have been so bad. But my senior position was salaried. When I did the math, I was making less per hour than the receptionist. I truly believed the sacrifices I was making for the job would pay off if we succeeded. And we did. By the end of the year, we managed to keep the doors open and even turned a profit. My reward? A twenty-five-dollar Best Buy gift card—just like everyone else in the office, except for the few at the top whose jobs we'd saved. Life just isn't fair, and God knows it.

To borrow from St. Augustine, God loves each of us as if there were only one of us. It's never about earning God's love. It's always about receiving it with open hands, knowing that it is always enough for each of us, as if we were the only one that mattered to God. In the kingdom Jesus is ushering in, love and grace are not columns on a spreadsheet—if only because they are boundless, limitless, and perfectly sufficient for every need.

Jesus' parable blows up everything we think we know about fair compensation. As Philip Yancey puts it, "What employer in his right mind would pay the same amount for one hour's work as for twelve?"[*] The answer is simple. God would. God's fairness looks nothing like ours. The world teaches us to measure everything in terms of time and effort. You get what you put in, as the saying goes. But the truth is most of the people around me get more. It's hard to see the subtle difference until we've stood in the shoes of those hired last.

Imagine it's five in the afternoon. You've been standing in the hot sun, hoping for work, praying for a chance to earn enough to survive another day. Finally, a truck pulls up, offering you a job. It's not much, but it's something. Still, there's a lingering fear inside you. The hour is late; will you even earn enough for a ride home? Never mind the fear most of these laborers face, will you even get paid for the work you do? Again, God is unfair because humans are. Still, you feel your

---

[*] Phillip Yancy, *What's So Amazing About Grace?* (Grand Rapids: Zondervan, 1997), 61.

stomach growl, and you know the only choice is to get in the truck, trusting everything will work out in the end.

When the vineyard manager sees the workers still waiting for a job at the end of the day, he's not there to judge them but to hire them. He doesn't view them as lazy or unworthy—that's not why no one hired them. Instead, he sees men in desperate need of a chance, and he responds to their silent pleas with compassion. He understands their struggle to feed their families, so he offers them work, knowing that providing for them will come at the cost of his own resources.

No one likes to be overlooked or passed by while others are being chosen. It does something to our psyche. The fear and pressure of survival can chip away at a person's sense of worth. But the kingdom of heaven has never been about who's in and who's out. No one gets overlooked. All are chosen. Jesus is telling us to let go of our anxiety and the fears of getting through the day. We all have need, but God has plenty to give—enough for us all.

God's economy doesn't run on merit, but on God's own faithfulness and generosity. It's not about who's deserving; it's about who's in need. The landowner upholds his end of the agreement, paying every worker the same wage—not because it's fair, but because it's what they need. As Philip Yancy reminds us, God isn't interested in what we've earned because "God dispenses gifts, not wages."* God's love is not a paycheck. It's something much better. It's grace. And thank God for that.

We will always see life as a "fair pay for fair work" kind of game until we come to grips that grace is the currency in God's economy. I actually believe Jesus tells us this parable to show us that God has already affirmed our worth, not based on what we've done or what we can do but based on who God is and what he can do. God's love is not conditional. When God calls us into the vineyard, whether we've been there all day or just showed up, we are loved the same. No one is

---

* Yancy, *What's So Amazing About Grace?*, 62.

ever last. The last shall be first, because God's grace is for everyone, no matter when we come.

Jesus offers us a place where timing, competence, and merit don't define us. A place where starting with a disadvantage—the color of your skin, education, language, nationality—don't set you back. This kingdom he ushers in is where God is always faithful, always generous to everyone. Nothing is calculated on a timesheet. Nothing is held over our head as a bonus or reward based on merit. God's love and grace are freely given to anyone willing to enter the vineyard.

A man in one of my bible study classes once joked, "God's a lousy bookkeeper because he adds infinity to every check he cuts." I can live with that. Infinite grace. Infinite love. Infinite forgiveness, healing, joy, hope, and so on. And no matter how many times God gives and gives and gives to us, the checks never bounce.

We're all trying to find our way in the vineyard. Some of us just happened to get a head start. But God's love isn't about that. God welcomes everyone into the vineyard—anytime, every time. This is God's kingdom, not ours, and God—who is generous beyond measure—can do whatever God wants even if that means "paying scoundrels twelve times what they deserved."*

The landowner goes out five times to gather workers. I suspect if he went out a sixth or seventh time, the story wouldn't have changed. Instead of fixating on who gets what or when, let's focus on the simple truth: God's love is for everyone, and everyone benefits equally from it—even a dying gang member tattooed head to toe in swastikas.

Jesus reminds us to be gentle with those at a disadvantage. God loves and welcomes everyone into the vineyard, no matter when they come. And we should be deeply grateful for that—grateful for a God whose love is not about math or merit, but about generosity and grace.

---

* Yancy, *What's So Amazing About Grace?*, 62.

21

YOU WANNA TALK ABOUT MONEY? LISTEN TO THIS SHIT!

> *"You cannot serve God and wealth."*
> —Luke 16:13

I really hate to admit it, but I'm cheap. Like, truly, epically cheap. I don't like spending money if I don't have to. My wife knows that even if there's something I really want, she'll have to buy it, because I refuse to spend money on myself. My thriftiness has become the punchline of every Scottish joke you can think of. But, hey, it's also given me the financial freedom to follow my call. And Jesus had a lot to say about money. Spoiler alert: He wasn't like me.

Jesus is good with money, but he only has one use for it: to give it all away. When a rich young guy asks what it would take to inherit eternal life, Jesus tells him to follow God's commandments (Mark 10:17–21). The man, proud of his spiritual résumé, assures Jesus he's already doing just that. Jesus nods and says, "Great. Now sell everything you have and give the money to the poor." That's how Jesus sees wealth—as something meant to be emptied into the hands of those who had nothing. Easy for him to say. He had no attachment to material things. The rest of us? Not so much.

You've probably already figured out that Jesus rarely speaks in absolutes. But when he does, it's usually about one of two things: the poor or money. That should tell us something about this hard line he draws. "You cannot serve both God and wealth." Another spoiler: he knows which side most of us will fall on.

Jesus tells this parable about a rich man who has a house manager (Luke 16:1–13). This guy's been skimming off the top of his employer's assets. Knowing he's been caught and is about to lose his job, the untrustworthy employee suddenly starts to panic. He's too weak to dig ditches and too proud to beg. So he starts making shady backroom deals, slashing the debts of everyone who owes his boss money, buying himself some goodwill for when he's out on the street. Oddly, Jesus doesn't condemn him for doing this. Instead, he tells those who are listening, "Remember, you can't serve two masters. You'll love one and hate the other" (Luke 16:13).

Jesus knows we need money to live, but he's pointing to something deeper: the sickness that grows when we love money too much. The obsession, the hoarding, the scheming. People back in his day called it "mammon illness." And it still infects us.

I have a friend who quit acting to raise a family. She has a brilliant mind, with hyper-focus. Maybe a little too much hyper-focus. She watches the market like a hawk, waiting for just the right time to strike or sell. She rides the highs and lows, both emotionally and financially. It's a lot for her sometimes simply because of the very nature of the market. She's like most of us who stretch every dollar, stress over investments, and fixate on security. Pretty soon, our focus is no longer where it ought to be, which can make us do things—lie, cheat, steal—things that fracture relationships and hollow us out from the inside. We know the stories. Wall Street guys lining their pockets at the expense of the vulnerable. It's always been this way. Mammon blinds us to what actually matters: the people right in front of us, the love we were made for. We're all guilty of it—hoarding, stockpiling, always looking for ways to multiply what we have.

Mammon illness takes our eyes off what actually matters—God and love—and onto something meaningless to the kingdom. Money draws the lines, splitting the world into haves and have-nots. But

God? God refuses to divide. Love and mercy? Free for all. No price tag, no buy-in—just grace, poured out without a ledger. No keeping score.

Jesus lays it out plain and simple: You can't serve two masters. And just to make sure we get the point, he tells this parable—one of those stories that sneaks up on you and leaves you shifting in your seat (Luke 16:19–31). He says, there's this rich guy—dressed to the nines, eating like a king every day. He compares him to Lazarus, a beggar, who is slumped outside the rich man's gate, hoping for scraps. That's their whole relationship—one feasting, the other starving. And then, as things tend to go, they both die.

Lazarus is carried off to Abraham's side (let's call that heaven). The rich man? He wakes up in Hades (whatever your opposite of heaven is). And wouldn't you know it, in his misery, he finally notices Lazarus. The rich guy is the one begging.

"Father Abraham, send Lazarus to dip his finger in water and cool my tongue—I'm burning up here."

Abraham shakes his head. "Remember? You had everything. He had nothing. Now the tables have turned. And besides, there's this great chasm between us—no one can cross it."

The rich man panics. "Then send Lazarus to warn my brothers so they don't end up here."

Abraham shrugs. "They've got Moses. The prophets. Let them listen to them."

But the rich man pleads, "No, no—if someone comes back from the dead, they'll believe!"

Abraham sighs. "If they won't listen to Moses and the prophets, they won't listen even if someone rises from the dead."

Jesus isn't being very subtle here. He smashes the illusions that make us see money as a life insurance policy. But money is only good in the short-term. Once we die, what use is it? Money lulls us into a false sense of security, a belief that we're untouchable, that our wealth makes us powerful. But Jesus flips the script. In this story, the poor man has a name; the rich man does not. The poor man is carried away by angels; the rich man is buried. And that chasm? The one between him and Lazarus? It was there the whole time. He just never saw it—until it was too late.

Jesus is making a point, and it's a big one. The division between rich and poor? It's man-made. And it's killing us. But despite what you might be tempted to think (about heaven and hell), Jesus isn't warning us about some distant, future reckoning. He's pointing to right now. If we don't close the gaps between us—if we let money convince us we're fine while others suffer—we're the ones who'll end up lost. Because real security isn't found in the bank. Only love saves. Only God saves. And God? God's always on the side of the ones lying at the gate, waiting to be seen.

If Jesus ever made a political statement, *this is it*. The stark contrast and disparities in this story aren't just for effect—it's a call to action. Jesus wants us to respond—emotionally, mentally, spiritually. The kingdom of heaven is here, and it matters how we care—for our own souls and the souls of others. And the ever-widening economic gap is still one of the biggest issues of our time.

Jesus is practically shouting, "Stop it!" Stop widening the divide. Stop pretending suffering isn't our problem. Stop stepping over people to get ahead. Stop being blind to the world as it actually is. Because God's will isn't some far-off dream. It's right here, right now. *On earth, as it is in heaven.* And it starts with us.

Paul tells his student Timothy not to put his faith in wealth or power—because they don't last. They slip through our fingers, especially when it matters most. Instead, Paul points to something real—generosity, love, the kind of faith that actually does something (see 1 Timothy 6:17–19). Both Jesus and Paul get at the same truth: real power isn't found in hoarding, but in giving ourselves away. This is how we store up our treasures in heaven. Love is the only currency that holds its value—God's love. How we live out that love matters as much as the person lying at the gate that we step over.

In Matthew 25, Jesus says it's him. He's the one lying there, hungry and thirsty. He's the one locked up, cut off from the decent folks. He's the one we've shoved to the margins, the one sleeping on the sidewalk, who we step over on our way to brunch. He's the guy on the evening news, tired of being shot at. The kid in the schoolyard, pushed around and ignored. The one holding the cardboard sign at the freeway offramp, grateful for that granola bar you forgot was in your glovebox. He's the bruised and broken woman in the shelter, running from fists that once promised love. He's God's own beloved son, standing outside the door—not hoping for the scraps that hit the floor, but for a seat at the table. He may not look like us, or sound like us. But if we're paying attention—if our eyes are clear—we'll recognize him instantly. Because he looks exactly like God. And yet, mammon keeps us blind. It keeps us grasping at wealth, convinced it will empower us. But what good is power if it turns against us? What good is money if it tricks us into thinking we're better, safer, untouchable? "When did we see you hungry and refuse to feed you?" they ask. And Jesus doesn't hesitate: "Every time you ignored that poor person over there, you ignored me" (Matt. 25:44–45).

To borrow from Mother Teresa, if you want to know God's will, go and love someone who is hurting. If you want to hear God's voice? If you want to see God, look in the face of your neighbor. Listen to the cries of the poor, the lonely, the broken—and respond. "Each one of them is Jesus in disguise."*

Richard Rohr wrote, "Love is not merely something we are called to do. Love is someone each one of us must become."† It's either love or money. You can't serve both.

While watching a political rally some years ago, I saw a person wearing a red shirt that read, "Jesus Votes Republican." I'd bet you some mammon that somewhere out there is a blue shirt that says, "Jesus Votes Democrat." But Jesus? He wouldn't be caught dead at the ballot box. He wasn't interested in our political tribes. While he might be hard to pin down politically, he's pretty clear about bringing together the most unlikely people. And money seems to be the bridge.

---

* Mother Teresa, *Come Be My Light: The Private Writings of the Saint of Calcutta*, ed. Brian Kolodiejchuk (New York: Doubleday, 2007), 186.
† Richard Rohr, *The Universal Christ: How a Forgotten Reality Can Change Everything We See, Hope For, and Believe* (New York: Convergent Books, 2019), 33.

Some of the religious elites once tried to box Jesus in. They set up the perfect trap, asking a simple question: "Is it lawful to pay taxes to Caesar?" (Matt. 22:17). No matter what your political leanings are, I think we can all agree that no one wants to pay taxes. Again, this is another wonderful example of mammon illness. We want to keep all our money in our pocket.

So it's a very clever political conundrum they've set up. It's designed to be that "gotcha!" moment that gets Jesus in trouble. If he answers yes, it is lawful to pay taxes, then the religious elites will paint him as a sellout. If he answers no, then they will paint him as a revolutionary. But Jesus, as always, sidesteps the nonsense. Leave it up to him to find a loophole.

His response is to ask for a coin. They hand him one. It's a Roman denarius, not a Jewish coin. It has Tiberius Caesar's face stamped on it, along with the blasphemous title, "Son of God." No good Jew would be caught dead carrying one because it would be the equivalent of having a false idol in your purse. But it's interesting how a Pharisee had one handy. Jesus holds the coin up, and asks, "Whose image is on this?" (Matt. 22:19–20).

"Caesar's," they say.

"Then give to Caesar what is Caesar's," Jesus replies, "and to God what is God's" (Matt. 22:21).

Boom. Mic drop.

He doesn't actually answer their question. He leaves it for them to decide who gets what. Tertullian, writing a couple centuries later, spells out what Jesus was getting at. Give Caesar his stupid coins—he stamped his image on them. But give yourself to God because you bear God's image.* That's the real flex for both Jews and Gentiles alike. Every human being carries the divine inscription of God, etched into our very being. This divine inscription gives us our worth and purpose. That's worth more than any amount of silver or gold.

---

* Tertullian, *On Idolatry* (Latin: *De Idololatria*), chap. 15.

God doesn't want to see your coins. God wants to see your heart, your compassion, and not your complicity with the mammon used to harm in the kingdom of heaven. Jesus reminds us that we belong to God. And yet, we continue to chase after that which is Caesar's. We strive to make gods out of coins, but struggle to allow God to be made fully manifest in us. Talk about being infected by mammon.

Rohr awakens our hearts to this truth. "There is that in you that no one can destroy or diminish because it belongs completely to God."* Why do we still chase after what belongs to Caesar when Jesus tells us where to bank. He says coins, crowns, robes—they're just things. Rust eats them. Thieves steal them. Moths chew through them. You and I don't belong to Caesar. We belong to the God who breathed life into us. Caesar takes; God gives—again and again, without keeping score.

Rulers don't want us to be like them. They want us to be afraid so we'll serve them. But God? God wants us to be who we were destined to be—bearers of God's image, of God's love. While Caesar's economy runs on taking from others, stealing, hoarding, demanding what isn't his, God's economy runs on giving, giving, giving. Jesus isn't worried about taxes because he's more focused on our love. This is not our paycheck but our inheritance.

Love is our greatest wealth. It's also the best investment we can make. It is the currency and social capital in the kingdom of heaven.

A large majority of people throughout the world don't have IRAs or stock portfolios. What little they have isn't being shuffled through the market. Most folks are just trying to get by, hoping their car doesn't break down this month. But what they do have is each other—family. "You have to love and honor your parents because they're all you've got. And parents have to love and respect their children because they're going to take care of them in their old age. That's their insurance plan."†

---

* Richard Rohr, "Money," *Center for Action and Contemplation*, September 22, 2019, https://cac.org/daily-meditations/money-2019-09-22/ (accessed on September 16, 2022).
† Rohr, "Money."

Life in the kingdom of heaven runs on love—on relationships. Love is always personal. Always relational. But mammon? It only knows how to count. It measures, weighs, calculates. And before long, "it becomes the way we relate to one another."* We meet someone and immediately do the math: What can she give me? What does he have that I need? Jesus says, Stop counting. Stop measuring. Stop keeping score. Love doesn't add up; it pours out. We can't hoard God's love—it's not ours to stash away. It's only ours to give away.

Mammon whispers the lie of scarcity: there's never enough. Not enough money. Not enough resources. Not enough for *them*. It pits us against each other, keeps us clutching what we have. It turns families into battlefields when the will gets read. It convinces us that our worth is tied to our bank accounts, and that security is something we *own*. But God doesn't deal in scarcity. God is infinite—limitless grace, boundless love, mercy that won't run dry. If God's love can't be measured, why are we still keeping score? That's mammon thinking. Jesus invites us into a kingdom where we stop measuring who deserves what, where everyone gets their fill of grace. We can't serve both. It's impossible. It just simply doesn't work.

As St. Thérèse of Lisieux would come to discover, "There is a science about which God knows nothing. Addition and Subtraction."† This is the economy of grace. And the good news Jesus ushers in. With God, even the tiniest drop of infinite love is still infinite. More than enough for you. More than enough for me. More than enough for *everyone*.

Mammon tells us there's never enough. But God says, *I am enough.*

Jesus meets us in the space between scarcity and abundance, between God and mammon, and he invites us to step into the infinite. To live in a world where love doesn't get counted—just given. Where our hearts crack open and grace flows freely. Where fear of not

---

* Rohr, "Money."
† St. Thérèse of Lisieux, as quoted in Richard Rohr, *The Universal Christ: How a Forgotten Reality Can Change Everything We See, Hope For, and Believe* (New York: Convergent Books, 2019), 147.

having enough gets replaced by the joy of knowing God is already giving *everything*.

22

PEARLS, PIGS, AND PUNK ROCK

*"Do not give what is holy to dogs,
and do not throw your pearls before swine,
or they will trample them under foot and turn and maul you."*
—Matthew 7:6

In the movie, *Pirates of the Caribbean: The Curse of the Black Pearl*, Captain Jack Sparrow stands aboard the deck of the *Black Pearl*, addressing his ragtag crew.[*] With dramatic flair, he boldly declares, "The code is the law! We abide by the pirate's code, or we're no better than common thieves." His ragtag crew, filled with mischief and hope, nod as if they have just learned the gospel. The pirate's code—an oxymoron if ever there was one—sounds noble coming from their eccentric captain. But when a desperate sailor points out that Jack himself had just ignored the code, their leader waves off their acute understanding, confessing, "The code? The code is more what you'd call 'guidelines' than actual rules." It's a moment as deliciously contradictory as life itself.

---

[*] *Pirates of the Caribbean: The Curse of the Black Pearl*, directed by Gore Verbinski (Burbank, CA: Walt Disney Pictures, 2003), film.

We all have our own little rules—principles, ethics, pearls of wisdom—which we uphold when it's convenient. But when circumstances challenge our comfort, we also find ways to bend them, justify them, or toss them into the wind like pearls before swine. Life is mostly this back-and-forth between what we aim for and what actually happens. Take a parent who preaches honesty but also nudges their kid to say, "Thanks, Grandma, I love the itchy sweater." It's not hypocrisy; it's survival in a complicated world. Even Jack Sparrow, our favorite swashbuckling philosopher, knows this dance. He shouts about the pirate code one minute and shrugs it off the next. He wants loyalty but also the freedom to do whatever he pleases. This tension leads him to alternate between enforcing the code and disregarding it. As amusing as it is, Jack's contradiction exposes one of the ways we justify shifting between our highest ideals and the messy reality of being human. But instead of getting stuck in guilt, we can let these contradictions lead us somewhere deeper. If we're paying attention, they don't just expose us; they guide us. And if we're lucky, they might just point us in the direction of grace.

One of my favorite things about the Bible is that it's full of contradictions. If you don't believe me, then you probably haven't read it. I mean, why would you? It's full of contradictions. But that's exactly the thing I love about it. Because right out of the gate, in the very first chapters of Genesis, we get two different versions of how humans showed up on the scene. Did humans arrive as a matching set, male and female, after all the other stuff got made, like in Genesis 1? Or was the man sculpted from dust first, with the woman showing up later, fashioned from a spare rib, like Genesis 2 tells us? Hard to say.

And then there's Noah. In Genesis 6, he's told to bring two of every kind of animal. Seems straightforward. But by Genesis 7, the instructions get a little more specific—seven pairs of the clean animals, two of the unclean. So, which is it? Did the elephants get plus-ones while the pigs had to fend for themselves? Even Jesus falls into this category—telling us not to be mean to others, then calling people names like "wolves in sheep's clothing" (Matt. 7:15) and "brood of vipers" (Matt. 12:34).

The contradictions don't bother me. They delight me. Because they remind us that faith isn't about having airtight answers—it's about diving headfirst into the mystery. The Bible, after all, isn't an instruction manual; it's a conversation. And lucky for us, God isn't afraid of a little inconsistency. I'm not here to argue about whether the Bible is inerrant or errant—flawless or full of errors. That's a debate for people with too much time on their hands.

I'm just saying that, on the surface, even the holiest, most sacred texts don't always line up neatly. And that's a good thing. It requires us to rethink any rigid expectations of the Bible, which I believe invites us to see it not as a rule book or an error-free manual but a collection of ancient, inspired, and very human writings that reflect the messy, evolving relationship between God and humanity. Teacher and podcaster Pete Enns often argues that the contradictions in scripture aren't a problem to be solved, but an invitation to deeper engagement. For Enns, the Bible isn't meant to give us clear, consistent answers—it invites us into a conversation, a journey of faith where wrestling with the text is part of the point. If we don't take the time to understand the context of the ancient world that these words were written in, we'll end up forcing ancient words into modern molds they were never meant to fit.

These contradictions don't weaken scripture—they invite us deeper into it. They ask us to trade easy certainty for wonder, to let mystery have the last word. And if we're paying attention, they don't just challenge us—they change us. So I welcome them—embrace them, even—because they rattle the cages of the buttoned-up, overly certain, rule-loving religious folks who act like faith is a Scantron test with only one right answer. But more than that, it forces me to actually engage with the text, to sit with it, to wrestle with it like Jacob grappling with the angel in the dark (Gen. 32:24). It makes me slow down, dig into different translations, and ask bigger questions. It's not so much about answers as it is about trust. Trust that God knows what God is talking about. And Jesus invites us to ponder it further.

Of course, Jesus isn't always clear either. Thus, the title of this book. But his goal is to inspire us and encourage us to see the world through a different set of lenses. He teaches us how to gaze at one another through God's eyes first. This will, without a doubt, contradict how we have been taught to see and hear and do.

A rabbi friend of mine told me this wonderful story. In it, a young man full of passion and certainty approaches his wise old rabbi with a question.

"Rabbi, does the Torah contradict itself?" he asks, arms folded, certain he was about to expose a flaw. The rabbi nodded. "Yes, of course it does."

The young man, triumphant, smirked. "Ah-ha! Then how can we trust it?"

The rabbi smiled. "Come back tomorrow, and I'll explain."

The next day, the young man returns, eager for the rabbi's wisdom. "Rabbi, does the Torah contradict itself?" he asked again.

The rabbi shook his head. "No, of course not."

The young man blinked, confused. "But yesterday, you said it did!"

The rabbi chuckled. "And today, I say it doesn't. You see, my son, wisdom is not about choosing between contradictions. It is about holding them both and learning to listen."

The young man frowned, thinking. Then the rabbi pats his shoulder and adds, "If you can understand this, you are ready to begin." *Where was my rabbi when I was a kid?*

Jesus says, "Do not give what is holy to dogs, and do not throw your pearls before swine, or they will trample them under foot and turn and maul you" (Matt. 7:6).

Jesus has just spent most of his time teaching everyone how to love their enemies, forgive well beyond what the law states, and seek the kingdom of God. Now he slips in this strange little gem of a command as if he's got a personal vendetta against dogs and pigs. Does Jesus hate animals? I mean, sure, pigs were unclean in Jewish law, so I get that one. But dogs? Have you ever met a Labrador? Maybe he knows something we don't. When my dog Cali was a puppy, she chewed through everything I owned—my hat, my belt, even my laptop charger. Maybe Jesus had a run-in with a first-century golden retriever and thought, *Yep, this is why we can't have nice things.* So don't give them anything precious if you don't want it destroyed. The same could be said about pigs. There is nothing they won't eat; including one another.

But obviously, Jesus isn't talking about actual animals here. He's talking about people. And this is why context is everything when reading scripture. If we take it as a literal rule book, we miss the poetry, the humor, and the nuanced wisdom buried in every line. Jesus isn't telling us to exclude people—he's actually calling us to something deeper. He's talking about discernment—what Paul calls seeing with "the eyes of the heart" (Eph. 1:18).

The pearl, of course, is the gospel—the radical, scandalous truth of God's love. We need to be very careful with it and how we share it. In another parable, Jesus calls the kingdom of heaven *a pearl of great price*—so precious that it's worth selling everything to possess it (Matt. 13:45). So when he warns us not to throw pearls before swine, I would argue he's telling us not to waste the sacred on those who aren't ready to receive it. Not because they're unworthy, but because some truths have to be discovered, not force-fed.

Imagine trying to talk a conspiracy theorist out of their wildest theory—the one where they believe the moon landing was faked, birds aren't real, and their neighbor is a reptilian spy. You can bring them all the evidence in the world, present every rational argument, even wave around Neil Armstrong himself—but they're too deep in it. They don't want truth; they want certainty. And at some point, you just have to let it go. Jesus himself says, "If they won't listen, brush the dust off your sandals and move on" (Matt. 10:14). Some people just aren't there yet. And that's okay.

I learned this lesson the hard way when I was thirteen. I decided I was going to be a rock star, so I signed up for guitar lessons, fully expecting to be playing The Clash and Ramones songs by the end of the week. Instead, my teacher had the audacity to suggest I start with basic scales and chords—as if I had time for all that nonsense. I had read stories about punk rock legends who picked up a guitar and were playing gigs a year later. I was impatient, convinced that I already knew what I needed to know. Or to put it differently, I wasn't ready to hear what my teacher was getting at, much less pointing me toward. I was still in the dream stage, not the learning stage. Frustrated, I quit after a few lessons. I didn't pick up a guitar again for almost twenty years when I was actually ready to learn.

Sharing the truth of God's love is kind of like that. You can't force someone to see what they aren't ready to see. You can't make someone understand God's redemptive love and grace when they're still convinced they have to earn it. Some people need time. Some need to struggle. Some need to sit in the mess for a while before they're ready to reach for something more. The key is discernment—knowing when to offer what is holy, when to hold back, and when to trust that God is still working, even when someone isn't yet ready to listen. Because grace isn't something we shove down people's throats—it's something they have to be hungry for.

Jesus is the pearl. He models this truth perfectly. When he meets the woman at the well, he listens, engages, and offers her *living water* (John 4). He meets her where she is—with her questions, her history, her thirst for something more. But when he stands before Herod, he says nothing. No debate, no defense, no pearls thrown before someone who isn't ready and doesn't want what is offered. Herod is too caught up in his own power to recognize God's presence even when it's staring him in the face (Luke 23:9). Like the poet in Ecclesiastes reminds us, "There's a time for everything under heaven...a time to be silent and a time to speak" (Eccles. 3:7).

The thing is, if you share the gospel in a way that alienates people, you've already lost them. The goal isn't to alienate. It's to draw people toward the truth, which you can do by embracing Jesus' patience and wisdom. In other words, the best way to *share* the gospel is to *be* the gospel—meet people where they are, because that's where they're most open to hearing something real. Or to quote the pearl of wisdom my wife teaches her students: "You catch more bees with honey than vinegar."

We are the pearl as well. I learned this in seminary when I found myself in a rather spirited "discussion" (read: heated argument) with some classmates who were big on street evangelism. I asked them a pretty straightforward question. "What's the best way to teach someone about Jesus who doesn't believe in Jesus?"

Without hesitation, they started rattling off scripture—*"Jesus is the way, the truth, and the life!"* (John 14:6). Which, of course, I immediately shut down.

"Great," I said, "but if someone doesn't believe in Jesus, why would they care what your book says about him?" As you might imagine, that didn't go over well. They kept trying to prove their point with more scripture, and I kept pushing back like someone who wasn't ready to hear what they were offering—which, honestly, was the whole point. This continued until another classmate, clearly fed up, blurted out: "Look! You don't tell them who Jesus is—you show them." That was my point. Well, not mine per se. It really belongs to Jesus.

Again, this passage is more of a warning than a command. Some people simply can't *hear* the good news until they *see* it in action. This could be you. But my street evangelist classmates were so focused on "winning souls" that they missed what Jesus was actually asking of them. The Bible isn't a weapon to beat people into heaven. It's the living word of God, meant to meet us exactly where we are—and beyond.

Jesus doesn't send us out into the world to win arguments. He doesn't commission us to shove doctrine down people's throats or make sure we're always right. He sends us out to love, to awaken hearts—not to shut them down; to embody the pearl, not just talk about it.

Which is exactly what St. Francis of Assisi meant when he said, "Preach the gospel at all times, and if necessary, use words."

If our mission is to love God, love others, and serve both, then that's exactly what we should do. Not talk about it. Not argue about it.

Not weaponize it. Just do it. Loving God doesn't mean we have all the answers or hold the keys to every mystery of the divine. Loving our neighbor doesn't mean shoving Bible verses down their throats or burying them in theological debates about atonement or regeneration. (And if you don't know what those words mean, congratulations—you are in very good company. Look them up if you want, but I'm not here to teach you systematic theology.) But what good are those big words if we're not going to live them out ourselves, in real spaces in real time? What good is anything Jesus says if he's not going to live them as the embodiment of God's love?

Here's what I *do* know: our love for God and for one another *is* the good news. And Jesus has asked us—no, commanded us—to share that love with every single person on this planet and beyond. But love can't just be a word we toss around. It has to be lived, breathed, embodied. Jesus didn't just call a few professionals to be the light of the world. He called every single person who hears his words to go and live them out. To be a beacon in the darkness. Even when you don't fully understand. Even when you're not totally sure you believe.

Jesus says, "Go and share the good news to all the nations" (Matt. 28:19), which might sound like a contradiction. I mean, share it with everyone, even the ones who are not ready to receive it? But is it really a contradiction? Or is Jesus just saying to go out and bring God's love to every city, every home, every heart that's open. And the hearts that are closed? That's where discernment comes in. Some people aren't ready. Some aren't listening. And that's okay. Jesus doesn't ask us to *force* it. Sometimes, we have to step back and trust that God is working in ways we can't see. The seeds we plant now might not sprout until much later. And even in the waiting, we are called to be faithful.

The Apostle Paul—who, let's be honest, had some pretty solid wisdom to share—puts it like this: "Walk in wisdom toward outsiders, making the best use of the time. Let your speech always be gracious and seasoned with salt, so that you may know how you ought to answer each person" (Col. 4:5–6). In other words: Be wise. Be patient. Be gracious. Don't force the pearl into hands that aren't ready to hold it. Instead, let your *life* be your testimony. Let your *actions* be the sermon. And as you go, hold onto this promise from Jesus himself: "I am with you always, to the very end of the age" (Matt. 28:20). Carry that promise with you. Step out in faith. Love people like crazy. And watch what happens when you let your life be the gospel—the kind that doesn't need words to be heard.

23

WAIT—HATE EVERYTHING IMPORTANT IN YOUR LIFE?

> *"Whoever comes to me and does not hate father and mother, wife and children, brothers and sisters, yes, and even life itself, cannot be my disciple. Whoever does not carry the cross and follow me cannot be my disciple. For which of you, intending to build a tower, does not first sit down and estimate the cost, to see whether he has enough to complete it?"*
> —Luke 14:25–28

This is one of the craziest things Jesus said. It seems like the antithesis of everything this book is about, and yet it's exactly what this book is all about. To fully understand it—if that's even possible—we need to remember that Jesus doesn't mince words when he calls people to follow him. In his radical invitation, he warns, "Whoever comes to me and does not hate father and mother, wife and children, brothers and sisters—even life itself—cannot be my disciple" (Luke 14:26). Not the best recruitment sales pitch I've ever heard. At least, not for the kind of people we would like to work with.

At first glance, these words strike us as harsh—a demand to set aside everything we hold dear. Yet this is exactly the heart of discipleship: a call to measure what we are willing to give up for a love that transforms us. This familiar truth was echoed by Dietrich Bonhoeffer when he wrote about the cost of discipleship: "According to our text, there is no road to faith or discipleship...only the obedience to the call of Jesus."* Following Jesus isn't a path paved with easy comforts—it's a journey where we burn our boats, leaving no room for retreat. It's a pilgrimage into vulnerability, where the very things we cling to must be reexamined and sometimes left behind.

Cost, by its nature, demands sacrifice, effort, and the surrender of what is familiar. Jesus invites us—like a master builder surveying his plans—to tally every brick and beam required to build a life that reflects the kingdom. On the surface, it might seem like he's asking us to despise all that we love. But the truth runs deeper: a life steeped in love may require us to let go of the comforts, prejudices, and attachments that keep us from fully embracing another kind of love—a love that challenges us to be more than we ever imagined.

In the 2008 film *Sunshine Cleaning*, Amy Adams plays a woman whose job is to clean up scenes where people have died—including suicides and murders.† Yes, this is a real job. There are people whose work is to step into the aftermath of human tragedy and restore order from chaos. It's a job most of us wouldn't choose, yet it hints at the raw, unvarnished reality of following Jesus. His path isn't designed to be attractive in the conventional sense. Instead, it's a call to forsake the safe and the known, inviting us to face ridicule, loss, and even the threat of death itself, all for a chance at something far greater.

If this was an ad to attract people to be a part of his ministry, I suspect every church in the world would see a radical decline in attendance. Jesus isn't recruiting us for a comfortable ministry. He's issuing a clarion call for a countercultural life—a deliberate, transformative choice we're called to make. Amid the competing voices of a noisy world and the gentle, persistent call of God, we must ask: if love

---

* Dietrich Bonhoeffer, *The Cost of Discipleship* (New York: MacMillan, 1949), 48.
† *Sunshine Cleaning*, directed by Christine Jeffs (Los Angeles: Overture Films, 2008), film.

demands such a cost, do we dare to pay it? Judging by the items on Jesus' list, I find myself wondering how anyone can afford it.

Jesus calls us to follow him with eyes wide open and hearts fully engaged. He doesn't expect blind obedience but demands that we truly see what the journey entails—letting go of the familiar comforts of family, the safe routines of daily life, and even our own carefully constructed identities. Discipleship isn't a trendy diet or a fleeting experiment; it's a radical, all-in commitment that reshapes every fiber of our being. The very idea makes most completely uncomfortable.

This passage stares us in the face with a challenge that cuts deep. It asks us to reconsider everything we cling to—our families, our jobs, our communities—even our nation. It demands that we push away those we are more inclined to embrace, and the everyday things in our life that we willingly or unwillingly put above our loyalty to God. But is Jesus really saying I have to hate my wife and kids? Is he expecting me to sell our home and belongings, leaving our families exposed to the hardships of life? That doesn't sound like love to me. It's not a world I want to belong to. You're probably thinking the same thing. Is it possible, then, that Jesus is just using vivid language to challenge our priorities and fortify our resolve? Are these commands meant to be taken literally, or do they serve as a metaphor for the uncompromising focus required to actually hear what he's telling us?

At its core, Jesus wants commitment—a wholehearted devotion that places God above all else. God wants to be our number one for no other reason than because we are inherently precious in God's eyes. Yet, embracing this truth comes with a steep price.

When my wife and I first married, I was climbing the corporate ladder and earning a comfortable salary that allowed us to build a comfortable life for our family. But when I answered the call to ministry, I never fully grasped the cost—how it would alter my marriage, reshape my relationships with our children, and upend the life we had known. It took years for Kathleen to accept she was not my first love—God is. That was a tough pill for both of us to swallow.

Then when I decided to leave behind a secure church salary—and even a free home—I was forced to confront the truth of this question: Am I willing to pay the full price of following Jesus? Could I really plant a church with the modest support of a few kind souls? Could I pull over and help a drunk stumbling into the road? Or give the actual shoes off my feet for someone who had greater need than me? The answer has always been unequivocally, "Yes." And yes, at times it has cut deeply into the fabric of my life, my family, and all the things I once thought were non-negotiable.

In her reflection on this text, pastor and author Melissa Early writes, "You can't mitigate the cost of discipleship with budget spreadsheets and good project management. Jesus warns the crowds that following him will cost them everything. Other relationships have to come second. It's about sacrifice—not just of comfort and companionship but of one's rootedness in a community, one's present circumstances, and one's future."* In this uncompromising call, Jesus isn't trying to thin the ranks or scare us off; he's inviting us to a transformation that redefines what we value most.

When I read this passage to a group of seniors at an assisted living facility, one resident asked, "Can I still be a Christian if I'm not able to do what Jesus is asking?" Of course. Just keep in mind, no one dives into the deep end of a pool and instantly swims. First, you learn about the water—how to stay afloat and not drown. Then, in time, you'll learn some strokes. And before you know it, you're moving through the water with ease.

Following Jesus begins with a decision—a choice to hear what he says and then go and do it. To truly follow him is to live a life shaped by his example—a life where doing the will of God is the single most important thing we can do.

Those first disciples—the Twelve—didn't get it all at once. Over time, they learned that aligning their hearts with his takes instruction, practice, and patience. In that space between our human frailty and divine love, we discover what we are called to do. Who we are called to be. How we are called to live. We are God's beloved, called to

---

* Melissa Early, "Reflections on the Lectionary," *The Christian Century* 136, No. 18 (August 28, 2019): 18.

practice and live out the will of God's radical hospitality, sharing God's inclusive and steadfast love with one another. If you ask me, this is what it means to take Jesus at his word, knowing and truly believing him when he says, "For where two or three are gathered together in my name, I am there with them" (Matt. 18:20).

Following Jesus doesn't come easy. It takes practice. Like understanding what he says, it takes a new mindset, a new way of seeing and doing things. It requires a change of heart and behavior. It demands that we let go of the self-centered ways that keep us clinging to our comfort zones—our ego, our anger, the divisions that blind us to the love we're called to share. If we are to make God our number one priority, we have to stop pretending that God loves us more than those people over there. God's love isn't reserved for a select few; it's for everyone. This is where the real costs begin to add up. It's easy to love people who are like us. It's not so easy when their culture or accented speech is different and hard to understand.

"Whoever does not carry the cross and follow me cannot be my disciple" (Luke 14:27). This doesn't sound like good news, does it. But notice Jesus says, "carry the cross." He uses the singular—he's referring to his cross. Jesus isn't calling us to shoulder the burden or bear an unbearable weight on our own. He's inviting us to take hold of his cross, to walk alongside him, and to help usher in the kingdom of heaven.

My friend's husband Charlie can lift six hundred pounds of dead weight on his own. That is something I can't do. Most of us aren't like Charlie. But when two or three of us lift together, the load is easier to manage. When we join forces, with each other and with Jesus, the load becomes something we can bear. And in that unity, each of us finds the strength to keep walking.

There's a story about an island that barely survived a massive storm—one that destroyed most of the island's infrastructure and broke the people's spirit. One day, a young girl slumped over in the square, too weak from despair to get up. Seeing her struggle, an elder knelt beside her, offering his strength to steady her, but he too was weak. Seeing him struggle, another neighbor leaned in to support the two. One by one, all the villagers joined. Together, they lifted one another in their grief. Years after the storm, this act remained a ritual. Whenever someone fell—physically, emotionally, or spiritually—the community gathered and shared the weight of the burden. From the strongest to the weakest, no one stood alone. Every gesture of care became a brick in an invisible structure that held them together against every storm.

The early church was just like this—a community that lifted the weak, comforted the grieving, and rejoiced together in hope. "They shared everything, so no one was without" (Acts 2:45). In living out Jesus' sacrificial love, they showed the world that it's possible to offer ourselves to one another, following Jesus' way of love and reconciliation and hope. They reminded us that the church is not some run-down building that only sees people once, maybe twice a week—it's a collection of fragile, imperfect souls bound by Christ's love. When we hold each other up, we become the hands and feet of Jesus, giving the world a glimpse of heaven, the kingdom he ushers in.

The more of us there are in this family, the easier it becomes for each of us to "burn our boats" and become little reflections of Christ. C. S. Lewis wrote, "the whole purpose of becoming a Christian is to become a little Christ."* I believe that. But I also know this is more than just believing it to be true. It takes instruction, practice, patience, and time—often more than we think we have. But as we watch Jesus in action and strive to mirror his way of life, our love, forgiveness, hospitality, kindness, and willingness to share becomes as natural as breathing.

Discipleship, we will discover, is a journey that starts with one small, brave step and grows with every stumble and every victory until it becomes a comfortable stride spent in the presence of God. If you want this walk to be truly meaningful, if you want to get a big return on your investment, then each step must lead us to a closer, more intimate relationship with God. That's the way of Jesus. That's

---

* C. S. Lewis, *Mere Christianity* (New York: MacMillan Publishing: 1978), 153.

the path he walks. And this is where all his stories and all the shit he says leads us—to the very heart of God.

Following the way of Jesus means putting God's will above our own, even when that decision unfolds over a lifetime. It calls us to examine what in our lives—our families, our careers, our personal desires, even our loyalties to church or nation—are pulling us away from truly living out God's will. And what is that will? Jesus was pretty clear about that too. Love. To love is to know God, see God, feel God, and be close to God.

Love isn't something we are simply called to do or practice. Love is exactly who we're called to become. In order to make God's love our greatest priority, we have to make God our greatest investment. God must come first—in our hearts, our minds, and our every word. Everything else is sacrifice. As John the Baptist declared, "I must decrease so Christ can increase" (John 3:30). This is the cost of our faith—a cost that, though heavy at times, yields rewards beyond measure.

Jesus says, you're blessed when people laugh at you, hate you, or even kill you for choosing God's way over the world's. He doesn't say you will be blessed. You *are* blessed. Following him comes with a cost, but the reward is greater. What you pay for now, you receive now. Instead of letting that pain break you, let it lift you up with gladness and joy, because your reward in heaven is immense (Luke 6:22–23). Heaven has come. And you are already in it. So what's stopping you from loving your way through it? Love as if your life depends on it. Even if this means hating the things that stop you from doing just that.

24

WHERE'S YOUR FAITH, DUDE?

"You of little faith, why did you doubt?"
—Matthew 14:31

I can't tell you how many times I've said it or heard it said to be, but it all comes down to faith. But what is it? In the simplest terms, faith is trust—pure and unfiltered—in someone or something. You sit in a chair without a second thought, trusting it won't collapse beneath you. You bite into an apple, assuming there's no hidden worm waiting to surprise you. It really is that basic. But faith can also stretch into the deep end—like trusting when you show up at work, you'll still have a job. That kind of faith isn't just about believing in your own competence—it's about trusting that your boss does too.

Faith is what gets us out of bed in the morning. It's what keeps us married. It's what allows us to step into the unknown with some measure of confidence. And yet, as plenty of blindsided spouses will tell you, just because you've been operating with trust doesn't mean the other person has. Betrayal has a way of shaking faith to its core.

Now, when we talk about faith in the religious sense, it's similar—but different. Spiritual faith asks for trust in something unseen, unheard, and often unprovable. Take Moses, for example (Exodus

3:1–15). He's out there, shepherding his father-in-law's herd, when he sees this bush burning. Nothing unusual perhaps until he realizes it's not burning up. And just when you think it can't get weirder, the bush begins to speak. It calls his name and tells him, "I am the God of your father, Abraham, Isaac, and Jacob. Go back to Egypt to free my people." Talk about a test of faith.

Now, I know a lot of folks who like to think that, if God spoke to them like that, they'd jump without hesitation. Not Moses. He's more like, "*Hold on a sec—you want me to do what? And who are you, again?*" He doesn't have faith so much as he has questions. He pushes back, testing the waters. And God? God just says, "*I am who I am.*" Somehow that's enough, and Moses goes.

But here's the thing—faith is rarely this tidy. The people Moses leads out of Egypt have even *less* faith than he does. They grumble, doubt, push back. Turns out, faith isn't a straight line. It's more of a forward stumble—trusting just enough to take the next step.

At its heart, spiritual faith is letting go of needing to know everything and trusting in the mystery of it all. It's believing in something beyond what can be seen or proven. I have a very dear friend who constantly tells me that he only has faith in science—because it's measurable. But even scientists, for all their formulas and findings, lean on a kind of faith too. Not blind faith, but a trust in the scientific method, in the possibility that today's unknowns might become tomorrow's discoveries. They run experiments not just to prove what *is*, but because they believe there's more to be revealed. That's faith in a different language.

St. John of the Cross wrote, "To come to the knowledge you have not, you must go by a way in which you know not."* His words inspire us all to move forward into the unknown—not because we know where we're going, but because we trust enough to take the next step. In this forward motion, the mystery begins to make itself known.

---

* St. John of the Cross, *The Ascent of Mount Carmel*, in *The Collected Works of St. John of the Cross*, trans. Kieran Kavanaugh and Otilio Rodriguez (Washington, DC: ICS Publications, 1991), Book I, Chapter 13, Section II.

CHAPTER 24

Whether it's in science, in God, or in the unseen, faith moves us forward. It allows us to stretch beyond our place of comfort, to venture into the unknown, to do things we never thought possible. It's not just belief—it's action. It's stepping out, not because you *know*, but because you *trust*. And that kind of faith? It changes everything.

When we lived in Michigan, my wife and I took the kids to one of those zip line obstacle courses out in the woods—the kind advertised as fun for the whole family. It didn't take me long to discover this was a gross misrepresentation. The place was called Treetop Adventures, but a more accurate name would have been Phobia Forest. An intricate web of ropes and wires connected to trees and rickety platforms high above the ground, where only squirrels and bad decisions belong. The concept? Strap yourself in, defy all survival instincts, and swing your way through increasingly terrifying challenges.

If you know my wife, it won't surprise you that she made me go first—not because she's cruel, but because she knew I'd never leave the ground otherwise. So up the rope I went, trying to act normal, praying my kids wouldn't see the panic in my eyes.

Ahead of me was a young couple. I noticed the guy was putting on a brave face for his date and yet still took the steps, trying not to let his fear be seen. She, on the other hand, not so much. It was painfully clear that she shared my fear of heights. Eventually, she and I ended up together on a tiny, wobbly platform, staring down at the only way forward: a thin rope that we were supposed to trust with our lives. Her companion was on the ground, making promises, coaxing her to jump. But she refused. I did my best to help, but outside of pushing her off...I had nothing. Fear had gotten the best of her. And me.

Long story short, she eventually closed her eyes, took the leap, and floated down into the young man's arms—where she immediately burst into tears. It was a beautiful, heartfelt reunion. And then, as fate would have it...it was my turn. Down below there were no arms waiting for me. Just the hard, unforgiving ground. No coaxing, no encouragement. Just my kids yelling, *"Hurry up, Dad!"* I won't tell you how long I stood there or the terrible things they said. But eventually, I jumped. And just before my feet hit the ground, something unexpected happened—a surge of life rushed through me. Adrenaline. Exhilaration. Maybe even joy. Whatever it was, it was enough to move me forward to the next challenge. And that's faith, isn't it? It will either scare the hell out of you...or fill you to the brim with life.

The disciples are out on the water, struggling against the wind, when they see someone *walking on the waves (Matt. 14:24–31)*. Naturally, they assume it's a ghost—because, well, what else could it be? But then Jesus calls out, "Take heart. It's me. Don't be afraid." And Peter is the first to react. He blurts out, "Lord, if it's really you, tell me to come to you on the water."

Jesus says, "Come." And Peter does it. He actually steps out of the boat and starts walking on water. But then, reality catches up with him. The wind, the waves, the sheer absurdity of what he's doing—it all hits at once. Fear takes over. He starts to sink. "Lord, save me!" he cries.

And Jesus, without hesitation, reaches out and grabs him. *"You of little faith, why did you doubt?"*

This is Peter's zip-lining faith in action. Like the young woman on the platform, paralyzed by fear, or me, standing there while my kids heckle me. Peter steps out, trusts for a moment, and then fear creeps in. But Jesus doesn't let him go under. He grabs him.

"Where is your faith?" Of all the questions Jesus asks, this is the one I never quite know how to answer. I've lacked faith when I've doubted from time to time. And I've been in that boat with Jesus—spiritually speaking—facing my share of storms, both literal and metaphorical. More often than not, I've walked straight into them myself...like climbing that cursed rope ladder onto that first terrifying platform.

In this story, though, it's Jesus who pushes the Twelve out onto the water. *By themselves.* He stays back, spends time with the people, then heads up a mountain to pray (Matt. 14:22–23). Did he know a storm was coming? Maybe. Most of these guys were fishermen. I'm sure they'd handled storms before. Still, why would Jesus endanger them like that?

The Hebrew word for water—*mayim*—comes from a root word meaning *chaos*. Jesus pushes them straight into it. Is this some kind of test? Or his way of reminding them that the mission ahead won't be smooth sailing—that sometimes it won't be wind slapping them in the face, but fists? That storms will come out of nowhere, without warning and without mercy? Maybe this isn't just about faith. Maybe it's about learning to live with doubt.

As most of us have experienced, doubt and faith will always collide. Like high and low pressure clashing over the Midwest, they create spiritual storms. But in this story, Jesus isn't just conquering the chaos—he's showing us that faith can actually *steady* us when we're in that chaos. There will be moments when we stand at the edge of something terrifying, faced with a choice: stay frozen or take the leap. That's the thing about faith—it's always a *going-forward* kind of deal. Like those poor Israelites when they got to the Red Sea, standing there with an escape route literally opened before them, yet terrified to take that first step. *"Do not be afraid,"* God tells them. But many of them still wanted to turn back.

History is filled with these moments. When ordinary people—full of fear, full of doubt—step forward anyway. Those who drafted the Constitution, who shaped and outlined a future they'd never live to see. They weren't fearless. They just kept their eyes in front of them, looking faithfully ahead to the next generation to carry this movement forward.

Where we get stuck—where I get stuck—is when doubt paralyzes us, leaving us stranded on the edge of the platform with nothing to trust but ourselves. And if I've learned anything, it's that when I sit too long in my doubt, I spin out. I can't move. I can't even make a simple decision. Like that young girl at *Phobia Forest*, frozen in fear while her boyfriend begged her to jump. I stood there beside her—just as scared, just as stuck. And in that moment, I had to believe that I couldn't be *both* on the platform and on the ground to catch myself. But God could. And God *does*. God meets us in those *both/and* moments—in the fear *and* the faith, the doubt *and* the trust.

Because faith, without God, has no real purpose or meaning. It can't save you—only God can. I think this is what Jesus wants the disciples to grasp. They can't rely on their own skills, their own knowledge, or their own abilities to read the waves and predict the wind. Because the real chaos—the unpredictable, gut-wrenching storms they'll face in their mission—won't be found on any weather map. Jesus needs the disciples to have faith in the one who sends them. In the one who catches them. In the one who will never *ever* let them drown.

Another fun Hebrew word is *emunah*. It's often translated as "faith," but it's more than something you have—it's something you do. It literally means "to take firm action." Faith moves; it doesn't loiter. Up there on that rickety platform at Phobia Forest, I had all kinds of faith. I believed the wooden planks beneath me were solid. I believed the ground was safer. But that belief alone wasn't faith. The only way to get where I needed to go was to jump. And until I did, I would never know the joy of having both feet planted on solid ground again. That's what faith asks of us. Not just to believe in God, but to trust—to take that terrifying first step into the unknown, trusting that God will meet us there. And for some mysterious reason, God often does this by dragging us right to the edge of our comfort zones and whispering, "Jump."

Jesus builds this kind of faith in us because he knows what he's asking isn't easy. Love the unlovable. Forgive the unforgivable. Make peace when the world is hell-bent on war. Faith doesn't sit trembling in the boat. It doesn't cling to safety. It steps out. It takes action. It leaps—sometimes into chaos, sometimes into peace, but always toward Jesus. And when it leaps into action? It changes everything.

Peter gets this. Well, *eventually*. At first, he does what most of us do—he hesitates. He's standing at the edge of the boat, in the middle of a violent storm, seeing what he thinks is a *ghost* walking toward him. A reasonable person would just stay put. But Peter, like Moses before him, does what we all do when we're unsure. He asks for proof. *"If it's really you, tell me to come"* (Matt. 14:28).

Jesus simply says, *"Come."*

So Peter steps out. And for a moment, he *walks on water*. That's what faith does—it moves us into the impossible. Until fear creeps in. Until we start noticing the wind and the waves instead of the one who called us forward. And that's when Peter sinks. Not because he doubted, but because he let fear have the final word. God's kingdom doesn't run on fear, but trust that you are safe exactly where you are. Faith can scare you, or it can transform and empower you, strengthening you to do what you never thought was possible.

We all get to this moment sooner or later—the edge-of-the-platform moment. Some of us will jump fearlessly. Most of us will jump reluctantly, knees shaking, voices cracking, hearts pounding. And that's okay. Faith isn't about *never* doubting. It's about knowing who's waiting for you when you doubt. Jesus will call out our lack of faith, sure—but not to *test* us. He does it to show us what God can do *for* us and *through* us. God doesn't test us. God *loves* us. And love—especially the radical, terrifying, change-everything love of God—will push us right up to the edge.

Jesus says some pretty wild things, and none of them are easy. *Repent. Forgive. Love. Heal. Feed. Create. Thrive.* Then, just to top it off, he adds: *If you want to follow me, take up your cross and let's go.* Jesus doesn't just tell us to have faith. He tells us to have *courage*. To *move*. To *act*. To trust that the Spirit of God is already at work in us, propelling us forward, giving us exactly what we need for the road ahead. When we don't trust, that's when we sink. That's when we fail. But when we leap? We *live*.

If we're supposed to be the hands and heart of Jesus—meant to step into this world as light, a beacon on a hill, letting heaven break through us—then we need a faith that doesn't flinch. God pushes us to the edge because that's where we're needed most. Not in the center, where it's safe and familiar, but out on the margins—where the lost, the left-out, and the looked-over live. That's where Jesus always goes. And that's where he sends us. God pushes us to the edge to show us what we're capable of. To make us ready for the things we never imagined ourselves doing—things we'd run from if left to our own devices. But if we trust God—if we actually believe the wild, impossible, countercultural things Jesus says—then our faith will hold up, even in the hardest places. Even when we feel like we're free-falling.

Because in the end, it's not about *our* faith getting the job done. It's about *God's* faith in *us*.

This is what it means to follow *the way*, to root ourselves in Jesus, the foundation that steadies us. Jesus doesn't draw cultural battle lines in the sand. He doesn't pick fights on Facebook or craft the perfect clapback on Twitter. He doesn't try to control the narrative or make it about himself. He does what we *hope* he would do—he loves us where we are. He breaks through the sacred barriers we build, the ones that separate the haves from the have-nots. He steps into the storm and the chaos, calling us into something greater—a community where compassion and sufficiency are enough for both the oppressed *and* the privileged.

Meister Eckhart helps us realize faith isn't a single leap, but that we must, "Be willing to be a beginner every single morning."* Faith is a daily practice, a continual stepping out onto the water, again and again, even when we don't feel steady.

Peter and the other disciples get shoved into a boat and pushed out to sea, because there's work to do. There's no time for rest, or even a little breather. There are only more people to love, more wounds to heal. This is salvation-at-hand kind of work, awakening others to the heaven Jesus ushers in. The pace is relentless. It knocks them down—physically and spiritually, over and over again. This is a warning to us all. Faith takes effort, sacrifice, and a few bruises along the way.

Another thing about Peter is he's the expert at messing up. He trips over his own feet—when they're not already in his mouth. Jesus calls him out for his lack of faith more than once. He denies even *knowing* Jesus—*three times*. And yet...he never walks away. Through hell and high water, Peter keeps going. He carries his cross, stumbles forward, and keeps moving forward. By Pentecost, Peter is a spiritual giant—the rock the Church is built on. But this Church isn't built on Peter's *perfection*—it's built on his *faithfulness*. His doubts, his missteps, his failures—they don't disqualify him. They *shape* him.

---

* Meister Eckhart, quoted in Matthew Fox, *Meditations with Meister Eckhart* (Rochester, VT: Bear & Company, 1983), 44.

And they shape *us*. Every church is filled with imperfect people. Lucky for us, Jesus isn't asking for perfection. He's asking us to keep showing up, day after day. Take the leap. Love *daringly,* recklessly, and freely. This is how it's done in God's kingdom.

Peter jumps at this crazy invitation by Jesus with what little faith he has, without hesitation. And somehow, that's enough. He takes that first terrifying step toward Jesus, locking eyes with his teacher. The wind slaps him in the face, the raging water rises around him, but his first instinct isn't fear—it's faith. His spiritual muscle memory instinctively kicks in, and he cries out, *"Lord, save me" (Mark 14:30).* And immediately, Jesus is there.

True, Peter never quite gets it right. He stumbles. He doubts. He sinks. But he *knows* who Jesus is. And his default response is to rely on him. That's faith. And it's all that you need to do this kingdom work. When it's hard to love someone, let Jesus love them through you. This way of faith might scare you, but it will always save you. Jesus isn't calling us to be perfect; he's calling us to be faithful. And the more we practice faith—by stepping out onto the ledge of life—the more it becomes instinct, just a part of who we are.

Rumi writes, "As you start to walk on the way, the way appears."* What beautiful encouragement to get out there and practice faith. Taking the first step without knowing exactly where your foot will land, trusting that the path will unfold beneath you.

This reminds me of a story my grandfather told me about a traveler who comes to the edge of a massive canyon. On the other side, there's this breathtaking city—golden towers, lush gardens, everything he's ever wanted. But between him and that city there is...*nothing*. No bridge, no path. Just a whole lot of open air. As he stands there, staring at the impossible gap, he notices an old man sitting nearby, just watching him.

"How do I get across?" the traveler asked.

The old man smiled. *"You walk."*

---

* Jalāl al-Dīn Rūmī, quoted in Deepak Chopra, *The Love Poems of Rumi* (New York: Harmony Books, 1998), 45.

The traveler laughed. *"You must be joking! There's no bridge, no path—just empty space!"*

The old man nodded toward the canyon. *"Take the first step. The way will appear."*

The traveler hesitated, then, gathering all his courage, lifted one foot, and stepped forward—fully expecting to plummet. But as his foot touched down, a single stone appeared beneath it. Shaking, he took another step. Another stone. With each step forward, the path unfolded beneath him—stone by stone—until he reached the other side, breathless and amazed.

That's how faith works. It doesn't hand you a blueprint. It doesn't give you a bridge. It just asks you to take a step—trusting that the way will appear *only* as you move forward.

Some days, it will feel like you're stepping into an abyss or drowning in a sea of despair. Earthquakes of grief shake your foundation. Tornadoes of bitterness leave destruction in their wake. Hurricanes of physical or mental pain batter you relentlessly. Nights of depression press in—dark and isolating. Floods of helplessness cut you off from everyone. Avalanches of anxiety crash down, faster than you can outrun. Storms *will* come. And when they do, Jesus is already reaching for you. When the waves rise and fear crashes in, you can bail out at the first sign of trouble...or hold tight to the one who never lets go.

Jesus doesn't just calm storms—he teaches *us* how to ride the waves and harness the wind. He gives us the courage to take that first shaky step from weak faith to the kind that moves mountains, heals wounds, casts out demons, forgives the unforgivable, and loves even those who hate us. So don't freak out if your faith feels shaky. Don't quit when you trip. Weather the storm. Keep moving. Keep building your spiritual strength. Because when you do, you'll find that the impossible was possible all along.

25

I HAVE A QUESTION

He said to them, "But who do you say that I am?"
—Matthew 16:15

By now, you've probably figured out that Jesus says some pretty wild things. But let's not forget he also asks some strange questions. And this one—this moment right here—is a big one. "But who do you say that I am?"

The story unfolds as Jesus and his disciples are wandering through Caesarea Philippi—a lush, vibrant community about twenty-five miles north of the Sea of Galilee. This was a Roman resort, think first-century Hamptons, where the elite would come to relax and flex their wealth. The city was built around a massive rock spring, its waters feeding the Jordan River, which sustained the land and the people. And in the middle of this grand, bustling backdrop, Jesus decides to take the conversation in an unexpected direction. He asks his traveling companions, "So, what are people saying about me?"

Why does Jesus care what people are saying about him? Is he checking to see if he's trending? Maybe he's just curious. Or perhaps he's taking the spiritual temperature of the crowd. Was he curious about his polling numbers, how the people were identifying with his talking points? I suppose they could have been walking past one of those grand shrines to the Greek god Pan (they were in his stomping grounds, after all), and maybe the question just popped up. Or maybe someone muttered something under their breath as they walked by, prompting Jesus to wonder aloud, "Who do people say that I am?" (Matt. 16:13).

The disciples answer with some interesting guesses, "Some say John the Baptist. Others say Elijah. Or Jeremiah. Or one of the prophets" (v.14).

Jesus doesn't seem to actually care what others think of him, because he quickly asks the Twelve the same question, "But what about you? Who do you say that I am?"

I suspect the disciples clam up right about now—because now it's real. It's one thing to talk about what everyone else is saying; it's another thing to say it out loud, to stake your claim. Then Peter speaks up. Good ol' Peter—always the first to blurt something out: "You are the Messiah, the Son of the living God" (v. 16).

And Jesus beams. "Blessed are you, Simon son of Jonah! Flesh and blood didn't reveal this to you, but my Father in heaven" (v. 17). And then, the famous line that has separated Christian denominations for centuries: "And I tell you that you are Peter, and on this rock, I will build my church" (v. 18).

I love this moment because Peter gets it right—and yet, not really. He names Jesus as the Messiah, although his idea of what that means is still unfolding. But this isn't just about Peter. Or even the Twelve. It's about all of us. Because Jesus isn't done asking the question. He still asks it of you and me: "Who do you say that I am?"

Go ahead and gulp. It's okay if you sweat a little under your arms —most of us would. Some of us answer with certainty. Others hedge. Some want to give a respectable, intellectual response: "A great teacher." You might say, "A wise man." Maybe even, "A deeply religious figure, like Moses or Buddha." Most of the people I know only know his name as an expletive when they stub their toe. But Jesus isn't asking for sound bites. He's asking for something deeper. Who.

Do. *You.* Say. *I Am?* What do you actually believe? Get it right and... what? You win the lottery, right?

We will all have to answer this question if we are going to take anything this man says seriously. This question isn't just some theological pop quiz; it's the heartbeat of the Christian faith. It's the thing that anchors and orients everything. And how we answer? Well, that changes everything.

Peter, in classic Peter fashion, blurts it out first: "You are the Christ" (Matt.16:16). Four words. That's it. But those four words become the bedrock of faith—a confession that ripples out and reshapes the world. And here's the kicker: Peter doesn't even fully get what he's saying. But he knows it in his bones—that Jesus is the fulfillment of God's promise, the one who draws us into God's redemptive love.

Long before Christ became an identifying marker for followers of Jesus, it carried deep, historical weight in Judaism. The Messiah, the Anointed One, the one who would make things right. In *The Universal Christ*, Richard Rohr describes *the Christ* as the divine presence that has existed since the beginning of time. It's the one thing that permeates all of creation. He sees Christ not just as Jesus of Nazareth but as the eternal, cosmic reality through which God loves, sustains, and transforms the world.* Peter may not have grasped the full implications, but in that moment, he knew Jesus was the embodiment of something bigger than himself. He knew Jesus was the real deal.

If Jesus is what God looks like in the flesh, then sign me up. Because Jesus moves through the world with mercy, justice, and radical compassion. He loves the ones no one else sees. He stands with the outcasts. He forgives without keeping score. If that's who God is, then don't you think Jesus' words are worth being etched in your heart?

For two thousand years, the church has stood on this truth: Jesus is the Christ, the Son of God. And today, our job is to bear witness to

---

* Rohr, *The Universal Christ*, 5–7.

that reality—not just with our words, but with our lives. Not by making the right theological arguments, but by living like Jesus lived. With tenderness. With courage. With a love so big it makes people stop and wonder. Because at the end of the day, this isn't just about Peter's answer. It's about yours and mine. Who do you say that he is? And maybe even more importantly—what does your life say?

Following this confession, Jesus does something wild—he hands Peter the keys to the kingdom of heaven (v. 19). Now, I don't know if you've ever handed car keys to a brand-new teenage driver, but let me tell you, it's a terrifying moment. You hesitate, because this is a powerful machine, and once they're behind the wheel, you can't control what happens. And Peter? He's just like that teenager—overconfident, quick to speak, prone to missteps. A few verses later, Jesus calls him Satan for trying to block the road to the cross. This guy just got the keys, and he's already swerving into oncoming traffic.

So why does Jesus trust him? Maybe because Peter's faith isn't about perfection—it's about relationship. It recognizes who Jesus is and steps forward, however wobbly, in that truth. The kingdom of heaven isn't built on flawless people. It's built on the ones who keep showing up, who keep saying yes, who keep confessing—even when they don't have it all figured out. And that's us. Because the way we live, the way we testify to Jesus at work in our lives, is how others come to know him—and to see their own worth in this sacred space.

Our identity matters. The labels we wear, the communities we claim, even the bumper stickers on our cars—they all tell a story. While historically, this passage has been used to justify all sorts of claims to authority, I think we've gotten it wrong. We've looked at it through human eyes, not God's eyes. It's not about who holds the keys, but about what Jesus is inviting us into—a life that reflects God's merciful, just, reckless, unstoppable love. That's your testimony! That's also your confession.

Years ago, a coworker invited me to lunch. She was feeling stuck in her career and needed advice. Somewhere in the conversation, she asked what I'd do if I weren't in advertising. What she didn't know was that I was in the middle of my own crisis, restless and unfulfilled.

Instead of answering, I asked her what she thought I'd be good at. She glanced away, then said, "I think you'd make a great minister. My uncle is one, and you remind me of him." That confession was powerful. She had no idea I had already applied to seminary, but her unexpected yet simple testimony helped me see God's hand at work in my life.

Jesus hands us the keys to the kingdom—not as a souvenir to tuck away in our pockets, but as an invitation to unlock something new. They're meant to be used, to open doors to a new way of living. And that new way looks like showing up. Like being the hands and heart of a God who meets us exactly where we are and loves us just as we are. That's heaven-on-earth kind of stuff.

It's on us to proclaim God's love—not with grand speeches, but by being like Jesus. By embodying justice, compassion, and mercy in a world that desperately needs these virtues. Because let's be real—there's a whole lot of pain out there. You don't have to own a television or smart phone to know how much hurt lives in our communities, our families, even within ourselves. But as Mother Teresa so wisely put it, "Help one person at a time, starting with the person nearest you."

Maybe that's the whole thing right there. Jesus hands us the keys, and we use them one act of love at a time.

Like a dad watching his kid drive off for the first time, Jesus gives us that look that says, You know what I'm asking of you, right? It's like he's telling his disciples to be alert and on their best behavior because, "When you step into the world—especially in my name—the way you love will testify to who I am." We can pretend. Or we can love. Who do you say that I am?

That's the question for all of us. How will I move through this world with heart and hands wide open, so that the love of God is unmistakable in me? How will I love with such reckless mercy and forgiveness that people can't help but see God's light and love shining through? Journalist and theologian Jason Byassee writes, "God desires a people of mercy who adore the poor, who treasure creation, who notice the dignity in every single human face. Not because it's nice. But because God has a human face."*

Jesus invites us all to be the rock others can lean on. Stand firm in love. Be the rock of his salvation, healing and restoring and redeeming. Make your love his confession. Love is your testimony. Love is the key to the kingdom. And when we love like that, nothing—not even the gates of hell—can stand against it. Love stops you from hurting someone intentionally. Love compels you to lift up your neighbors. Love is the foundation of everything good and holy.

In these times—when fear builds walls and division runs deep—God needs you to love like you've never loved before. God needs you to show up—to be a visible sign, a walking billboard that proclaims to the world: You Are Loved! And when you doubt or feel small, remember this: The Church of Christ is not a building made of bricks and mortar, but living stones, held together by love, by honor, by the kind of respect that sees the divine in one another (1 Pet. 2:5). We are those stones. Little pebbles. Doesn't matter if you're marble or limestone, a gold nugget or a simple garden variety rock. To God, you are a diamond in the rough, precious beyond measure. Jesus is asking "Who do you say I am?"

And maybe, just maybe, the best answer is the life you live.

---

* Jason Byassee, "What Are We Baptized For?" *Sojourners*, May 2017, 44.

26

I HAVE ANOTHER QUESTION

"Who is my mother and brother and sister?"
—Matthew 12:48

I always like this question. But before we can answer it, let's give it some context. Jesus is in a packed house, teaching. People are spilling out into the streets, desperate to hear him, to be healed, to be near him. His family is out there too, somewhere in the crowd. Maybe they think he's lost his way. Maybe they're just trying to keep him safe. Then someone pushes through the bodies, interrupting him mid-sentence. "Your mother and your brothers are outside" (Matt. 12:47).

Now, imagine someone interrupting you to tell you that someone you love is just outside. You'd get up, right? Even if it were my mother-in-law, or any one of my many brothers-in-law or sisters-in-law, I would at least feign some interest or ask, "Where are they?" But Jesus doesn't do that. He doesn't rush to the door. Doesn't send someone to escort his mother in. He just asks a question: "Who is my mother? Who are my brothers?" (v. 48).

That might not sound like much to us, but in his world, family was everything. It was who you were. Your safety net. Your identity. To even ask the question was to shake the foundation of belonging. It's like Jesus is rewriting the rules in real time. Then, without waiting for an answer, he stretches out his hand, motioning to the people crammed into the house, the ones hungry for something true. He says, "Here is my family. Whoever does the will of my Father—whoever loves and cares for others—that's my mother, my brother, my sister" (vv. 49–50).

And then, just like that, Jesus proclaims something profound and radical: God is for everyone. Let me say that again. God is for everyone! This is not a rejection of others. It's an expansion. Jesus isn't saying family doesn't matter. He's saying it's bigger than we thought. That the borders we draw—bloodlines, tribe, nationality—don't define who belongs. Love does. Compassion does. Doing the will of God, which is always about caring for one another, does. Compassion is the way God widens the circle.

This is the thing about God's family—it's never exclusive. In fact, it's the opposite. It keeps getting bigger, keeps drawing people in—not because of birthright, but because of love. That's the only requirement. Show up with love. Show up with mercy. Show up with open hands. Welcome the stranger. Care for the wounded. See the people the world refuses to see. Do that, and you're already home. You're already family.

Jesus redefines family—not by blood but by love. He invites us to see beyond the narrow confines of biology, culture, and status. In his kingdom, the only name that matters is "child of God," and the only way to claim it is by doing God's will—caring for each other, showing mercy, loving without condition.

In first-century Palestine, family was everything. Your name was your worth, your security, your social currency. Marriages were arranged for power, not love. Kids were economic assets. And then Jesus says, "None of those things matter. The only real family is the one built on love and justice." You could almost hear the collective gasp.

Take the rich young man in Mark's gospel. He asks Jesus, "What must I do to inherit eternal life?" Jesus gives him the standard list—

don't kill, don't steal, honor your parents. The man is thrilled. "I've done all that since I was a kid!" (Mark 10:17-20)

Then Jesus, looking at him with love, drops the hammer: "You lack one thing. Sell everything, give to the poor, and follow me" (Mark 10:21).

The man walks away grieving. Because Jesus isn't just asking him to give up his money—he's asking him to abandon the identity his wealth secured, and that's terrifying. Wealth, status, even your family name—Jesus says, let it go. "Do not store up treasures on earth…but store your treasures in heaven" (Matt. 6:19-20). What you own, where you come from, none of those things define you. Love does. Kinship in God's family isn't about privilege, it's about how you show up for others.

It's a tough call. The rich young man knew his life would never be the same. And maybe that's the point. The way of Jesus transforms us from the inside out. It rewrites the rules, shifts our loyalties, and expands our circles. Family isn't about blood—it's about who we choose to love.

Jesus gets it. He had a family. He likely knows about the squabbles, the teasing, the rivalries. He also knows family is hard, that belonging takes work. And yet, he calls us to something bigger—a family without walls, without borders, without conditions. This is the family God is building. That's the one that lasts forever.

Although Jesus pushes the boundaries of our conventional wisdom, it's not all for nothing. Jesus says, "Everyone who has left houses or brothers or sisters or father or mother or wife or children or fields for my sake…will inherit eternal life" (Matt.19:29). This was a powerful thing to say. Although we all come from different backgrounds and hold different opinions and politics, Jesus reminds us that in God's family, we are all equals. We must set aside our petty differences and family squabbles and bend to the will of God.

According to the prophet Micah, "What does the Lord require of you but to do justice, to love kindness, and to walk humbly with your God" (Mic. 6:8).

Jesus wants mercy, justice, kindness, and love to be our new names. Not Jew or Gentile. Not sinner or saint. When our name is synonymous to God's inclusive love, then we know we are doing God's will. Faith is not passive—it's love in action. And it must be lived out as if it's the only thing that keeps us alive. We belong to God's family. And as St. Irenaeus put it, "What God creates, God loves. What God loves, God loves everlastingly."*

God's love has already named us—but it also asks something of us. It's a call, a mission. At his baptism, when Jesus heard God name him "Beloved," his life was forever changed. His purpose took shape: to transform us, redefining who we are to God and to each other. To claim this name is to open our hearts, to live deeply, and to act with kindness and justice. It's the way of Jesus—the way of God.

To be beloved isn't just to be loved—as we have been learning, it's to be the love of God in the world. Love is our identity. Love is our name. Love is our purpose. Love is the way people should recognize us. Love is the family name we carry. Jesus reminds us that each one of us is God's beloved child. And as God's child, you are invited into an intimate relationship with the one who created you from love—and given you the purpose to love.

This changes everything about how we live. If God loves us like this, then we are called to reflect that same love, to trust in it—even when things are hard—and to extend it to others. It's not about religious obligation. It's about being known and cherished by the one who created us. And if God is our Father, then we are all family. Jesus didn't just teach this; he lived it. Looking at the ones who left everything to follow him, he says, "Whoever does the will of my Father is my brother, my sister, and my mother" (Matt. 12:50).

Love, not blood, defines belonging. And the will of God? It's simple. "Love one another as I have loved you" (John 15:12). "There is no greater love than to lay down one's life for one's friends" (John 15:13). This is faith in action. The more we live it out, the more we find ourselves choosing peace over retaliation, reconciliation over

---

* Irenaeus of Lyons, *Against Heresies*, Book 5, preface, as quoted on Wikipedia, s.v. "Irenaeus," https://en.wikipedia.org/wiki/Irenaeus.

revenge, self-giving over self-serving. The more we love, the more we become who we were always meant to be—God's beloved children.

By surrendering to God's will, Jesus doesn't just redeem us—he remakes us into one family through his body and blood. And just as we inherit this great kinship, we are called to extend it, to see and do what Jesus does, to become givers of a life filled with his love and grace. Jesus looks to God as Father. But he looks to us to be mothers. Like the great German mystic Meister Eckhart wrote, "We are all called to be mothers of God, for God is always waiting to be born."*

Jesus takes what we think we know about family and flips it inside out. He invites us into the greatest family of all—God's. Our biological families can bring both joy and heartbreak. But in God's family, everyone is welcome. No jealousy, no competition, no keeping score. Just love.

By doing the will of God, we get a taste of heaven now—boundless love, overflowing grace, joy that doesn't run dry. Fear loses its grip, and we finally come alive.

This is who Jesus is. It's why we tune our ears to listen to what he has to say. This is why we are here—to bear God's love, grace, and peace into the world every day. To choose kindness, seek justice, walk humbly. To keep Jesus' mission alive.

Jesus entrusts us with great power and responsibility. Through him, God's love lives on in us—moving, healing, restoring. Until one day, in the fullness of eternity, the mother of all love is revealed.

---

* Meister Eckhart, *The Complete Mystical Works of Meister Eckhart*, ed. and trans. Maurice O'C. Walshe (New York: Crossroad Publishing, 2009), 197.

27

LOVE IS THE WOOD, THE NAILS, AND THE FLESH

Then he called the crowd to him along with his disciples and said:
"Whoever wants to be my disciple must deny themselves
and take up their cross and follow me."
—Mark 8:34

"When we consider how much our educational, political, religious, and even social lives are geared to finding answers to questions born of fear, it's not hard to understand why a message of love has little chance of being heard. Fearful questions never lead to love-filled answers."[*] That's a great quote by Henri Nouwen, who—as you've probably already figured out—has had an enormous influence on my own ministry. It's also such an obvious observation: Fear makes love almost impossible to understand.

Fear corners us, builds walls, and forces us to clutch at power, control, and certainty. Love? Love moves in the opposite direction. "There is no fear in love," John writes, "but perfect love drives out

---

[*] Henri J. M. Nouwen, cited in *Fear Never Gives Birth to Love*, sermon excerpt, *Sermon-Illustrations.co.uk*, drawing on Nouwen's unpublished letters and reflections.

fear" (1 John 4:18). Love is the antidote to fear. It is the key that unlocks the very mystery of God. Or at least the shit Jesus says.

Love is evolution. Love is revolution. It pushes us forward, carving a path through whatever stands in its way. Love isn't a transaction; it's the very reason for our being. Money won't get us there. Power won't either. At best, those are just stand-ins, distractions, things we think will give us life. But "without love," the Apostle Paul writes, "I have gained nothing" (1 Cor. 13:3). Love is the raw material we were made from, which means it's also what we're made for.

Of all the crazy things Jesus says, each word makes a very strong case for love. "You are blessed…" because you love. "You are salt and light…" because love is meant to illuminate and preserve. "Don't hate your brother…" because it is not love. "Do not seek revenge…" because love doesn't play that game. "When you give…" do it from love. "Forgive one another…" because you have been forgiven in love. "Do not be so flashy about your religious rituals…" instead, outdo each other in generosity. "Do not judge…" just love, because that's the only thing you'll be judged by.

Love is Jesus, the incarnation of God's reckless, boundary-breaking, always-expanding being. John calls him God's Word. Paul calls him Christ. I call him Love.

Seeing Jesus through this lens—through love—changes everything. It makes his words more than just a checklist of things to do or not do. Love isn't a set of requirements; it's the roadmap that leads us forward. It's the greatest commandment, the foundation of it all. "Love the Lord your God with all your heart and all your mind. And the second is like it: Love your neighbor as yourself" (Matt. 22:37-39). Love is the healing balm that makes all things new. It is the redemption plan that has been in motion since before time began (Eph. 1:3-4). It shouldn't surprise you by now that is why Jesus sends his people out into the world saying, "Proclaim the good news, the kingdom of heaven is at hand" (Matt. 10:7). The heartbeat of that kingdom is love.

Martin Luther King said it best. "Love is the only force capable of transforming an enemy into a friend."* Jesus knew this too. That's why he tells his friends, "Abide in me, and I will abide in you" (John 15:4). Not strive. Not hustle. Not stress. *Abide.* Stay close. Stay rooted. Stay open. Because love, like fruit, grows in those conditions. Love produces more love. An orange tree doesn't force itself to produce oranges. It stays planted, open to the sun, drawing from the soil, and in time, oranges appear. Jesus tells us the same thing: Stay close to him, to his love, and love will grow in you. No stress. No grinding. No performance. Just an open heart, ready to receive and give love freely—love that flows from the deep soil of grace. This is Eden, heaven's garden.

The Apostle Paul tells us that this grace, this love, was set in motion "before the foundations of the world, to be holy and blameless before him in love" (Eph. 1:4). Love has always been the goal. Love has always been the way. Love is what all of creation is about. It's what we were made from. It's what we were made for. Jesus knew this better than anyone. So *abide*, pay close attention to the weird shit he says, and watch love bloom.

Jesus knows the world will struggle with this idea. He knows where this road leads. And still, he sits with his friends and says, "No one has greater love than this, to lay down one's life for one's friends" (John 14:13). Love. That's it. That's the whole message. Love is both the gift received and the gift given. And to think it was all there in chapter one. I hope you've committed it to memory.

Daryl Davis is a black musician who has played alongside many of the greats. His fingers have spent a lifetime coaxing stories out of the piano, but the most important stories he's ever drawn out didn't come from black and white keys. They came when he befriended members of the Ku Klux Klan.† He didn't argue or condemn. He just asked, *"How can you hate me if you don't even know me?"* And then, he listened.

---

* Martin Luther King Jr., *Strength to Love* (New York: Harper & Row, 1963), 47.
† Daryl Davis, *Why I, as a Black Man, Attend KKK Rallies*. TED, Sept. 2017, https://www.ted.com/talks/daryl_davis_why_i_as_a_black_man_attend_kkk_rallies.

Time and time again, these men, steeped in racism and hatred, found themselves confronted—not by retaliation or condemnation—but by love, curiosity, and respect. Some remained hardened. But soon over two hundred Klan members ended up leaving the hate group and handing their robes to Davis as a symbol of their transformation. Initially, Klan leader Roger Kelly rejected Davis. He spewed hatred, tried to intimidate him, and even refused to shake his hand. But Davis kept showing up, kept engaging, kept loving. That love paid off. Kelly's heart eventually softened. He left the Klan. He even invited Davis to be his child's godfather. That is the holy power of love. It disarms. It reshapes. It flips the whole world upside down. *And most importantly,* love always wins.

The world has trouble understanding this because it has been led by hate for so long. Jesus doesn't sugarcoat it: "If the world hates you, be aware that it hated me before it hated you. If you belonged to the world, it would love you. But because I have chosen you out of the world, the world hates you" (John 15:18–19). And still, Jesus sends them right into the middle of it. Right into the mess. "Love one another so the world will know you belong to me" (John 13:35).

But the truth is we *do* belong to this world. We live here. Work here. Raise families and form communities here. We exist in this world, but we're meant to live in it differently. Love, Jesus says, stands in contrast to the way the world operates. And yet, this is the very place we're sent to love. Jesus isn't naive about this. He knows exactly what we're capable of—both the good and the heartbreaking. He knows we belong to God—and that we still have to move through a world that rarely reflects that truth. He's aware of the tension, this paradox of being both *in* the world and not *of* it. From the very beginning, Jesus has called people to repentance—not just a change of heart, but a change in how we live, how we move through the world. But he doesn't just tell us what to do; he shows us. Shows us how to let go of our old patterns, our old ways of thinking. Shows us how to embrace God's radical, inclusive love—a love that refuses to put up barriers or withhold itself from anyone.

David Mathis tells us, "Being 'not of the world' is not the destination; it is the starting place."* This is our jumping off point. We are salt of the earth kind of people, the kind whose light cannot be hidden (Matt. 5:13-16). Jesus doesn't leave us guessing on what that looks like. He calls us to hunger and thirst for righteousness. Be merciful. Be meek. Be humble. Seek reconciliation and peace. Jesus says, "You are blessed when you are persecuted for living this way." But he also promises, "The kingdom of heaven will be yours." Read it for yourself in Matthew 5!

Jesus spends his entire life cultivating this kingdom way of living. He invites us to, "Seek first the kingdom of God. And everything else will fall into place" (Matt. 6:33). As I've said, faith is an action. It's a call to follow the way of Jesus who "came to serve, and not to be served" (Matt. 20:28). He feeds the hungry, heals the sick, welcomes the stranger. Jesus doesn't want you to escape the world. He wants you to engage with it, like he did, with your sights set on the kingdom he ushered in. So, pick up your cross and get to it.

Eugene Peterson poignantly stated, *"We want to follow Jesus, but like Peter we also want to tell Jesus where to go. Jesus does not need our advice; he needs our faithful obedience."* † I think this is another great quote. I know I'd do better listening to Jesus than trying to get him to listen to me. So many of my atheist friends would agree. They find it kind of funny that most Christians talk a big game but rarely does one get off the bench and play.

The Episcopal Church once ran a powerful ad that said, *You Can't Worship a Homeless Man on Sunday. And Then Completely Ignore Him on Monday.* Nowhere in the gospels does Jesus say, "Worship me." But over and over, he says, "Follow me." This is where the rubber hits the road. Deny yourself. Pick up your cross. Follow me.

Real change—true transformation of the heart—begins with hard sacrifices. Perhaps this is why people resist change. Change

---

* David Mathis, "Let's Revise the Popular Phrase 'In but Not of the World,'" *Desiring God*, August 29, 2012, https://www.desiringgod.org/articles/lets-revise-the-popular-phrase-in-but-not-of-the-world.

† Eugene H. Peterson, *A Year with Jesus: Daily Readings and Meditations* (San Francisco: HarperSanFrancisco, 2004), 143.

demands sacrifice. And sacrifice? It's hard. It's painful. It asks more of us than we want to give. But if we want to live by the words Jesus teaches, we've got to stay on the page with him. We have to walk away from our own self-centered ambitions, goals, and choices, to walk the way of Christ.

St. John of the Cross wrote, "To reach satisfaction in all, desire satisfaction in nothing. To come to possess all, desire the possession of nothing."* The path of Christ isn't about getting ahead—it's about laying ourselves down. It's subtraction, surrender, and the willingness to let go of what we think we need so we can receive what God is offering—even the cross.

Jesus isn't telling you to go find a cross. He asks you to pick up the one you already have. Yours might be a handicap or disability; chronic pain or depression; conflict in your family or work. Too many in our country bear a cross simply for the color of their skin or the person they love. We don't choose these crosses, but they're ours to carry. We can ignore them, reject them, refuse them, and even hate them. Or we can lift them up and follow the one who gives our suffering new life, new purpose.†

We all make sacrifices—for our kids, our spouses, our jobs. I can't even imagine the sacrifices my wife makes being married to me. But that's not what Jesus is talking about. He's not talking about skipping dessert to shed a few pounds. He's talking about giving yourself away for the sake of others. This is kingdom building stuff. "Whoever wants to save their life will lose it" (Matt. 16:25). I suspect this is exactly why Paul confesses in his letter that, "The message of the cross seems like sheer madness. But to us who are being saved, we know it is the power of God" (1 Cor. 1:18). And what is this power of God? Love.

Love has been present since the very foundation of the world. It's the centerpiece of all the richness and mystery of heaven and earth.

---

* St. John of the Cross, *The Ascent of Mount Carmel*, trans. E. Allison Peers (New York: Image Books, 1958), Book I, Chapter 13.
† Henri J. M. Nouwen, *Bread for the Journey: A Daybook of Wisdom and Faith* (New York: HarperCollins, 1997).

It's God's heart. And what does it mean to follow Jesus if not to embrace and embody the heart of God? Which means, letting go of whatever we're holding onto that isn't love. For most of us, I could narrow that down to one thing: ego. To love like God loves requires a shift, a sacrifice. The ego has to get out of God's way.

Love makes us surrender the need to be right, to be better than, to win. It reshapes us, rewires us, teaches us to let our hearts lead. Deny yourself. Pick up your cross. Follow me.

In San Fernando, Pampanga, Philippines, the Passion of Good Friday isn't just remembered—it's felt. Devotion takes on a physical weight, as some carry heavy wooden crosses through the streets, embodying Christ's suffering. Others take it even further, voluntarily enduring actual crucifixion—real nails, real pain, real sacrifice—as a profound act of penance. It's unsettling, to say the least. I'm not sure this is exactly what Jesus meant, even if it's deeply reverent.

When Jesus tells us to pick up our cross, he's not asking for a show of suffering. He's inviting us into something bigger: to be the visible incarnation of God's love, compassion, and justice—just as he was. To walk the way of radical generosity. Forgiveness. Mercy. No half-measures. No hoarding grace. What good is our sacrifice if we're still holding on to past grudges? What good is following Jesus if we're going to keep ignoring the needs of others? We cannot shine his true light if our hearts are full of darkness and deception. Like Jesus warns the Pharisees—"You are like whitewashed tombs"—we can appear to others "as righteous but on the inside…full of hypocrisy and wickedness" (Matt. 23:27–28, NIV). It's in giving our hearts unselfishly that the world sees God in their midst. It's in the way we love and serve one another that the kingdom of heaven comes alive right here, right now.

Nouwen reminds us about the cross we carry. He wrote, "We can ignore them, reject them, refuse them, and even hate them. Or we can lift them up and follow Jesus, who gives our suffering new life and new purpose."* What we give up or let go of becomes the key to

---

* Nouwen, *Bread for the Journey*.

unlocking our true selves and our true faith. This requires us to place real trust in a God whose merciful grace overcomes death with life. Jesus assures his disciples—and us—that whatever we give up will pale in comparison to what we will gain: *a foretaste of heaven, here and now*. It might seem foolish or hard at first. And yet, "what will it profit you to gain the whole world but lose your soul?" (Mark 8:36).

To follow Jesus is to make a daily decision to devote our hearts, hands, and words to God's will, rather than ours. But let's be real—are we actually ready to stop clutching at control and sacrifice our will for God's? Jesus calls out the half-measures: "Why do you call me 'Lord, Lord,' and not do what I tell you?" (Luke 6:46). If we're unwilling to let go of the world's fleeting successes, we might lose the one thing that actually lasts—our souls.

Look at Jeffrey Epstein—a man who seemed to have everything. Money. Power. Influence. But he let his ego drive him into horrific darkness, using others and destroying lives. And in the end, all his wealth—all his control—couldn't save him from himself. As Michael Huffington put it: "Everything we think we own is only being loaned to us until we die. And on our deathbed, at the moment of death, no one but God can save our souls."*

Our souls need nourishment just as our bodies do. And that nourishment? It's love. God's *love for us and our love for one another*. God is love—the very force that sustains us. And the cross? The cross is proof of just how far God will go to show his love for us. Jesus gave everything—his life, his dignity, his very breath—because love demands everything. And once you've let that love take root in your heart, there's no going back.

The disciples knew Jesus wasn't just talking about change—he was making it happen. He didn't just forgive people; he loved them into transformation. He healed individuals, and in doing so, he healed entire communities. And the same power of God's love that

---

* Michael Huffington, "For What Profits a Man If He Gains the Whole World but Loses His Own Soul," HuffPost, April 26, 2008, accessed April 26, 2028, https://www.huffpost.com/entry/for-what-profits-a-man-if_b_98783.

moved through Jesus? It moves through us too. If we dare to take Jesus at his word, then our actions must match our words. We can't love with conditions. We can't divide people into worthy and unworthy. We have to participate fully in this kingdom Jesus ushers in. If our actions are fueled by love—real, reckless, boundless love—then we too can take part in this transformation. To summarize the highly influential Buddhist teacher Thich Nhat Hanh, "Our faith must be alive. This implies practice, living our daily life in mindfulness. Praying not just with hearts and minds, with our actions in the world."*

God's love is always a summons—a holy nudge, a relentless push beyond ourselves. It calls us out of comfort and complacency, out of the world's illusions of power and success, and toward the cross before us. It demands we show up as the visible presence of God's love in a world still gasping for justice. It asks us to break the hands of oppression that choke the life out of the vulnerable, to use whatever breath we have in us to speak love into the void. This is what Jesus means by bearing the fruit of the kingdom—real, tangible fruit. The kind that takes root in the ways we feed the hungry, clothe the naked, heal the sick, welcome the stranger, and forgive like our lives depend on it. He's not subtle about it—"For the measure you use will be measured to you" (Matt. 7:2)—and he doesn't leave room for loopholes—"What you do to the least of these, you do also to me" (Matt. 25:40). The way we love today shapes the world of tomorrow.

St. Ignatius of Antioch wasn't messing around when he said, "It is right, therefore, that we not just be called Christians, but that we actually be Christians."† Not in name only. But in how we show up. How we love. How we serve. To borrow an image from Paul, we are little Christs in the world—not *of* it, but absolutely *sent into it*. And what are we sent to do? To usher in the kingdom Jesus spoke of, where love is the only rule that matters. Where our differences aren't

---

* Thich Nhat Hanh, *Living Buddha, Living Christ* (New York: Riverhead, 1995), 135–136.
† Ignatius of Antioch, *Letter to the Magnesians*, in *The Apostolic Fathers*, trans. Bart D. Ehrman, Vol. 1 (Cambridge, MA: Harvard University Press, 2003), 195.

walls but bridges. Where we build relationships, serve our communities, and love people—no footnotes, no exceptions. Jesus promises that in doing this, *"We will have peace"* (John 14:27).

Nouwen reminds us: "We can really be in the world, involved in the world, and actively engaged in the world precisely because we do not belong to it. Because our home is in God, we can be in the world, and speak words of healing, of confrontation, of invitation, and of challenge."[*]

You are called to enter the world with love—not because it's easy, but because the world is aching for it. Love is the cross we must carry. It's the key to transformation. The key to healing. And the key to unlocking the kingdom of heaven.

---

[*] Henri J. M. Nouwen, "You Do Not Belong to the World," *Daily Meditation*, July 15, 2022, https://henrinouwen.org/meditation/you-do-not-belong-to-the-world/.

28

LOVE IS THE KEY THAT UNLOCKS IT ALL

"So he set off and went to his father. But while he was still far off, his father saw him and was filled with compassion; he ran and put his arms around him and kissed him. Then the son said to him, 'Father, I have sinned against heaven and before you; I am no longer worthy to be called your son.' But the father said to his slaves, 'Quickly, bring out a robe —the best one—and put it on him; put a ring on his finger and sandals on his feet. And get the fatted calf and kill it, and let us eat and celebrate, for this son of mine was dead and is alive again; he was lost and is found!' And they began to celebrate."
—Luke 15:20–24

By now, I sound like a broken record. But I warned you in the first chapter that there isn't much more you need to know than this: Love is how the kingdom of heaven takes root and flourishes. Nothing more. Nothing less. Love is everything. It's what it's all about.

Love breaks through in the most unexpected ways, not just as a balm to soothe our weary souls, but as the grace that keeps us moving, inching ever closer to God's heart. Jesus knew this. He had

CHAPTER 28

felt the love of God deep in his bones, so intimate that he called God, "Abba"—a child's tender word for their father. It seems so simple, and yet, for so many, love is the hardest thing to give or receive. We have certainly done a proper job of messing each other up—betraying love, twisting it, using it for gain. But that's not the love of God. And for that, we rejoice.

Gina is from a nowhere town in Ohio—a place with a single stoplight and a gas station that sells pizza. She has an older sister she's never really connected with. Her parents are conservative—like really conservative. Theirs is the kind of home where the Bible isn't just a book—it's the rule book. They try to mold her into someone she's not, wielding scripture like a hammer against the fire of her wild spirit. But the fire won't be tamed. The fights escalate. The walls close in. One night, Gina has had enough of it all. She slips out the door and runs toward freedom, toward something that feels alive.

One long bus ride, and Gina's in Chicago. The city is everything she dreamed it would be—and everything she didn't. On her second night, she meets a guy—charming, smooth, generous. He tells this wild spirit all the right things, makes her feel seen, like she's something special. For a while, life feels good—exciting, even.

He sets her up in a hotel, gives her cash, shows her how to "make it." She learns quickly that people will pay for what she has to offer. And at first, it feels empowering, like she's rewriting her own story. But the streets wear her down, stealing something from her piece by piece. When her pain becomes unbearable, she numbs it—first a little, then a lot. And when her new addiction becomes too visible, the nice guy disappears, along with the money. She becomes just another face on a corner. Every night is a fight—for a room, a meal, a fix. And it's never enough.

One night, a client drops her off in a quiet neighborhood. Houses line the streets, porch lights casting warmth over the darkness. A cat watches her from a window. Something about it touches a hidden nerve, and her mind drifts home—to the childhood cat buried in the backyard, to the porch light her parents left on whenever she came home late. Tears come, then a sob that shakes her whole body. She misses home. She misses *herself*. On the subway back to her side of town, she sends a text to her sister: "I can't do this anymore. Tell them I'm coming home."

The next day, she boards a bus back to Nowhere, Ohio. She carries nothing but the filth of the previous night. Every mile stirs a new wave of doubt. She rehearses what she'll say, how she'll explain...if they even let her in. If they even *want* her. When the bus hisses to a stop, she feels impossibly small. But she steps off anyway. The familiar streets she once ran from are the first to greet her. Her heart sinks. *What if they don't want me? What if they hate me?*

She turns the corner where she used to catch the school bus. The houses are unchanged—yet different. Shame washes over her. She wishes she could erase it all. But there's no erasing—only walking forward. And just as she's about to collapse under the weight of everything, the porch light flickers on.

The first one out the door is her sister. Then her mom, her aunt, her best friend from high school. But pushing past them all—*running*—is her dad. His eyes, wet with tears, lock onto hers. And before she can speak—before she can explain or apologize—he pulls her into his arms, holding her so tight she feels like she might disappear into him. Instead, all the shame, all the guilt and fear—*gone.*

She tries to speak, tries to say she's sorry, but he hushes her. *"Hush, kiddo. No time for that. There's a house full of people waiting for you."*

That's the story of God's love breaking through, finding us with nothing but love. The kind of love that refuses to let go.

In Luke's Gospel, Jesus tells a series of three great parables about things that were once lost being found. A lost sheep retrieved. A lost coin recovered. A lost child returned. "Rejoice with me," Jesus says on each occasion. "This is a time to celebrate."

Jesus told these stories while sitting with people like Gina. The first story is about a shepherd who loses a sheep and leaves the other ninety-nine to search for it (Luke 15:4–7). When he finds it, he throws a party, inviting all his friends and neighbors, just to celebrate that the one lost sheep was found!

Then he tells another story, this one about a woman who has ten silver coins but loses one of them (Luke 15:8–10). She turns her house upside down until she finds it. And then? She calls everyone she knows to come and celebrate. Another party for something that was once lost but is now found.

In our disposable culture, these illustrations can seem antiquated. We are more likely to replace things that could easily be fixed, throwing what is broken into the trash. In less than twenty-four hours, a replacement is delivered to our doorstep. But that's harder to do with a misplaced paycheck. If you've ever experienced that nightmare, you know the relief when it turns up. You rejoice. So does God. That's the good news here. God doesn't throw us away. God searches. Finds. Embraces. Celebrates. Love is the way the kingdom comes alive. Love is everything. Nothing more. Nothing less.

Because holy things always seem to come in threes, Jesus tells a third story, which is probably his most well-known (Luke 15:11–32). It is about a young, reckless kid who is full of himself. He demands his share of the inheritance, as if he's entitled to it. And in an act of love so illogical it would have turned heads in first-century Palestine, the father *gives it to him*!

The kid bolts out of the country with the cash burning a hole in his pocket. Then he spends it like a high roller in Vegas. He lives large. Actually, too large. The cash runs out—every last dime. Before he knows it, he's knee-deep in pig slop, starving, humiliated, and alone. With nowhere else to turn, he does the only thing he can: he heads home, rehearsing his apology and practicing his plea for mercy. Maybe his father will take him back as a hired hand. Maybe there's still a way to survive, even if he never gets to be a son again. But before he can even make it up the driveway, his father sees him. And runs toward him. And embraces him!

To us, that might not seem shocking. But for those listening in Jesus' time, it was outrageous. Men of honor don't run; it's beneath them. But this father? He doesn't care about appearances. He doesn't care about respectability. He doesn't care about the neighbors' whispers or looks of disgust. He runs because he knows his boy is a dead man walking.

By Hebrew law, his neighbors could have stoned this kid to death for the disgrace he brought on his family. The father doesn't just run to welcome him home—he runs to save his life. And when he reaches him, there's no scolding, no interrogation, no demand for an explanation. He wraps his arms around this ragged, broken kid, presses kisses into his filthy face, and calls for a robe and a ring, a symbol of his position in the family. And just like that, it's party time. Everyone is invited to celebrate! That's how it's done in the kingdom of heaven.

It's no wonder Charles Dickens called this the greatest short story ever written. It's our story, after all. You can't make it through this life without screwing up a little—or a lot. In my prime, I was one of the best. A gold-medalist of screw ups. Now, I am only so-so. And yet, no matter how good we mess things up, God is always better at forgiving.

This doesn't mean God loves our screw-ups—plenty of places in scripture make that clear. But God knows we're all runaways, that we're always finding new ways to get lost. And God still loves us. Not loves us in a distant, theoretical way. Loves us in a reckless, embarrassing, over-the-top way. A way that throws dignity out the window and sprints straight for us, arms wide open. A way that doesn't wait for our shame to subside before embracing us. A way that throws confetti instead of punishment.

Meister Eckhart reminds us that, "God is at home, it is we who have gone out for a walk."* Yet, according to Jesus and this prodigal, no matter how far we stray, we are never beyond the boundaries of God's love. The kingdom of heaven is all about the furious love of God. A love that breaks every rule, crosses every boundary, and never stops chasing us down.

Most parents have heard their kids say something reckless in a moment of frustration—maybe even words like "I wish you weren't my parents" or "I don't need you." And most of us, as teenagers, were

---

* Meister Eckhart, quoted in Matthew Fox, *Meditations with Meister Eckhart* (Rochester, VT: Bear & Company, 1983), 10.

guilty of shouting something we didn't really mean. But this was no childish outburst. For a son to demand his inheritance while his father was still alive was the equivalent of saying, "I wish you were dead." It wasn't just disrespectful—it was a grave offense. Like I stated, dishonoring one's father in such a way could get you stoned to death on the spot. The father in this story doesn't disown his son or demand retribution. Instead, in an act of love that defies logic, he grants his request. He takes on the shame, the humiliation, and even the financial loss—all for the sake of a son who only sees him as a means to an end.

Jesus isn't just telling a story about forgiveness. This is a rescue mission. The father runs with urgency, knowing his son's life is at stake. He shields and restores him before the village can cast judgment—before anyone can cast the first stone. Love chases us down and celebrates with joy! Rejoice! What was lost is found.

This is the radical, lifesaving love the kingdom of heaven is all about. This is how God chooses to reign over this kingdom, embracing us with tenderness and grace, even when we don't deserve it. We'd be wise to really listen to what Jesus has to say here because he's offering us a glimpse into the very heart of God—one that waits with open arms, longing for our return, eager to celebrate us with reckless joy.

What does this say? It tells me that God doesn't hesitate. God doesn't wait on a heavenly porch, arms crossed, demanding an explanation. God sees a hungry, exhausted, broken child and runs. There's no lecture prepared. No conditions to meet. No proving one's worth. Just an embrace that wipes away every ounce of shame and restores each one of us, fully, as beloved. God is not keeping score. God is not waiting for us to grovel. God is running toward us. Arms open, eyes full of love, ready to pull us close.

In God's arms, there is no list of past sins, no shame, no guilt—only love that "kisses the past into forgetfulness."* This is what makes

---

* Paraphrased from Charles Spurgeon, sermon on Micah 7:19, in *The Metropolitan Tabernacle Pulpit*, vol. 37 (London: Passmore & Alabaster, 1891), 310.

grace so scandalous. No one earns it. No one deserves it. No one buys their way into it. It is given so freely, so relentlessly, that anyone—anyone—who dares to return home will find the doors flung open and the arms of God waiting. Is this the picture you have of God?

In a time when society was fueled by honor and shame, this parable was so countercultural that Jesus had to add the jealous brother into the mix just to make it believable. What about the one who never left, who played by the rules? He sees the party, hears the music, smells the roasted meat, and seethes. "I've done everything right," he says. "I've worked hard. I've been good. And you never threw a party for me."

And the father, as if his love had not already been obvious, pleads with him too. "Everything I have is yours. But we have to celebrate. Your brother was dead. And now he's alive" (Luke 15:31–32).

Jesus teaches us that it's never about what we deserve. It's always about what God gives. A taste of heaven. A feast. Philip Yancey writes, "Jesus is pretty clear that there is nothing that can disqualify us from God's love. There is nothing we can do to make God love us more. There's nothing we can do to make God love us less."[*]

Let that sink in for a moment. Grace is not a reward for good behavior. It's not a prize for the pure. It's not dependent on what we do for God but on what God willingly does for us. God takes the risk, makes the first move, and becomes vulnerable—just to retrieve us and restore us to our rightful place in the family. And when we come home, God doesn't hesitate. God rejoices.

God is always calling us home. Always ready to run after us. Always upending the world, if that's what it takes to rescue us. Nouwen writes, "God rejoices. Not because the problems of the world have been solved, not because all human pain and suffering have come to an end, nor because thousands of people have been converted. No, God rejoices because one of his children who was lost has been found."[†]

---

[*] Yancy, *What's So Amazing About Grace?*, 7.
[†] Nouwen, *The Return of the Prodigal Son*.

And if you look closely at these three parables, you'll notice they all share the same thing: there's *no* catch. No "if you do this, then God will do that." No quid pro quo. No fine print. No contract. No secret conditions. There is no loophole, no failure, no brokenness that can disqualify us from God's love. Nothing.

Paul echoes this. "But God, who is rich in mercy, out of the great love with which he loved us even when we were dead through our trespasses, made us alive together in Christ—by grace you have been saved." (Eph. 2:4–5). At the center of everything—every parable, every gospel story—is this relentless, irrational, too-good-to-be-true-but-it's-true-anyway love of God. A love that Yancy notes is "so good that it must be true."*

God believes in you and me. We are important and worthy of love for no other reason than that's who God is. When we return to him, we might expect condemnation, judgment, and punishment. But Jesus tells us something completely unexpected. He says get ready for a party thrown in your honor. Expect rejoicing. Expect love that is bigger than your worst mistake.

The kingdom of heaven runs on love. It's fueled by love. It feeds off love. And it produces nothing but love. That's it. God's love isn't based on our economy or our understanding. It doesn't make sense in our scorekeeping world—because it runs on what God designed it to run on. Mercy. Grace. Love. Despite all our faults and messiness, God finds ways to love us. If you still don't believe this, then look again at Jesus.

In the words and stories about Jesus, we see how God comes to us. How God walks on the wrong side of town and talks with the wrong kind of people. Jesus shows us that God has no problem crossing lines, breaking barriers, dining at the wrong tables, touching the untouchable, and calling the outcasts home.

God doesn't just sit in temples or lofty places; God goes in the back alleys and rolls through the bars to be with those at the bottom of the ladder. God wanders around parking lots and midnight motels

---

* Yancy, *What's So Amazing About Grace?*, 49.

with open arms, finding the frightened runaway, embracing the dope-sick, and looking into the eyes of the unlovable. And then, God does the unthinkable. God loves all over them as if it's the only thing God knows how to do. Why? In case you haven't figured it out...love is the celebration of God's great joy.

If we take the words of Jesus to heart, we discover how God's love and grace is shockingly personal. There is nothing—nothing—that can disqualify any of us from being a beloved child of a beloved God, whose ears are always listening, whose eyes are always searching, and whose arms are always extended, always ready to embrace us at our worst, our messiest, our most shame-filled.

You are the lost sheep found. You are the coin trapped in the cracks and rejoiced over. You are the runaway child, covered in dirt, wrecked by your own choices. And still God sees you—really sees you just as you are—and embraces you. "God sees the shattered fragments of His image in us ... and cannot – will not – give up." * Jesus says all this shit because he wants you to know that you matter. God comes to you because you matter. Heaven is revealed to you because you matter. Heaven rejoices because you matter.

You are a beloved child of a loving God. That has been true, since the beginning of time—long before you ever took a breath. There was never a moment when God was not love. This is how it was. It's how it's always going to be. This love became flesh in Jesus, who came running after us—not to scold, not to punish, but to save and transform.

God takes the first step toward us for our own redemption. And even when we run, grace runs faster. God's furious love and endless grace chase after us—no matter who we are or what we've done. And when we finally turn toward home, God doesn't stand still. God runs. Because God's love is home. This home has an address. It's here. For wherever you find or share God's love, there you will find the kingdom of heaven.

---

* Yancy, *What's So Amazing About Grace?*, 50.

29

DON'T MAKE IT SO HARD

"Come to me, all you who are weary and are carrying heavy burdens, and I will give you rest. Take my yoke upon you, and learn from me, for I am gentle and humble in heart, and you will find rest for your souls. For my yoke is easy, and my burden is light."
—Matthew 11:28–30

I don't know about you, but the thing I hated most about kindergarten was nap time. You could have paste on your fingers or half a sandwich left on your napkin, but when the teacher said, "Nap time," that was it. You grabbed a thin, plastic-covered mat holding the germs of a hundred other kids. And you lay down adding your runny nose to the petri dish. And if you couldn't sleep, you faked it. Because that's what you did. By first grade, I missed naptime. *Naps were for babies*, they said. Big kids powered through the day. Today, a nap feels like a guilty pleasure instead of the necessity it is. Our bodies need rest. But we're conditioned to push through, to treat exhaustion like a badge of honor.

My dad has this saying that he loves to share whenever someone is listening. "At my age, happy hour is a nap." He's not wrong. That's solid advice. Rest isn't just *good* for the body—it's *essential*. It lowers stress, heals the heart, clears the mind, and even fuels creativity. Studies show people who nap live longer. So maybe there's something sacred in all this resting. Maybe that's why—out of all the laws in Torah—taking a day of rest made God's top ten list.

Still, we like to ignore rest. And so, God intervenes. Sometimes the intervention comes from our bodies just giving up and shutting down. Or sometimes, God takes more drastic measures. Remember 2020? Our overworked, over-stressed, over-tired world shut down, like God had unplugged the planet and done a hard reset. At first, we panicked. We tried to make sense of things. But after a while, something shifted. People started walking their dogs. Neighbors, masked and six feet apart, started looking each other in the eye. We slowed down. We breathed. And then—just as quickly as we had been forced to stop—we rushed right back into the grind. If it weren't for long weekends, would we ever stop to catch our breath?

In the kingdom of heaven, rest is essential. Jesus knows this. So, he asks those around him, are you burnt out? Worn thin by bad news? Exhausted by division and conflict? Tired of the endless cycle of work, bills, commutes, obligations—just trying to keep your head above water? If so, Jesus says, "Come to me."

Jesus knows how exhausting it is to be human. He knows what tired muscles feel like, what anxiety can do to the mind, what doubt can do to the heart. He's been there, done that. He sees the people around him, weighed down by burdens too heavy to carry, and he doesn't shame them for it. He doesn't tell them to try harder or push through. He names their spiritual state without adding anything else to the list and simply says, "Come. Bring it to me."

And yet, we ignore him. We hear those words and think, "That's nice, Jesus, but have you seen my schedule?" Like rest is a luxury we can't afford. Like the weight of the world is ours to carry alone. But Jesus says, "No. Hand it over. Let me take it. Let me lighten the load." Love does that. Love makes things lighter. And in the kingdom of heaven, love is always the way.

The late and wonderful teacher Rachel Held Evans captures this invitation beautifully. She wrote, "Jesus invites us into a story bigger than ourselves, yet one that affects our everyday lives. His invitation is to come and see, to follow and believe, to take up residence in the story of redemption and rest."*

Jesus says some really good shit. It would be a shame to just brush it off because it sounds too good to be true. I mean, doesn't he know? Doesn't he see how work, family, and even our own expectations can feel like a relentless weight? We barely have time to breathe, let alone tend to the things dragging us down. And then Jesus comes along and says, "Come on, hand those over to me. I see you. I know life's hard enough without you hauling all that extra weight around."

This passage gives us two things to chew on. First, life is hard—no way around that. It's full of all sorts of things that wear us down, things that make us weary. Which is why naps are totally sacred. We need rest—body, mind, and soul—if we're going to live a full life, the kind of life God dreams for us. Following Jesus? Yeah, it adds more to our plate. But it doesn't have to crush us. Heaven is...well, heaven. Not a burden. If all of my years of shouldering burdens have taught me anything, that's not heaven—that's hell.

The second thing Jesus tells us is that his yoke is easy. He wants to make things lighter. As Dallas Willard puts it, "Jesus brings us the easy yoke. The secret to a fulfilling life is not in trying harder, but in resting more deeply in his way of living."†

Think about all the stuff you carry with you every day. Maybe it's that coworker who makes you crazy. Maybe it's some tension at home—your marriage, your kids, the fact that no one ever remembers to take the trash out but you. Maybe you don't have someone special to share life with, and that ache is heavier than you let on. Or you're stretched thin, pulled in a thousand directions, keeping up with friends, family, work, and trying not to let anyone down. Maybe it's

---

* Rachel Held Evans, *Inspired: Slaying Giants, Walking on Water, and Loving the Bible Again* (Nashville: Nelson Books, 2018), 235.
† Dallas Willard, *The Spirit of the Disciplines: Understanding How God Changes Lives* (San Francisco: HarperOne, 1988), 9.

just the daily grind, the endless to-do lists, trying to hold it all together while feeling like you're about to come undone.

And then, there's the heavy stuff. The shame over something you did. The regret over something you didn't do. The burden you don't talk about because it's been buried for so long you don't know how to dig it out.

Episcopal priest Joshua Bowron writes, "Each of us is dealing with something, or a whole litany of somethings, that if we all had to wear them outwardly, I daresay we'd have a much more compassionate world."* And isn't that the whole point Jesus is constantly making? Be compassionate. That's the world Jesus is trying to create—one where we stop pretending we have it all together and actually show up for each other. Jesus doesn't ask us to hide our problems. He says, "Bring them to me and I will give you rest." He's not offering a soft pillow or a quiet place to lay our heads for a nap. He is offering us God's own heart—a welcoming sanctuary to let it all go without judgment or shame. While the world might offer us a long weekend here and there, Jesus offers true rest for our weary souls—a profound, eternal peace that comes from knowing we are with God, being loved and cared for. He's offering us heaven. So why keep living in this hell?

Jesus is always inviting us to experience a deeper, more meaningful relationship with God and one another—one that changes us from the inside out. This is all part of building up the kingdom of heaven, right here in the midst of all the struggles and stress and work and worry. I believe this to be true because real spiritual transformation begins by setting our eyes and our burdens on the broad shoulders of the one who says, "Give me your shit. Take my yoke. My way is far easier than the world's way."

I think it's worth mentioning that in ancient Judaism, a yoke is not the yellow blob inside an egg. And it's not just that heavy, wooden thing they slap on an ox's neck—though every Sunday School class made it seem that way. Sure, an egg yolk is a yolk, and an ox yoke is a

---

* Joshua Bowron, "Taking on Jesus' Yoke," *The Episcopal Church*, July 9, 2017, https://www.episcopalchurch.org/sermon/taking-on-jesus-yoke-proper-9-a-july-9-2017/.

yoke—but when Jesus talks about his yoke, he's talking about something else entirely.

A yoke, in rabbinic tradition, was a way of interpreting scripture, a way of walking in the world. Each rabbi had a different yoke—a particular way of understanding the Torah and applying it to life. And depending on the rabbi, that yoke could be as heavy as a boulder or as light as a feather. Some rabbis had pages upon pages of what you could and couldn't do. The dos and don'ts were endless. Imagine trying to live under all that pressure.

Jesus knows how suffocating all that rule-following can be. I'm sure he's met a few exhausted students along the way, the ones barely hanging on. He sees how the system crushes people with impossible expectations, so he offers something completely unexpected. A yoke that is easy. A burden that is light. Who's in?

Imagine that showing up on *Rate My Rabbi*. The class would fill up on day one. But here's the thing—it's not about being the "easy teacher." It's about authority. It's about authenticity. When Jesus speaks, folks lean in. "The people were astounded, for he taught them as one having authority, and not like their scribes" (Matt. 7:28–29). It wasn't just what he said. It was the way he embodied it. His way was radically different. And he had the proof—he lived it.

And despite what the Pharisees and scribes thought, Jesus wasn't out to embarrass or discredit them. He wasn't trying to make them look foolish. He wasn't playing "Gotcha" with the law. As far as Jesus was concerned, they were all on the same team—bound to God and to one another. But they didn't see it that way. They liked to accuse him of breaking the law and twisting the prophets' words. But Jesus makes it plain: "I have not come to abolish the law, but to fulfill it" (Matt. 5:17).

Jesus does uphold the laws—raising them to a standard that goes above conventional wisdom and beyond a call for strict obedience. He does this not by tightening the screws or demanding stricter obedience, but by returning to the heart of it all. Because anyone can memorize rules to pass a theology quiz. But Jesus? He's always asking the deeper question: *Why was the law given in the first place? What was God's dream behind it all?*

Jesus always points back to what's always been true: *The law was made for humanity, not the other way around.* If we want to see the kingdom of heaven crack open in the here and now, then we must not wield the law like a weapon. Instead, listen to the prophets who called out the religious elites for getting lost in the words while ignoring the cries of the suffering. They are the ones who still remind us, time and time again, that love always comes first.

In his Sermon on the Mount, Jesus says, "You have heard it said, 'Do not murder,' but I'm telling you—don't even stay angry" (Matt. 5:21–22). He knows that simply following rules won't stop you from getting pissed-off at the guy who cut you off in traffic. But love—love for God and neighbor—can help you let it go. It can help you breathe and stop you from carrying that burden of anger around like a weight strapped to your chest. Jesus says, "Love your enemy" (v. 44), because he knows love is the only thing that can stop hate. The only thing that can turn an enemy into a friend.

You've probably heard that old saying, "an eye for an eye." It comes from the ancient law of *lex talionis*—a principle not meant to promote revenge, but to place limits on it. Think of it like this: if you break my window, I break yours. Not exactly graceful, but at least we're not burning down each other's houses over something trivial. It's a kind of fair-and-balanced justice system—at least on paper. But Jesus takes it a step further. He reframes justice altogether, inviting us to step out of the tired loop of retaliation. "Don't fight evil with more evil. Turn the other cheek" (v. 39). Jesus sees what these cycles of revenge do to people, families, entire communities. Just look at gang culture—how many lives are lost in the name of "evening the score"? But time and again, Jesus shows us a different way. His way—his yoke—breaks the chains of violence, anger, greed, and lust. He doesn't just curb the retaliation; he transforms it into love.

Eugene Peterson paraphrases Jesus' words to his followers in *The Message* like this: "There's no time for tit-for-tat stuff. Just go and live graciously and generously" (v. 42). Studying God's laws is not going to cut it. We have to embody the Spirit of each one with every fiber of our being. "If your eye is healthy, your whole body will be full of light" (Matt. 6:22).

It's good to remember Jesus' yoke isn't about strict obedience to a rule book—it's about relationship and a way of living where kindness, forgiveness, mercy, and justice shape all our actions. Like Jesus told his students, "A disciple is not above the teacher. It is enough for the disciple to be like the teacher" (Matt. 10:24).

If we want to take Jesus seriously, we have to take on his way of living—where love isn't a burden but a gift. Because at the end of the day, Jesus isn't looking for people who are just *woke*. He's calling for people who will *work*. Who will keep pushing to wake the world up to injustice, inequality, and all the ways we fail to love as God loves. Including the way laws and systems keep certain people from thriving in God's glory.

Barbara Brown Taylor writes, "Salvation is so much more than many of us were taught. It is not about being delivered from pain but about being delivered through pain, not about being rescued from the world but about being remade through our engagement with it."* Her words remind us that Jesus invites us to rest, not escape. His invitation is a call to transformation. His call is simply this: Learn from me. Walk with me. Make life easier, not harder.

To take Jesus' invitation seriously—to make heaven a reality here and now—we have to extend God's radical, redemptive love to everyone. No conditions. No judgment. No shit. Do it without adding extra burdens on ourselves or anyone else. Let Jesus carry the weight. Let him handle them with divine justice—rooted in unconditional love. His yoke is a compassionate heart that frees you to love that person who annoys you. Or to welcome back the estranged friend you blocked on Facebook. By embracing Jesus' yoke, we begin to see everyone like he does. It's in this space that the words of Jesus ring true, "You will find rest for your souls" (Matt. 11:29).

This isn't about *doing* less. It's about *being* more. More present to

---

* Barbara Brown Taylor, *Learning to Walk in the Dark* (New York: HarperOne, 2014), 15.

God's love. More attuned to the rhythms of grace. More rooted in life as God's beloved. Because, just like a good teacher can inspire you to reach your potential, Jesus tells us, "You will do greater things than me" (John 14:12). His invitation isn't just to live—it's to thrive.

This is the message of love. The kingdom of heaven has come to us. All the shit Jesus says points and calls and invites and shouts, "Come! Thrive!" His words redeem us, change our thinking so our hearts can be healed and "saved" in our doing. When we follow his way, we love his way. When we take up his yoke, we love like he does. Our hearts are filled—and our communities transformed.

Jesus says it like this, "I have come as a light in the world so that anyone who believes in me no longer remains in the darkness" (John 12:46). In his light, our deepest pain, our darkest secrets, our heaviest burdens are not only exposed for what they are—but are also redeemed back into God's glory. Not just our burdens and fears and anxieties, but everyone's. Yours. Mine. The world's. I encourage you to accept the invitation of our gentle and humble Lord who calls out to us to embrace a life of love and service. His yoke is easy. His burden is light. And in him, we find rest for our weary, worn-out souls.

30

NOW WHAT?

Jesus said, "Feed my sheep."
—John 21:15–17

Love. Got it? That's the entire message of God. The entire Bible and all the shit Jesus says points to this truth. Love God. Love others. Love yourself. Love is the key that unlocks life. It's how we see and experience heaven here and now.

At the end of John's Gospel, the author tells us there are so many more things Jesus said and did; and "if everyone one of them were written down, I suppose that the world itself could not contain the books that would be written" (John 21:25). And so, the author chooses to end on this last story to not only encourage us, but to push us to take Jesus' words out into the world—"to shine into the darkness," like my good friend Bob Cooper offers in every one of his benedictions.

Let me set the final scene here. Forty days have passed since the disciples discovered that Jesus, their beloved teacher and friend, had been raised from the dead. And yet, they are already back at their old jobs. Not fishing for people, like Jesus called them to do. Instead, they are fishing for actual fish. And one last time, Jesus goes to meet his friends at the place where he first called them—at the beach.

I love this story on so many levels. It's profound, it's personal, it's intimate and inviting. It's also daybreak, my favorite time. It's quiet and calm; the world seems settled and manageable. The sun is just beginning to glow. The water is glassy and still. A light fog gives it an eerie calm, while a chill slices through the silence. There's a slow, melodic heartbeat on the shoreline. The steady rhythm of small waves lapping upon the rocks and shells. With the damp sand squishing between his toes, Jesus calls to the guys who are fishing about a hundred yards offshore.

Like he did when he first met them, he tells them where to cast their net. And a very naked Simon Peter is the first to react when they hear the familiar voice. Typical of him, he doesn't hesitate. He just takes off. Jumping overboard and rushing toward his friend. The others quickly follow, more sensibly taking the boat full of fish with them to shore.

I know I'm more like Peter than the others. I jump right in. That's my enneagram number—always rushing me here and there, with little regard to what's going on around me. The problem with rushing through a story like this one is we might miss the wonderful subtleties and profound symbolism that offer insight into the ways God works in our lives today.

For example, notice what Jesus is doing. He's sitting on the beach, waiting for his disciples to come home from work, which, by the way, is not going so well. So Jesus intervenes, helping them out by nudging them in the right direction to get their catch. What does this say to you about how Jesus works in your life? I like to think Jesus is waiting for me. And while he is waiting, he's watching over me as I go about my day. While he waits and watches, he guides me and helps me navigate the work he has called me to do. This simple story reveals a startling truth: God is intentionally present in our lives—waiting, working, and caring about our success.

Another thing John's story reveals to us is that Jesus is not just idly standing by, hoping to be noticed. He's been there for a while, making a fire and preparing breakfast for his friends. This task might seem mundane. But in scripture, fire is highly symbolic. It was a pillar of fire that led the children of Israel through the wilderness, and tongues of fire that leapt from the mouths of the disciples on Pentecost. Fire symbolizes the presence of the Holy Spirit. That says something about Jesus' presence on the beach. The one making the fire is also the one bringing the Holy Spirit to us.

And let's talk about that particular beach bonfire. It's not made with driftwood that's scattered on the shore. John makes the point of saying it was a charcoal fire. Charcoal is not commonly found buried in the sand, and given the early morning hour, we can assume the charcoal store was not open yet either. So Jesus had to haul it with him, lugging not only the fire but also the food for breakfast. The only other time we see a charcoal fire is in John's Gospel as well. It comes up earlier, in the courtyard where Peter pretended he didn't know Jesus. Three times he does this. Now, three times, Jesus redeems him as a perfect bookend to the Easter story.

This is what love does—it comes, it forgives, it rewrites the story.

The next symbol is the meal itself. It's not an elaborate feast. It's fish and bread, the same meal Jesus used to feed the multitudes. As the story goes, a massive crowd came to hear Jesus speak. Apparently, no one expected him to talk as long as he did, because no one but a little boy brought anything to eat. That boy offered Jesus all that he had. And what did he bring? A few fish and some bread. From this small gift of generosity, a miracle happened. Jesus turned it into a banquet of abundance. That's the way of the kingdom. God takes the little we offer, blesses it, and somehow it becomes more than enough. Leftovers, even.

This is what happens at the beach. Jesus doesn't feed his friends with his fish. He invites them to bring their own catch. If we're going to take Jesus at his word, and become fishers of people like he calls us to, then our work and our offerings matter. We have to bring what we have to him. Including people.

That's the call—bring what you have, and Jesus will multiply it. Peter gets this. He doesn't hesitate. He hauls the heavy net of fish—153 fish, to be exact—struggling but determined. I can't imagine that was easy. I've fished before, and if each fish weighed two pounds, that's a lot of weight to carry alone across the sandy shore. But that's what Peter did. And even though the net was weighed down and dragged over shells and rocks, it doesn't tear or break.

John's story reminds us that this call to love is work. It's not easy work either. It can weigh us down and drag us through uncomfortable situations. But it also stretches us and sends us out into deep waters. And still, the net doesn't break. This is what God's love is like. It holds. It sustains. It never tears. God equips us to do the work we're called to do. And like I said earlier, God does all the heavy lifting.

And that brings us to the last symbol: the bread being warmed by the fire. In the scriptures, bread is never just bread. It's manna in the wilderness. It's the bread of life, broken and given. It's Jesus saying, *"Take, eat, this is me."* Bread is God's word. It's nourishing and sustaining. And here, on the shore, warmed by the fire, Jesus breaks it again. Whenever we see Jesus and bread together, we know something holy and sacred is happening.

He wants us to know that this is who we are—people fed by love, people sent to feed others.

That's the whole thing. That's the work of the kingdom—not waiting for miracles, but *becoming* them. Not waiting for the world to change, but feeding the hungry, forgiving the broken, carrying the charcoal fire of love into a world starving for it. This is Jesus, still among us, still kindling fires, still setting tables. This is how the kingdom comes to life. "If you love me, feed my lambs. Take care of my sheep" (John 21:15–17). This is part of Peter's redemption, sure—but more than that, it's the marching orders for all of us who dare to follow Jesus. This is the heart of the church. This is what it means to be the Body of Christ in the world. To love and serve and feed and tend. To be people who *show up* for each other.

God is always present, always coming and caring for us, always equipping us, and always sending us to love and serve one another. The miracles of Jesus feeding the multitudes are examples that give us a glimpse of how God works. A meal becomes more than a meal. A small act of generosity—offering what little you have—somehow becomes a miracle like no other.

Miracles happen all the time. And most of the time, we don't even notice. We expect them to be grand, earth-shattering, sky-parting moments. But grace is quieter than that. Subtler. More woven into the everyday. Take gravity, for example. That everything in the universe holds together instead of unraveling into chaos? That's a miracle. That life keeps regenerating over and over again? That's a miracle. That love finds a way, that forgiveness cracks open hardened hearts, that wounds heal? All miracles.

And then there are the small, laugh-out-loud, God-is-in-the-details kind of miracles. Like the time I was at La Super Rica, my go-to taco joint, where the line is usually so long you start to wonder if tacos are worth this kind of devotion (they are). And I always, always forget they're cash only. Which means the inevitable scramble to find an ATM. But that day? Miracle number one—I get there, and only two people are in line ahead of me. That alone felt like God winking at me. Miracle number two? When I go to pay, I realize I have just enough cash in my wallet. I mean, I'm talking a nickel-to-spare kind of enough.

I don't think any of this happened because of some cosmic magic trick. We just happened to show up at the right time, order the right amount of food, and somehow, it all worked out. A fluke, maybe. But here's the thing—we get so caught up looking for the big miracles that we miss the small, everyday ones that are just as real, just as sacred.

And that's the problem when we rush, like Peter, to get through the story. We miss the little clues hidden in the miracle itself. What if what God wants us to see isn't the physics-defying, logic-bending act itself? What if the real miracle is what's happening beneath it—what Jesus is trying to reveal? If we get too hung up on whether or not Jesus actually walked on water, we might miss the bigger truth: that he walked toward his friends in the middle of a storm. That he showed up in their fear. That he reminded them they were never alone. And if we get too caught up in whether Jesus literally multiplied food out of thin air, we might overlook what's actually happening—where Jesus takes what's there, blesses it, and suddenly, it's more than enough. Sound familiar? It's what he's always doing—multiplying love, making sure the cup never runs dry.

Maybe this is why the feeding of the five thousand is the only miracle—aside from the resurrection—that's told in all four gospels. It's like the gospel writers are waving their arms at us, saying, "Pay attention! This is what it's all about!" Not magic. Not spectacle. Just a simple, stunning truth: In the kingdom of God, there is always enough.

The story goes something like this: a crowd has gathered, unplanned and unorganized. People heard Jesus was in town, and they showed up. Some just wanted to see him with their own eyes—to hear if he really spoke the way they'd heard. Others came hoping to witness the kind of miracle that had been making the rounds—water into wine, blind men seeing, the whole bit. But as the day stretches on, the disciples start getting nervous. No one expected the crowds to stay as long as they did. And it seems nobody thought to pack a lunch either.

So, naturally, the Twelve turn to their teacher. They've seen what he's done and know what he can do. You have a problem, you bring it to the man who can pull off a miracle. But Jesus isn't interested in wowing the crowd with a show. He looks at his disciples and says: *You give them something to eat.*

I imagine the confusion on their faces. I'm sure they shot him that *what-the-actual-hell* look my wife often gives me when I ask her to do the impossible. *We barely have enough to feed ourselves, Jesus.* Their eyes drop to their hands, to their empty satchels, to the pitiful sum of their resources. Jesus watches them for a moment, then asks: "What do you have?" They scramble for an answer. Not much. Five loaves. Two fish. Jesus says, "Bring them to me" (Matt. 14:18).

He takes these few, unimpressive, barely-worth-mentioning items, and he blesses them. And then—he hands them back to his disciples and tells them to start passing them out. And here's where it gets good. Because somehow, everybody eats. Not just a little bit. Not just a "take one bite and pass it down" situation. Everyone eats. And there are *twelve baskets* of leftovers.

Now, how did that happen? Did Jesus perform some divine math trick? Did the food literally multiply in their hands? Maybe. Or maybe—just maybe—it went down another way. Maybe the miracle wasn't in physics, but in the opening of hearts. Maybe it was the disciples stepping up and sharing what little they had that sparked something in the crowd. One small act of generosity lit the match, and suddenly, people who had quietly packed a bit of food for themselves saw what was happening and thought, *Well, shoot. I've got something too*. And suddenly, five loaves and two fish became bread and olives, and cheese and figs, and wine and—before you know it—*everyone* is full.

And maybe *this* is the real miracle. Not that Jesus could snap his fingers and create infinite loaves. But that one human could live in such a way—so generous, so abundant, so rooted in trust—that it called forth the same in others. Maybe we're not meant to read this as a miracle story but as a parable—one that tells us what we are called to do and who we are meant to be.

These poor, clueless disciples gave up everything they had—five lousy loaves and two small fish—because Jesus asked them to. And in that fearless, open-handed act of giving, they sparked something in everyone else. The crowd saw what they did, and something unlocked in them, too. What they had, they no longer hoarded. What was hidden, they now shared. And just like that, the kingdom of God showed up in the middle of a hungry, disorganized, unprepared crowd. And it was enough. It was always enough.

Love, when it's real, multiplies. This is how the kingdom breaks in. Not through spectacle, but through trust. Not by hoarding, but by giving it all away. The miracle isn't that *something* came from *nothing*. The miracle is that everything we need is already here—if only we dare to share it.

"Feed my sheep" (John 21:17).

Anglican priest and theologian Jason Cox reminds us that this story isn't so much about magic. "The magic has already happened.

God has already given us a world out of nothing—sun, earth, water, seeds. How much more magic do we need?" * Jesus doesn't conjure bread out of thin air. He doesn't snap his fingers and make food appear. Instead, he "takes what God has already provided. He draws out the resources that are already present in the community"†—the small, overlooked, not-enough offering—and draws out the abundance that was waiting in the community all along. That's the invitation. To see differently. To trust that what we have, when given away in love, will always be *enough*.

Jesus didn't come to pull off stunts. He came to usher in the kingdom of God—a world where heaven and earth shake hands, where love is multiplied, and no one is left out. This is what Jesus is inviting you to do! Stop waiting for miracles and start *being* them. "Feed my sheep."

If we were all willing to share what God has gifted each one of us, then perhaps there would be no hungry people in our neighborhoods, and no one in the world would thirst, or be without shelter and peace. If we dared to love like Jesus—recklessly, fearlessly, without worrying about whether it's enough, we would all have hope, and no one would be left behind. We all have something to share. There's plenty for everyone. And with leftovers to boot!

Jesus isn't handing out free meals. He's showing us how to break open our lives, our resources, our very selves, and pour them out for others. People followed Jesus because they wanted to *see* a miracle. They walked away realizing they were *called* to be one.

What if the real miracle isn't walking on water without sinking? What if it's showing up in the middle of someone's storm and calming their fear? What if it's not Jesus defying death but Jesus showing us that love is stronger than death? What if his message *is* that hope is always waiting on the other side of despair? And what if the most miraculous thing of all is that a little bit of love—a loaf of

---

* Jason Cox, "Take, Bless, Break, Give," *Episcopal Digital Network,* July 26, 2018, https://www.episcopalchurch.org/sermon/take-bless-break-give-proper-12-b-2018/.
† Cox, "Take, Bless, Break, Give."

bread, a handful of fish, a heart cracked open for others—can change everything? That when we give ourselves away, we don't run out. We overflow.

That's what God's abundance looks like. In real time. In real life. Through us. Jesus is what God's love looks like in human form. Following his way—his yoke—isn't about watching from a distance, nodding in approval. It's about rolling up your sleeves and stepping into the mess of loving people. It's less about admiring what he did and more about *doing* what he does. Jesus doesn't just open our eyes —he opens our hearts. He lets us see people the way God sees them. As beloved children!

From feeding the multitudes to making breakfast on the beach, Jesus moves through the world with one purpose: *to love*. Love doesn't keep walking when it sees hunger. Love stops. Love pulls up a chair. Love says, "Sit down. Let's eat." The people weren't just hungry for bread. Like so many of us, they hungered for the words of the one who said, "I am the bread of life. Whoever comes to me will never be hungry again" (John 6:35). Jesus gives us what we cannot give ourselves. He feeds our spiritual hunger. He nourishes our souls. Yet, Jesus doesn't feed our physical hunger. Instead, he entrusts his followers to do that for him. He didn't come to us to do all the work himself. Jesus turns to his friends and says, "Feed my sheep." He trusts *us* to carry this love forward, to put our faith to work, to make sure that no one is left hungry or forgotten or unloved. Jesus never says, "Stand back and watch." He says, "Go. Give. Love."

And that question he asked Peter—"Do you love me?"—is the same question he asks us. And if the answer is *yes*, then the response is clear: "Then feed my lambs. Take care of my people. Be love in a world that is starving for it."

The seed of love has been planted in you. Go and bear fruit. The kingdom of heaven has already begun. Go and make love grow. The invitation is there, waiting for your response. Go and feed that love to one another.

Meister Eckhart saw it like this. Within us is "the soil in which God has sown the divine likeness and image and in which God sows the good seed, the roots of all wisdom, all skills, all virtues, all goodness—the seed of the divine nature...This is the good tree of which our Lord says that it always bears good fruit and never evil fruit. For it desires goodness and is inclined toward goodness..."[*]

If the seed of God is in us, it will need to be cultivated and cared for in order to thrive. Jesus is the gardener, who tills the soul with his words. Fertilizes the heart with his compassion. Cultivates our faith and helps us grow closer to our divine truth whose seed is within us. "If the seed of a pear tree grows into a pear tree, a hazel seed into a hazel tree, the seed of God into God.... While this seed may be crowded, hidden away, and never cultivated, it will still never be obliterated. It glows and shines, gives off light, burns, and is unceasingly inclined toward God."[†]

God's love is abundant. Overflowing into us and through us. Love that is limitless and unconditional. When we stop hoarding God's forgiveness, kindness, and resources, we discover just how love begets love. The more we give, the more we realize we have. The closer heaven comes to us and the closer we come to God, whose fruit—whose love—grows within us all.

Jesus says some crazy shit, but nothing crazier than this: If you love me, you will love one another, you will love your enemies, you will love the wolves in sheep's clothing, you will love the marginalized, the silenced, the bigots, the racists, the queers, the noisy neighbor, the dentist with the heavy hand, the people you don't like, and everyone in the space between.

---

[*] Matthew Fox, *Passion for Creation: Meister Eckhart's Creation Spirituality; Selections from Breakthrough* (New York: Doubleday, 1995), 1–3.
[†] Fox, *Passion for Creation*, 3.

31

ONE LAST THING

Love. That's it.
   Just love.
   Without love, all the stuff Jesus says doesn't mean shit.

ABOUT THE AUTHOR

Before embracing a call to ministry, Ian Macdonald was an award-winning Creative Director and copywriter, who created campaigns for brands like The ACLU, American Express, Baskin-Robins, Mattel, Honda, Samsung, and Toyota.

His love of travel and passion for meeting people inspired *Jesus, not Jesús: Finding the Divine in the Space Between Us,* a blog where faith, doubt, and life collide.

Ian earned a Masters of Divinity from Fuller Theological Seminary. In 2017, he co-founded what would become Anamesa, an Internet/House church hybrid that invites people from all walks of life to explore faith and love through the words of Jesus.

He lives in Los Angeles with his wife, kids, a dog, and and the last surviving fish in the tank. When he's not practicing Jesus stuff, he's making noise on a guitar, scribbling sardonic love poems to the world, or cussing at the weeds in his garden—all of which, he's convinced, Jesus would do.

Visit his blog: jesusnotjesus.org

www.ingramcontent.com/pod-product-compliance
Lightning Source LLC
Chambersburg PA
CBHW032126160426
43197CB00008B/530